IMAGES
of America

RENO'S RIVERWALK DISTRICT

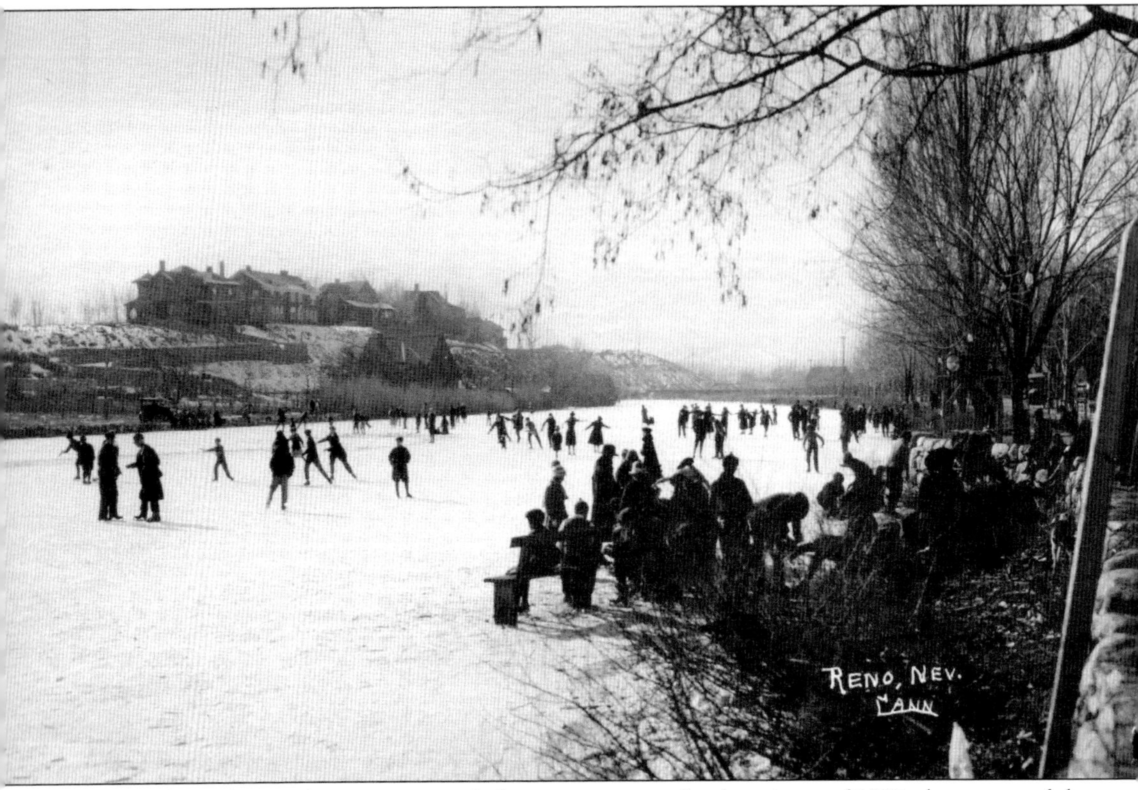

Reno braved many long winters and changing seasons. In the winter of 1919, the waters of the Truckee River were so cold that the top of the water froze solid enough for families and the community to ice skate on it. In this image, the bluffs high up on the hill are visible along with people standing on the banks of the river along Riverside Drive to the right. (WA-10684.)

ON THE COVER: Pictured is the historic Riverside Hotel and Reno's first trolley car crossing the legendary Virginia Street Bridge. The covered area above the water was once a lovely restaurant along Island Avenue, overlooking the banks of Truckee River in what would become one of the historical sites along the Riverwalk District. (WA-01544.)

IMAGES
of America

RENO'S RIVERWALK DISTRICT

Courtney Rhiana and Christopher Ryan Meredith

ARCADIA
PUBLISHING

ISBN 978-0-7385-9671-6

Published by Arcadia Publishing
Charleston, South Carolina

Printed in the United States of America

Library of Congress Control Number: 2012950195

For all general information, please contact Arcadia Publishing:
Telephone 843-853-2070
Fax 843-853-0044
E-mail sales@arcadiapublishing.com
For customer service and orders:
Toll-Free 1-888-313-2665

Visit us on the Internet at www.arcadiapublishing.com

This book is dedicated to the hardworking individuals who settled on the banks of the Truckee River, the Riverwalk Merchants Association, and our beloved family.

Contents

Acknowledgments

The concept for this book started with the initial contact of our Arcadia editor, Stacia Bannerman, who has patiently and kindly worked with us through the entirety of this process. We would also like to acknowledge our friends and families who supported us through the creation of this book. This publication would not have been possible without the assistance of the Riverwalk Merchants Association, whose members have provided detailed information about, and unique photographs of, their historic buildings.

The majority of the images used throughout this book belong to the photograph archive of the Nevada Historical Society (NHS), the Special Collections Department of the University of Nevada, Reno Library (UNRS), and the Library of Congress (LC). The knowledge and experience provided by the staff and volunteers of the NHS and UNRS were greatly appreciated, and this publication would not have been possible without their assistance. We are tremendously grateful for the expertise of Lee Brumbaugh, the NHS curator of photography, who scanned and processed the numerous images chosen for this book.

In researching the history of the Reno Riverwalk, we found particularly helpful the information, research, and articles of the following talented authors and organizations: Doris Cerveri, Lou and Phyllis Zauner, Mella Rothwell Harmon, Patricia D. Cafferta, Alicia Barber, Donnelyn Curtis, University Archives–University of Nevada, Reno (UNRA), the National Automobile Museum, the Historic Reno Preservation Society, the Nevada Historical Society Quarterlies, the Reno Fire Department and the International Association of Fire Fighters (IAFF) Local 731, First United Methodist Church, the Dave Stafford Collection, and Trinity Episcopal Church. Unless otherwise noted, most images appear courtesy of the Nevada Historical Society.

INTRODUCTION

When Charles Fuller established the first bridge to cross the majestic Truckee River, little did he know that it would mark the very location of Reno's inception and that the lovely river would became the centerpiece for the rich culture of the city. This book is a pictorial guide covering a selection of historic buildings and residences that exist in the picturesque Riverwalk District of downtown Reno.

The Reno Riverwalk District, with its numerous shops, urban renaissance, nationally recognized art, dining, and entertainment, is the core of the city. For over 98 years the area has thrived in the face of numerous floods, storms, and fires; it remains an ever-changing, beautiful, and exciting addition to the Silver State.

Charles William (C.W.) Fuller arrived in the Truckee Meadows in 1859 and purchased a small area of land on the south bank of the Truckee River. Fuller operated a log building on this land that assisted in providing food and shelter to gold seekers passing through the area during the "Rush to Washoe," triggered by the gold, and later silver, strikes of the famous Comstock Lode. By the early 1860s, Fuller had constructed a bridge and a small hotel; this area eventually became known as Fuller's Crossing.

In 1861, Honey Lake rancher (and acquaintance to Fuller) Myron C. Lake purchased the bridge after Fuller struggled with the constant rebuilding that was required because of continual flooding from the Sierra Nevada. Lake upgraded the property and renamed the area Lake's Crossing. With the help of the Nevada legislature, Lake was authorized to charge a comfortable toll of travelers crossing the bridge. The toll profit was to ensure that Lake would continue to maintain the bridge and the surrounding areas as a safe passageway over the river. The spot became an important station on one of the main routes between northern California and the silver mines of Virginia City during the big boom of the Comstock Lode. Today, the Virginia Street Bridge, as it would come to be known, is the dynamic centerpiece of the Riverwalk, connecting the city. Although it has been replaced a number of times over the years because of flooding and age, it serves as a focal point in this historical guide as a landmark of Reno's beginnings and as an iconic way to explore the core of the city.

In 1863, the excitement of the transcontinental railroad made its way towards the Truckee Meadows. The big four of railroading (Mark Hopkins, Collis P. Huntington, Leland Stanford, and Charles Crocker) searched for an adequate location for a new station, and Reno appeared to be the most attractive choice. Myron Lake sold much of his land to make way for the new depot, and soon plots of land became available for purchase during a live auction. Downtown Reno and the areas along the Riverwalk began to take form, and a clear divide was made regarding the boundaries of businesses and city amenities and the development of the first neighborhoods. High above the banks of the Riverwalk sat the bluffs, where the most prestigious aristocrats, politicians, performers, and city socialites would build their large and unique homes. This area became Newlands Heights and remains one of Reno's loveliest neighborhoods. Below the bluffs, along Riverside Drive, smaller homes were built, and an influx of Italian immigrants began to build their families. The homes in the area known as Little Italy (later the Powning District) sprang up quickly. Though they were modest in size, they allowed enough space for the Italian immigrants to build small vineyards and wine cellars in their yards and basements. These families would grow to become a large demographic of the community that set up shops in the popular Commercial Row area and along First and Second Streets.

The areas along the banks of the river made way for Reno's very first churches, coeducational schools, libraries, state buildings, theaters, fraternal orders, athletic facilities, and some of the area's most influential business owners.

Myron Lake's lodge and gristmill served as a temporary site for Reno's first school, which was moved to a more permanent location in 1869; the school would relocate a few times more before being renamed Reno High School. Four different churches would be erected along the Riverwalk through the years, and in times of disaster they would serve as facilities for other religious organizations and fraternal orders. Groups such as the Oddfellows, the Masons, Elks, and the Twentieth Century Club began to establish in small offices and retail establishments. As the population grew, so did the organizations, and soon they would raise capital to erect their own structures along the banks of the Truckee River. Some of Nevada's most iconic buildings took form along the Riverwalk, though few of them survive today. The organizations also expanded their causes; many of them assisted in planting trees and shrubs along the parkways and neighboring streets, provided educational resources to youth, and provided outlets for music, art, and history.

During the early 1900s, Reno became increasingly popular for the speed at which one could receive a divorce decree there. Divorces became so convenient to unhappy couples that many celebrities and others would create temporary or permanent residences within the city. The historic Mapes, El Cortez, and Riverside Hotels were some of the finest establishments populated by would-be divorcés. Nevada, quickly becoming known for its tremendous leniency in divorces, would revise its residency requirements to only a few weeks. The city's local economy was booming, and so was the nightlife.

By the mid-1900s, Reno had become famous for gaming and the glitz and glamour of the modern casino. The lovely river and the enchanting parks and walkways began to be showcased in numerous films and stories, leading to the development of new traditions and folklore. A handful of bingo halls, hotels, and casinos provided new growth, and Reno was becoming one of the most recognizable and popular cities in the West. Along Riverside drive, homes and neighborhoods continued to develop. Powning Square was developed as one of the only recreational areas in the center of the city. Shortly after that, Belle Isle was developed as an attractive amusement park featuring a dance area, live music, a Ferris wheel, and small-boat rentals for relaxing on the water. High up on the bluffs, overlooking the river, sat additional mansions and homes in Newlands Heights; they still serve as a reminder of the influence and glamour of Reno's high society.

It was not until the early 1990s that the City of Reno and the redevelopment agency officially created the Raymond I. Smith Truckee Riverwalk, which revitalized downtown Reno's scenic riverfront. The Riverwalk offered a scenic walkway that spanned the banks of the Truckee River and would stretch from the current location of the National Automobile Museum to McKinley Park School, built in 1909. Art and sculptures were introduced along the sidewalks, and seven fountains were installed along the walkway. There were also outcrops of gazebos, seating areas, and historical markers.

Today, residents and local merchants are proud to welcome back visitors to the Riverwalk District to celebrate the historic and culturally rich place of Reno's beginnings. The Riverwalk District covers a unique area of the city and encompasses Reno's most historic structures. At present, there are 12 registered listings on the City of Reno Register of Historic Places. One of the buildings is the El Cortez Hotel, which, at the time of its construction (1931), was the tallest structure in Reno. Another is the historic Riverside Hotel, located on the exact site of Reno's 1859 inception. Additional structures, such as the Mapes Hotel and the Wingfield Mansion, were lost to fires and demolition. Reno's first churches still stand, with the steeples stretching to heights visible from every area of the Riverwalk.

Shortly after the construction of the Riverwalk District, a collection of business owners came together to oversee and encourage the area's continued development. The boundaries of the Riverwalk Merchant Association span the area between Arlington Avenue and Lake Street, along the Truckee River. The Riverwalk District also falls within the boundaries of the Truckee River Arts District.

Many of the structures, theaters, and homes in this book have been destroyed as a result of devastating fires, floods, and storms, or have been demolished to make way for larger buildings, hotels, or casinos. Other establishments have simply closed due to struggling economies and changing times. Many of the buildings now act as newly renovated condominiums and housing structures.

The Riverwalk is a stunning and inspirational area providing tremendous views of the Sierras and the Truckee River. Along the Riverwalk, one can enjoy a variety of activities, including the White Water Park and the newly renovated bike and walking paths. The intention of this book is to provide an insight into the Riverwalk's rich past and, through the images, assist you in your travels along the pathways that so many pioneers, aristocrats, and famous politicians, actors, and inventors have also walked. We hope you enjoy reading through this book and that you are encouraged to research the areas farther north in Nevada, as well as your own community.

One

CROSSING THE TRUCKEE

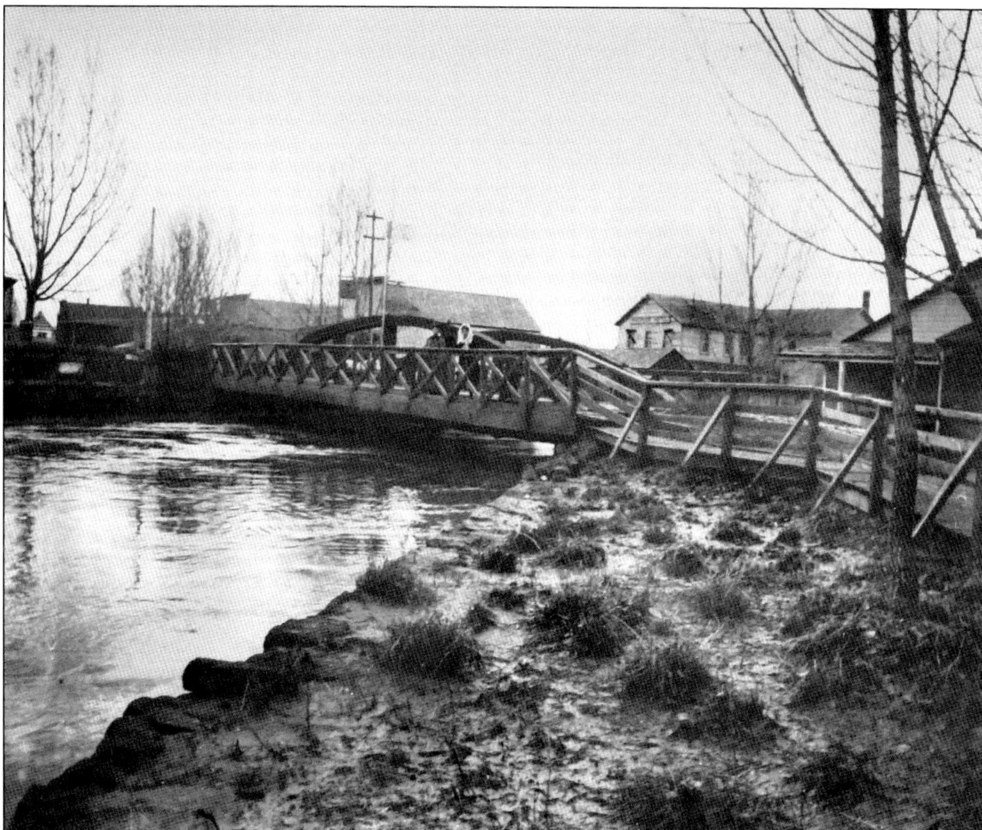

In 1859, Charles William Fuller laid claim to a small area of land on the banks of the Truckee River; there he built a bridge, about six feet downstream from the present-day Virginia Street Bridge in downtown Reno, declaring it Fuller's Crossing. In 1861, during the great Comstock Lode, Fuller was granted permission from the Nevada Territorial Legislature to collect a toll from travelers passing through. During later years, this area would come to be recognized as the ever-popular Riverwalk. (WA-07411.)

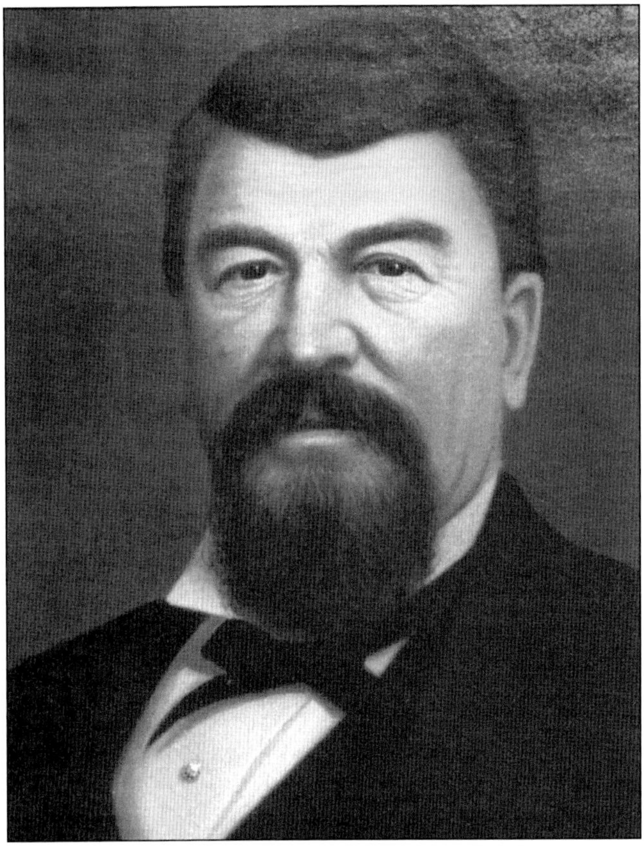

Annual flooding, caused by record snowfall in the Sierra Nevadas, repeatedly swept Fuller's bridge away. Fuller sold the bridge in 1860 to acquaintance and Honey Lake rancher Myron Charles Lake (pictured). Lake was a savvy businessman and, seeing the location's potential, constructed a much sturdier bridge. (BIO-L-5.)

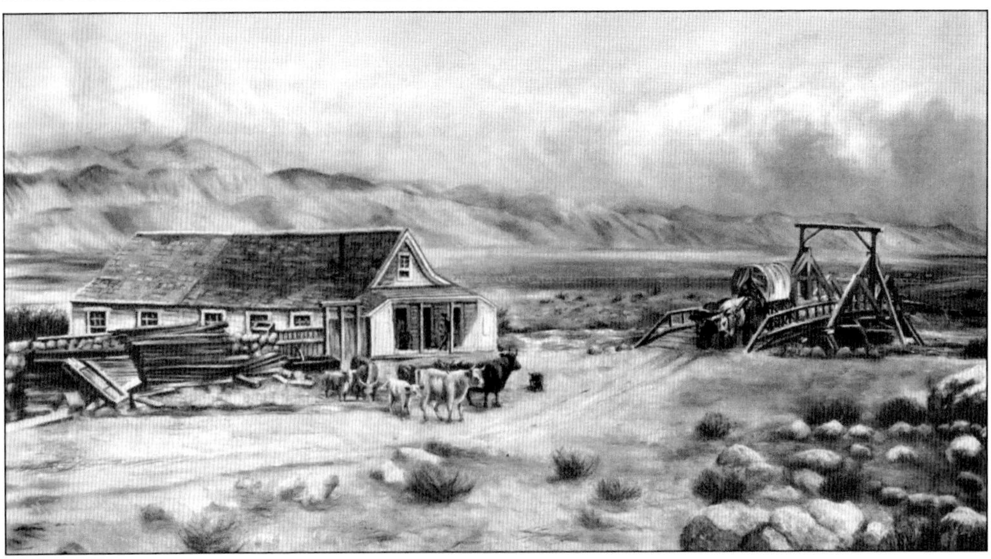

By 1861, Myron Lake had established a small hotel, catering to weary travelers and teamsters and offering meals for 50¢. The bridge was renamed Lake's Crossing and assisted in transporting tourists to the booming Virginia City and Carson City areas. This painting, by Nevada artist C.B. McClellan, depicts the location of Reno's beginnings and the modern-day Virginia Street Bridge. (WA-1282.)

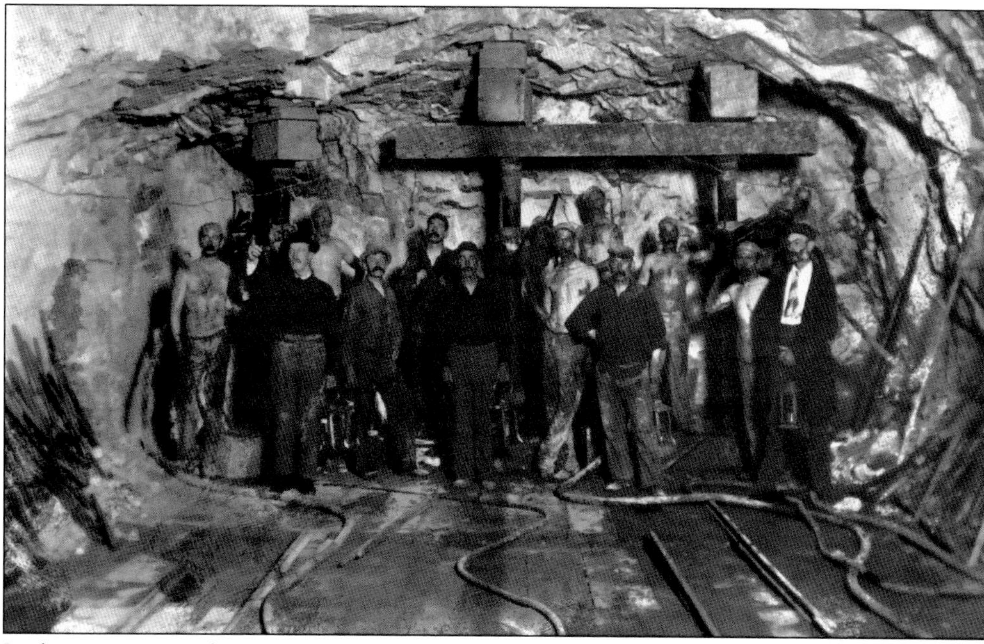

In the year prior to the creation of Fuller's Crossing, specks of silver and gold were discovered just 20 miles south at the peak of Six Mile Canyon (in present-day Virginia City, Nevada). Samples were reviewed by professional assayers and were found to contain levels of silver valued at $3,000 to the ton and levels of gold valued at $876 per ton. This marked the beginning of one of the richest silver strikes in North American history. The Comstock Lode, as it came to be known, rapidly accelerated the growth of the Truckee Meadows and brought with it an influx of settlers from surrounding areas, looking to stake their claim. A steady stream of suppliers and prospectors headed west, paying their toll to pass over Lake's Crossing on their way to the city of silver and gold. (UNRS-P1988-42-22, National Historical Society.)

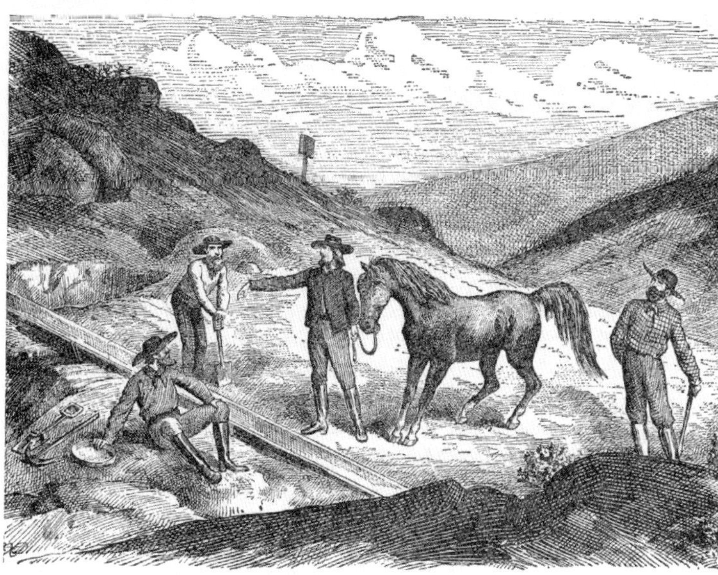

COMSTOCK DISCOVERING SILVER

Bridge and Hotel

AT FULLER'S CROSSING.

THE undersigned would respectfully inform the traveling public that he has purchased the hotel and bridge at Fuller's Crossing, on the Truckee river, and is now prepared to offer excellent accommodations to all who may favor him with their patronage. The house is large and roomy, and the table and bedding will be of the best quality. The road from the Northern Mines to Virginia and Carson cities is much nearer by this than by any other route.

Good stables are attached to the establishment, and a good supply of *Hay* and Grain is kept constantly on hand.

je29 3m M. C. LAKE.

For three months in 1861, Myron Lake published an advertisement in Virginia City's *Territorial Enterprise* announcing his purchase of the hotel and bridge that Charles Fuller previously built. Lake hoped to profit from the strategic location of the crossing, which was heavily traveled by people on their way from California to the booming Comstock.

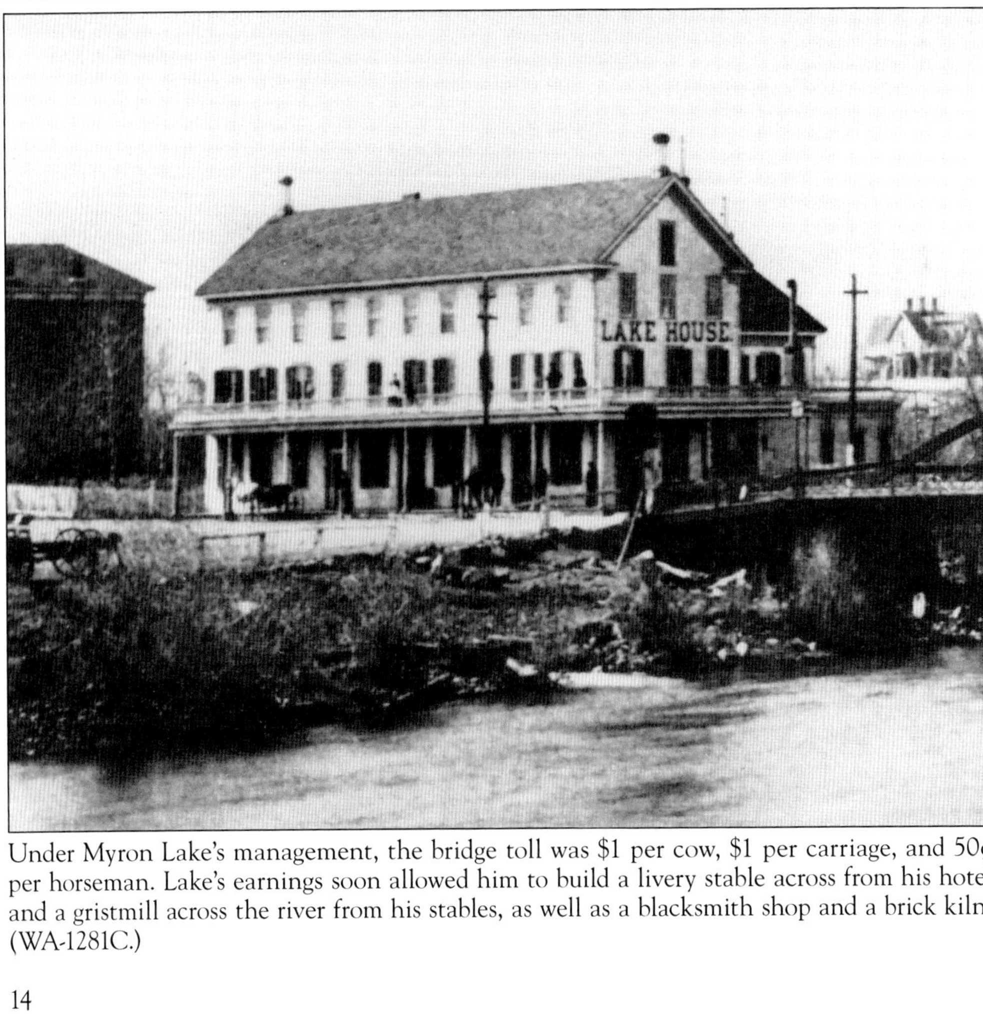

Under Myron Lake's management, the bridge toll was $1 per cow, $1 per carriage, and 50¢ per horseman. Lake's earnings soon allowed him to build a livery stable across from his hotel and a gristmill across the river from his stables, as well as a blacksmith shop and a brick kiln. (WA-1281C.)

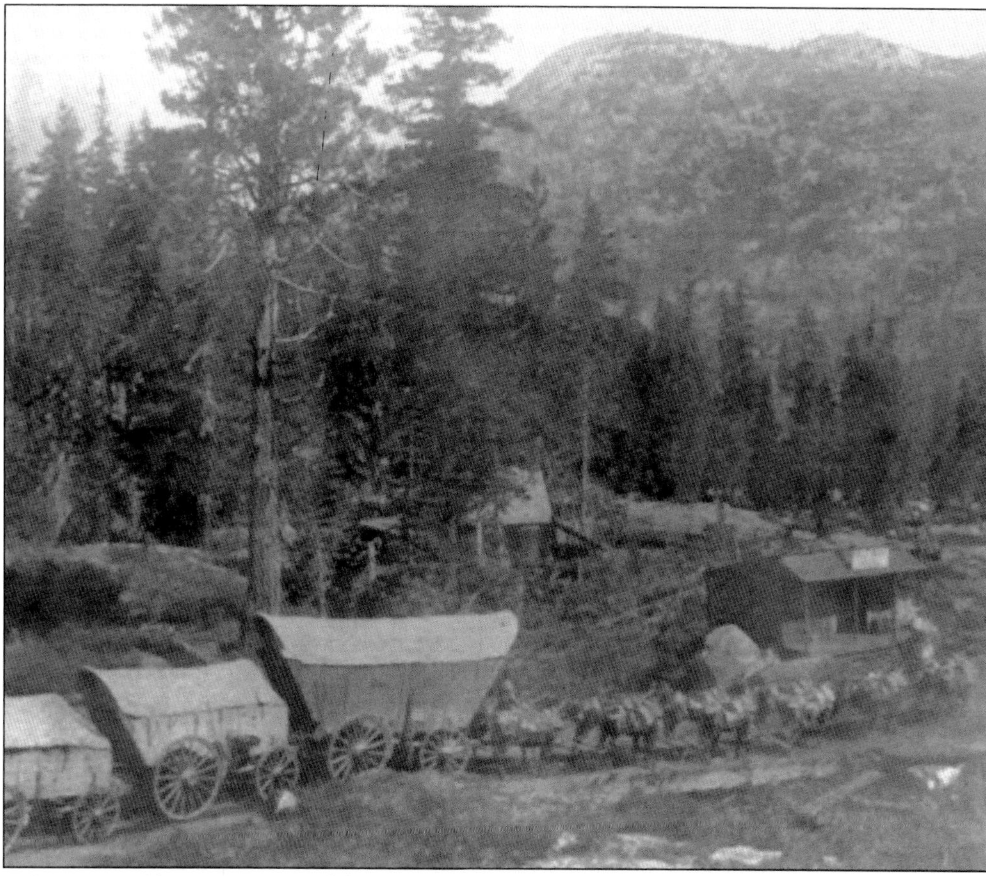

In January 1863, construction of the Central Pacific Railroad made its way east from Sacramento. Because of the difficulty of creating a route through the granite hills of the Sierra, it took nearly five years for the railroad to make its way towards Lake's Crossing. In 1868, the transcontinental railroad headed towards the Truckee Meadows. The big four of western railroading, Mark Hopkins, Collis P. Huntington, Leland Stanford, and Charles Crocker, were searching for an adequate town in western Nevada to serve as a depot. When the Central Pacific Railroad pushed its tracks into the Truckee Meadows, Myron Lake was waiting, eager to be part of the process. (LC-USZ62-27399, Nevada Historical Society.)

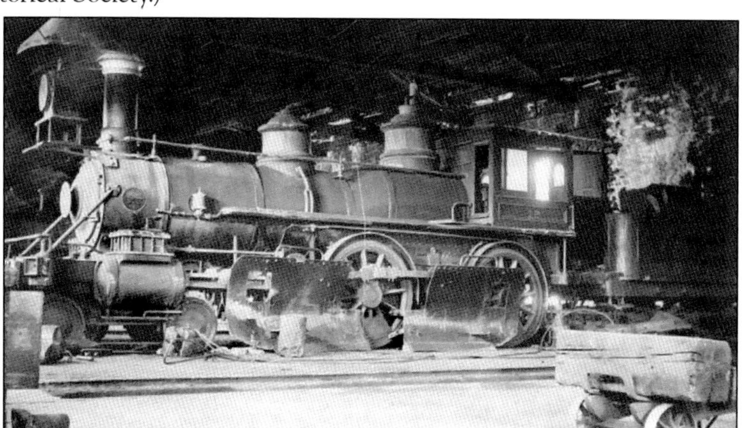

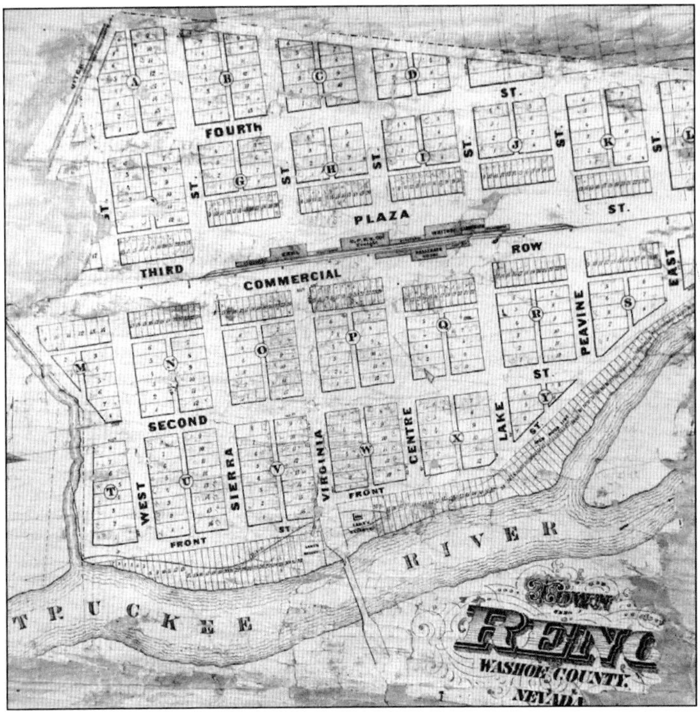

Myron Lake deeded 160 acres of his own property to serve as the primary township. He wanted to ensure that a train station would be built near Lake's Crossing. Charles Crocker surveyed the land and had it divided into 400 separate lots. In May 1868, the railroad held an auction in which only 70 lots were sold. The lots were sold for up to $1,000, with the first, located prominently on Commercial Row and Virginia Street, selling for $550. (WA-0138, 101RR.)

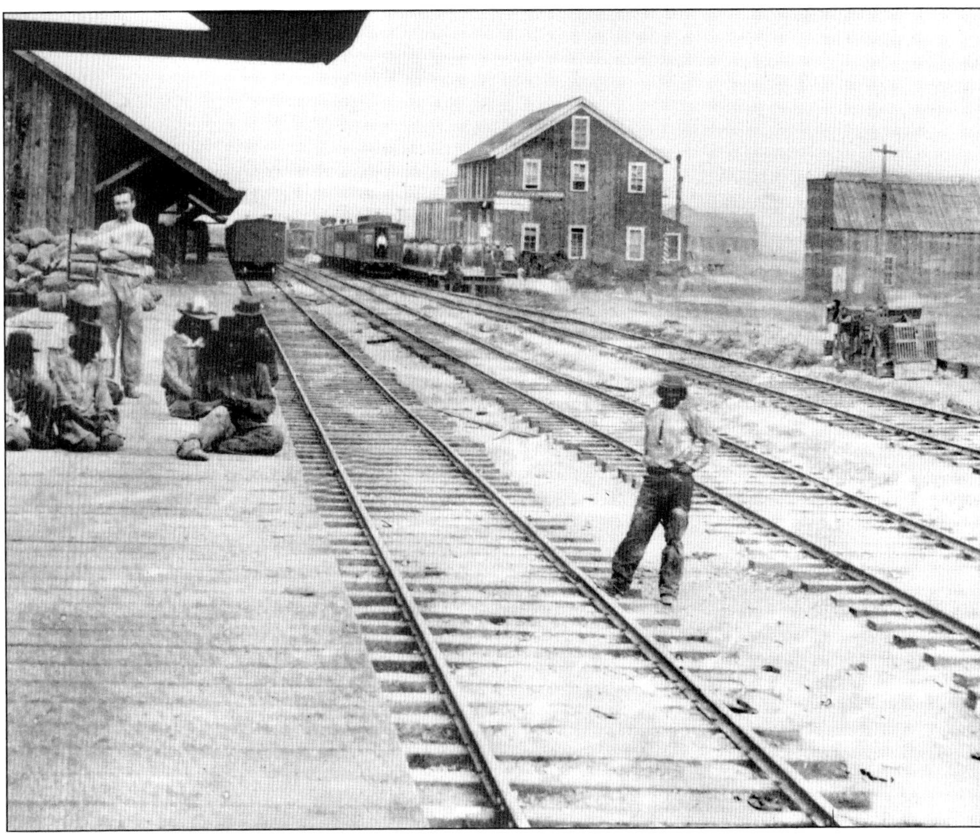

This 1868 San Francisco newspaper clipping announces Reno as the future railroad junction between the Overland Railroad and the future Virginia & Truckee Railroad (which would eventually transport individuals to the Virginia City mines). After news quickly spread about the auction of town lots, the area became populated with new travelers erecting makeshift homes, approximately 100 of which were constructed within a month's time. (WA-1307.)

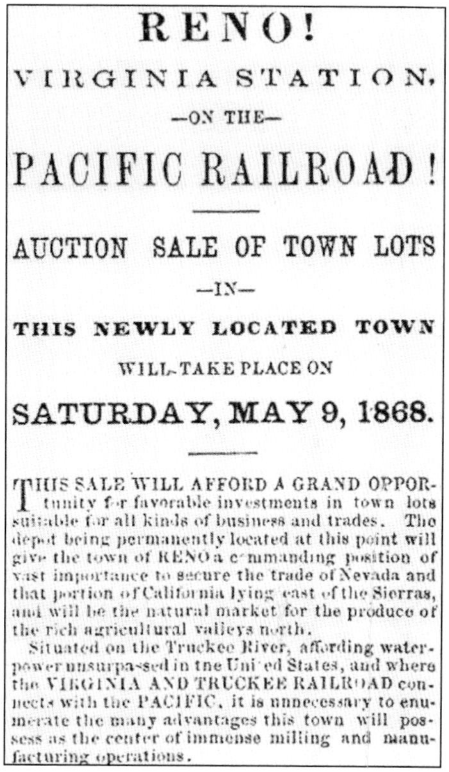

RENO!

VIRGINIA STATION,

—ON THE—

PACIFIC RAILROAD!

AUCTION SALE OF TOWN LOTS

—IN—

THIS NEWLY LOCATED TOWN

WILL TAKE PLACE ON

SATURDAY, MAY 9, 1868.

THIS SALE WILL AFFORD A GRAND OPPORTUNITY for favorable investments in town lots suitable for all kinds of business and trades. The depot being permanently located at this point will give the town of RENO a commanding position of vast importance to secure the trade of Nevada and that portion of California lying east of the Sierras, and will be the natural market for the produce of the rich agricultural valleys north.

Situated on the Truckee River, affording water-power unsurpassed in the United States, and where the VIRGINIA AND TRUCKEE RAILROAD connects with the PACIFIC, it is unnecessary to enumerate the many advantages this town will possess as the center of immense milling and manufacturing operations.

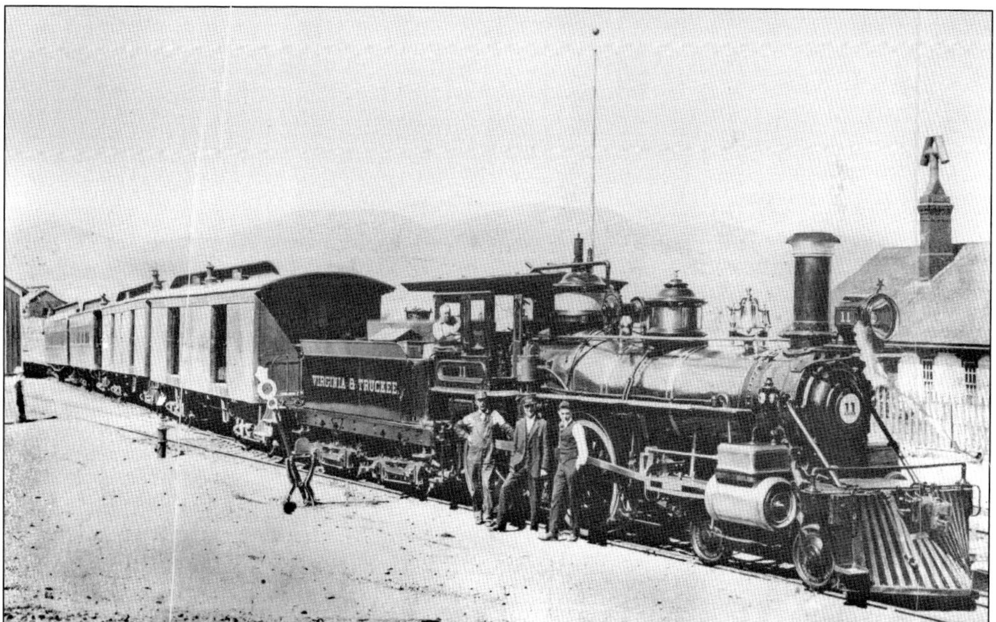

The railroad line to Reno was officially completed on June 19, 1869. Reno quickly became the epicenter for Nevada's agriculture, and, in the summer of 1872, completion of the Virginia & Truckee Railroad system allowed goods to be carried between Reno and Virginia City, ending the need for the local freight-wagon companies. (344RR.)

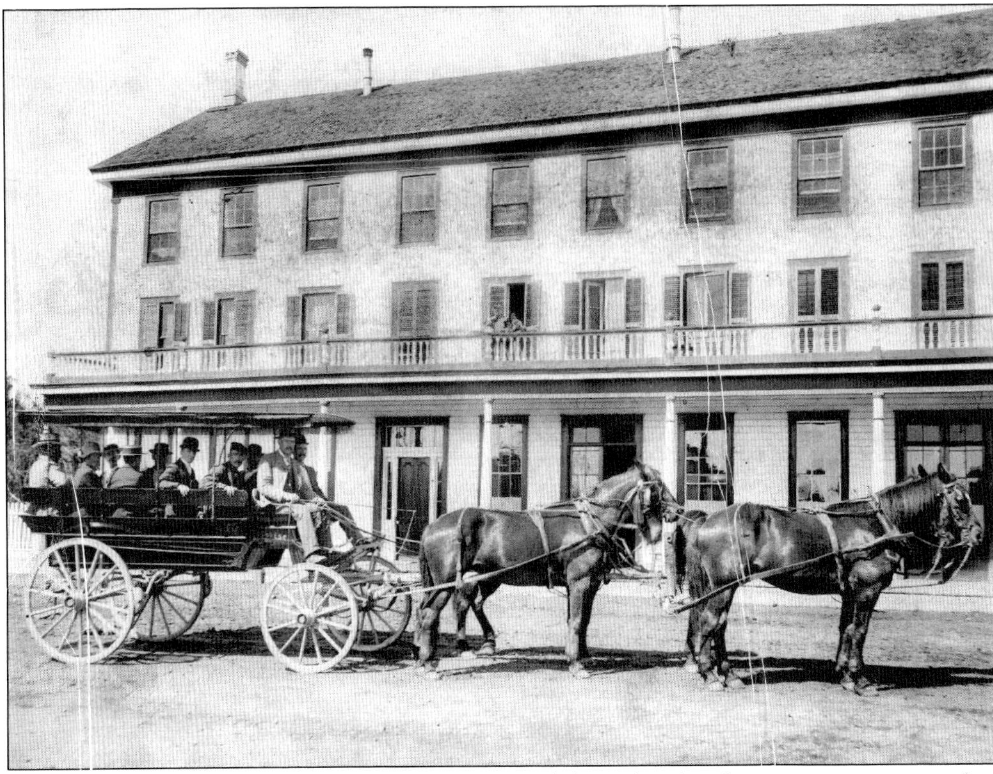

In 1869, Myron Lake rebuilt his lodge, creating a much larger hotel and an accompanying trading post. The hotel was renamed the Lake House and doubled as a temporary residence for Myron Lake and his wife, Jane. (WA-1491.)

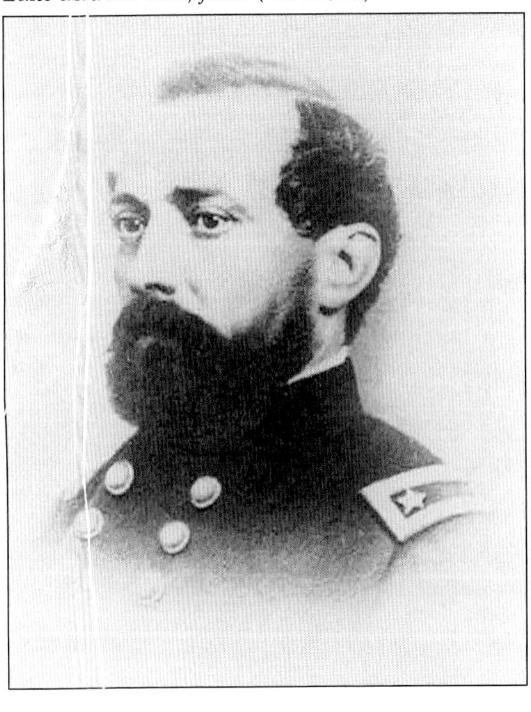

Many individuals, as well as the *Gold Hill Daily News*, temporarily referred to the new depot station as Argenta, meaning "Silver." The name was short lived, however, and the new settlement was ultimately called Reno in honor of Gen. Jesse Lee Reno (1823–1862, pictured), an officer in the Union army who was killed during the Civil War. (LC-USZ62-79466.)

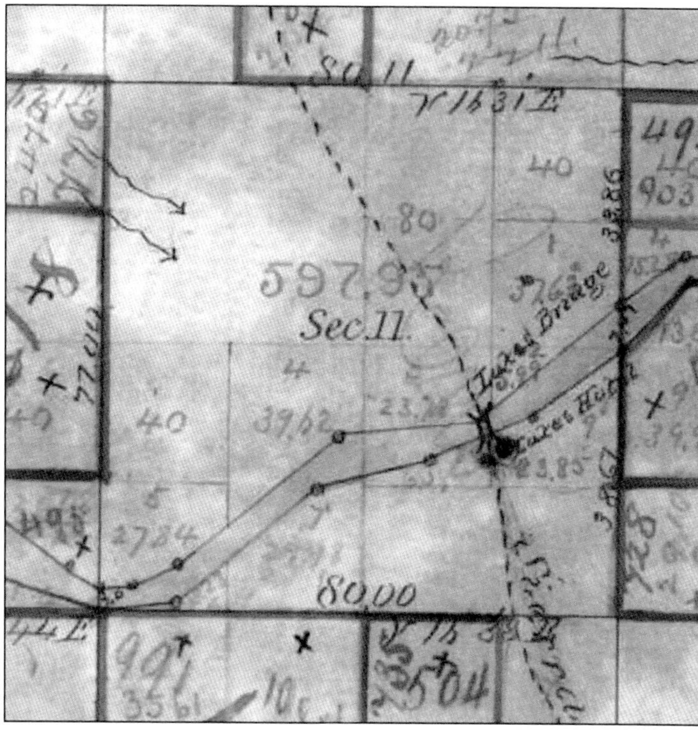

In the spring of 1871, the Nevada State Legislature approved the transfer of the county seat from Washoe City to Reno, where, in the previous year, the Virginia & Truckee Railroad had extended its tracks. This image shows the first 1868 plat of Reno on very old and worn vellum.

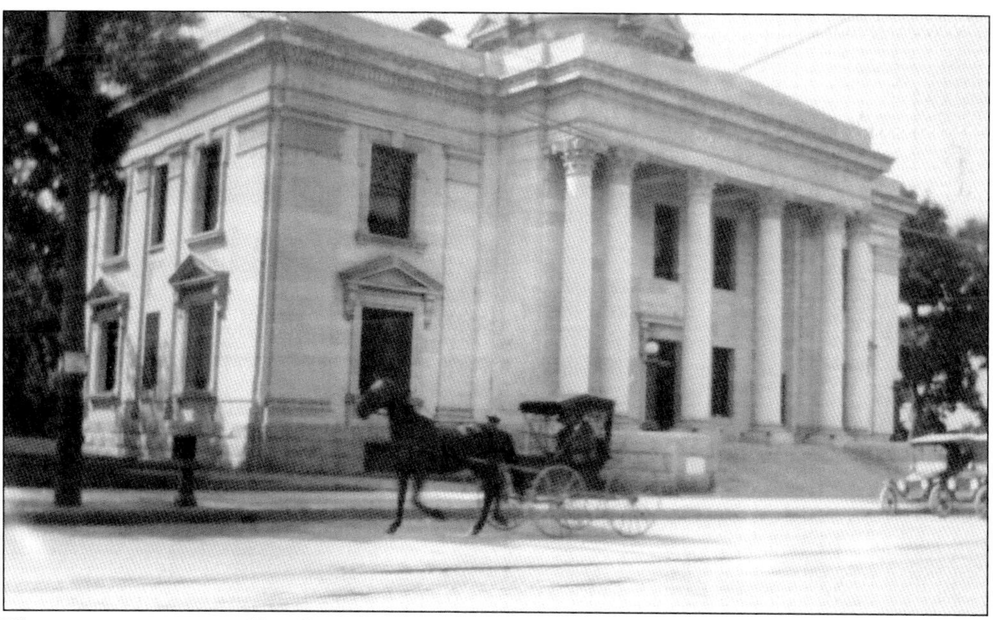

The county seat was officially moved to Reno on June 21, 1871. By July 1871, conversations progressed over the permanent location of the new courthouse. The County Commissioner's Office purchased one acre of land, on the south side of the river, from Myron Lake. Lake also agreed to provide $1,500 towards the construction of the new courthouse, in addition to supplying it with water and a public square. (UNRS-P1992-01-1194.)

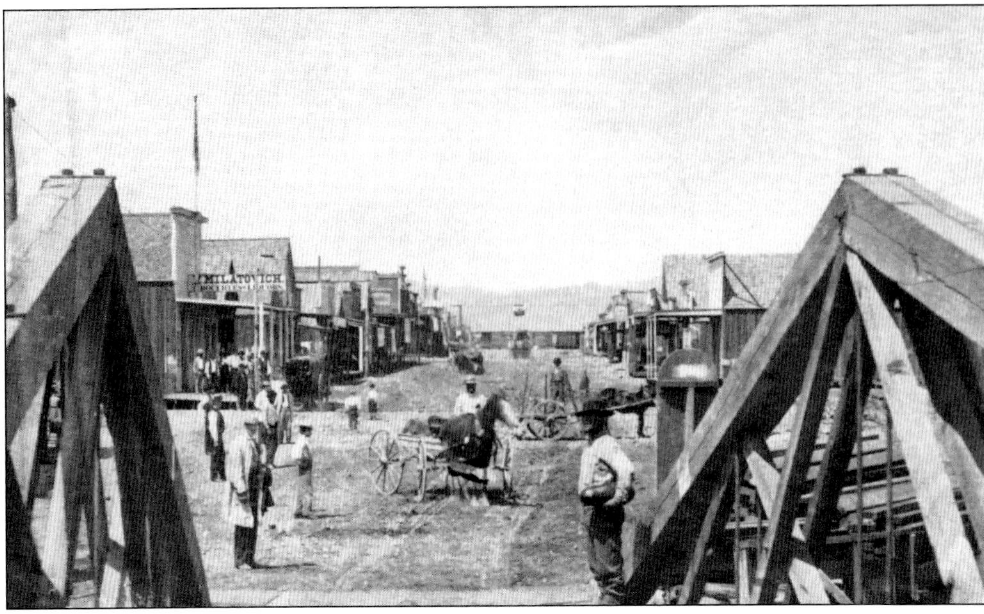

Reno played an important role as a primary transfer point between the transcontinental railroad and the Comstock Lode. In addition to the new courthouse and the depot, Virginia Street and Commercial Row had grown to include grocery stores, saloons, churches, schools, a quartz mill, a soap factory, flourmills, livery stables, a brewery, and a variety of other quaint shops necessary to support the newly developed town. By 1880, over 100 businesses, including 15 saloons, 10 hotels, 4 groceries, 6 different meat markets, and 5 churches had been established. (WA-02089, WA-07535.)

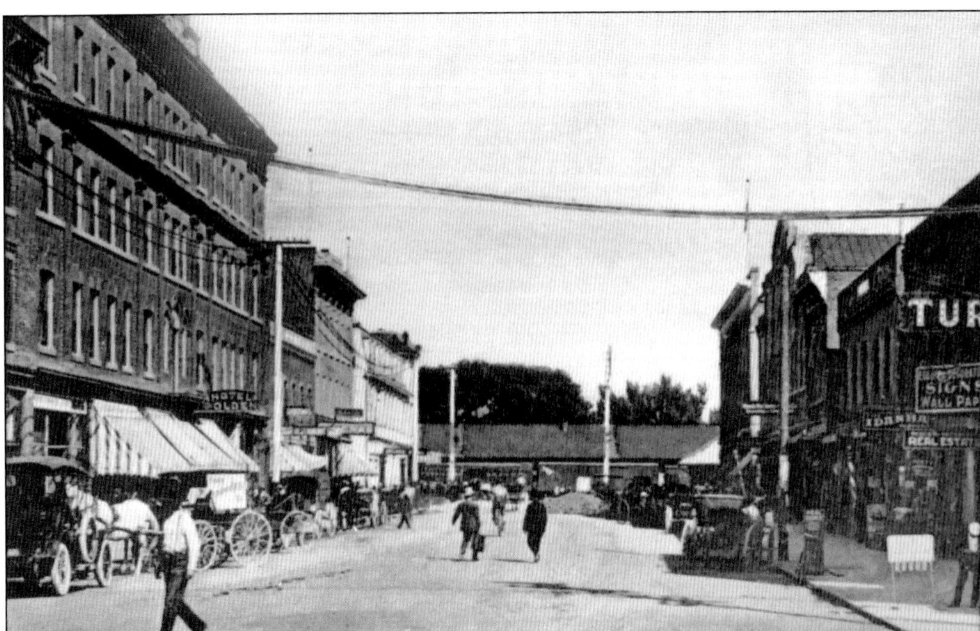

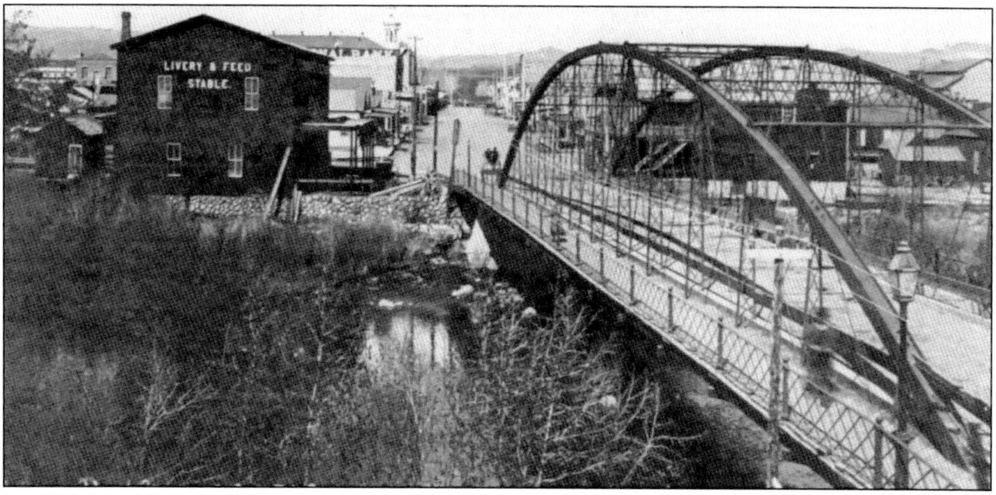

In 1872, the Virginia & Truckee Railroad constructed a second bridge, made of iron, across the river from Myron Lake's toll bridge. Lake, being unhappy with the development of another bridge, would go so far as to physically block any individual passing by. Later that year, the Nevada legislature revoked Lake's toll-bridge service, making all bridges free for public use. In 1877, the legislature replaced Lake's worn, wooden bridge with a new tied-arch bridge. In that same year, the primary road that crossed Lake's bridge was renamed Virginia Street, reflecting the heavy traffic headed towards the gold rush in Virginia City. West of Virginia Street, another crossing point was designated Sierra Street after the traffic arriving from the Sierra Valleys. (Courtesy of VSA arts of Nevada, Lake Mansion Collection.)

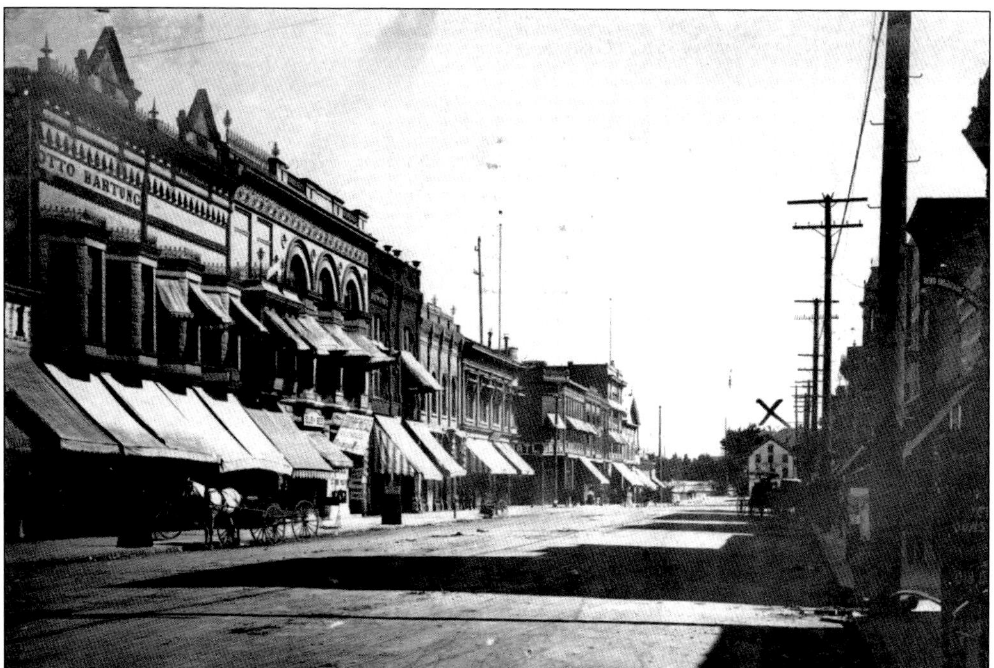

This postcard shows an early and desolate Virginia Street business block with horses and wagons in the street; the old Riverside Hotel is in the background. It was postmarked September 6, 1906. (Dave Stafford Collection.)

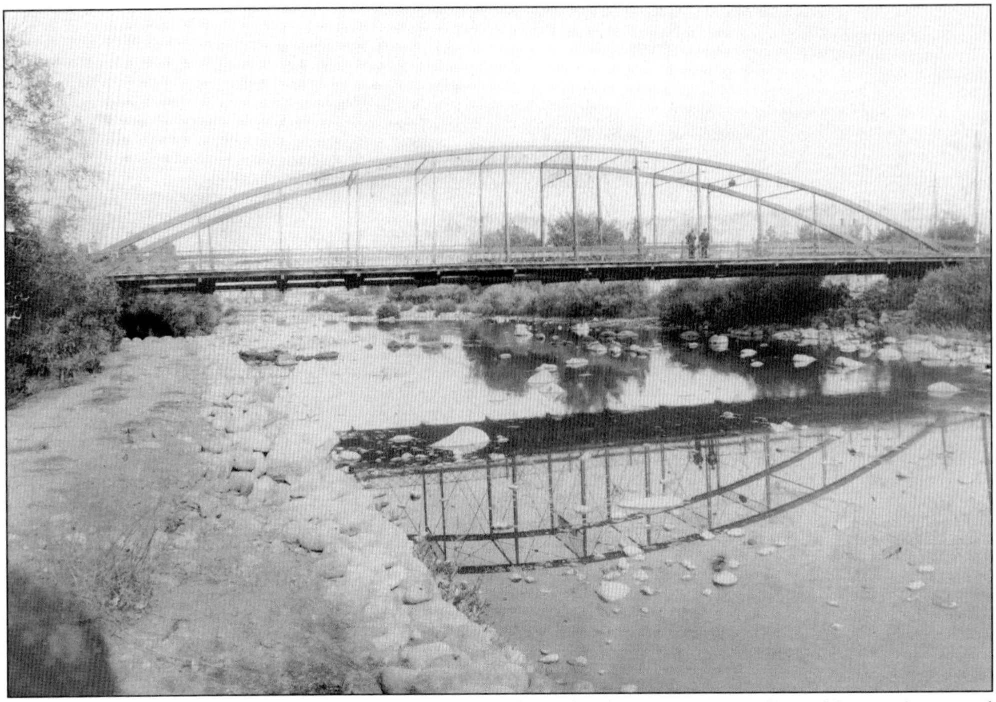

In 1905, the iron bridge was relocated to Rock Boulevard, where it remained until being destroyed by flooding in 1955. Myron Lake's bridge was soon replaced with a concrete bridge designed by San Francisco architect John B. Leonard. Leonard's Beaux-Arts design, which employed concrete that was scored to resemble masonry, was unusual in Nevada. This bridge, the fifth to be built in downtown Reno, was constructed by the Cotton Brothers and Company of Oakland, California. The Virginia Street Bridge is the oldest functioning bridge in Reno, and was one of the first reinforced concrete bridges in Nevada. (WA-04021, WA-1931.)

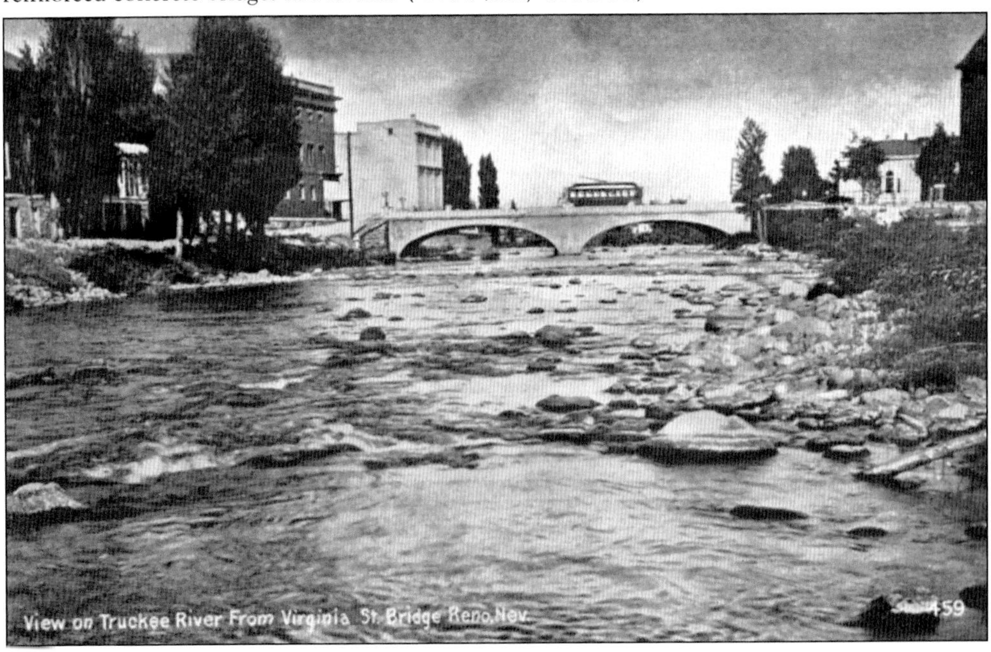

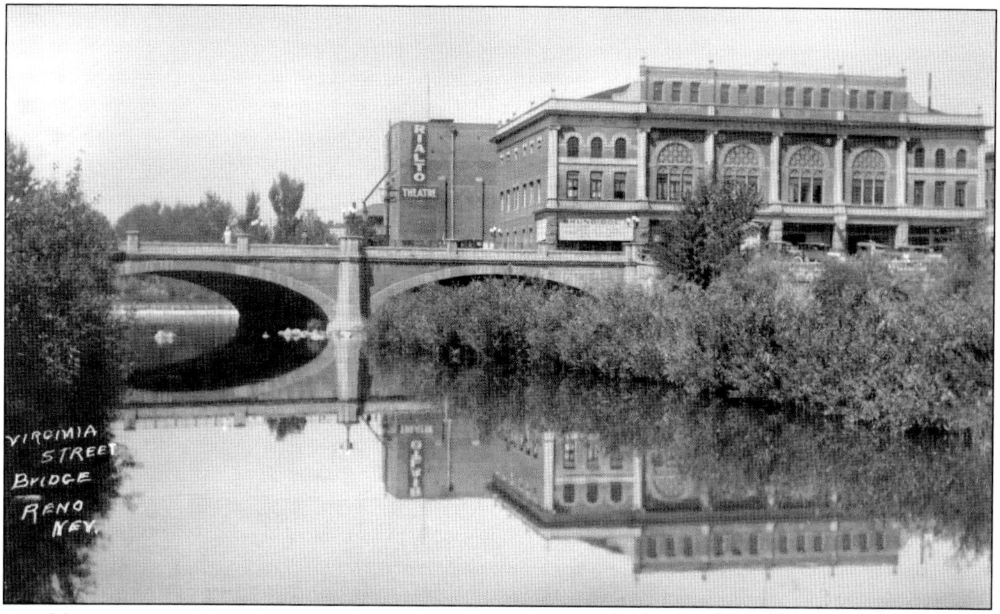

In addition to marking the very place where Reno began, the bridge has also been celebrated in folklore since the time of its construction. The bridge is often referred to as the "Wedding Ring Bridge" or the "Bridge of Sighs." It gained national recognition for its appearance in the 1961 film *The Misfits*, in which a character played by Marilyn Monroe tosses her wedding ring into the Truckee River. In 2002 and 2006, the bridge was listed as one of the 11 most endangered historic places in Nevada by a historic preservation organization in partnership with the University of Nevada, Las Vegas. (WA-3999, LC-198722.)

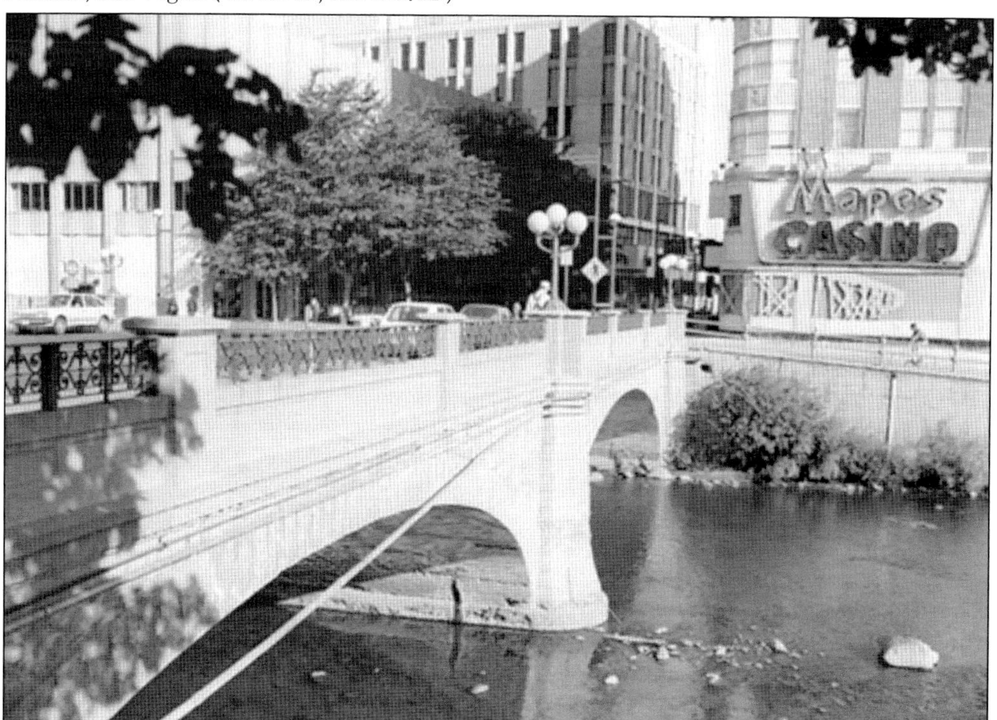

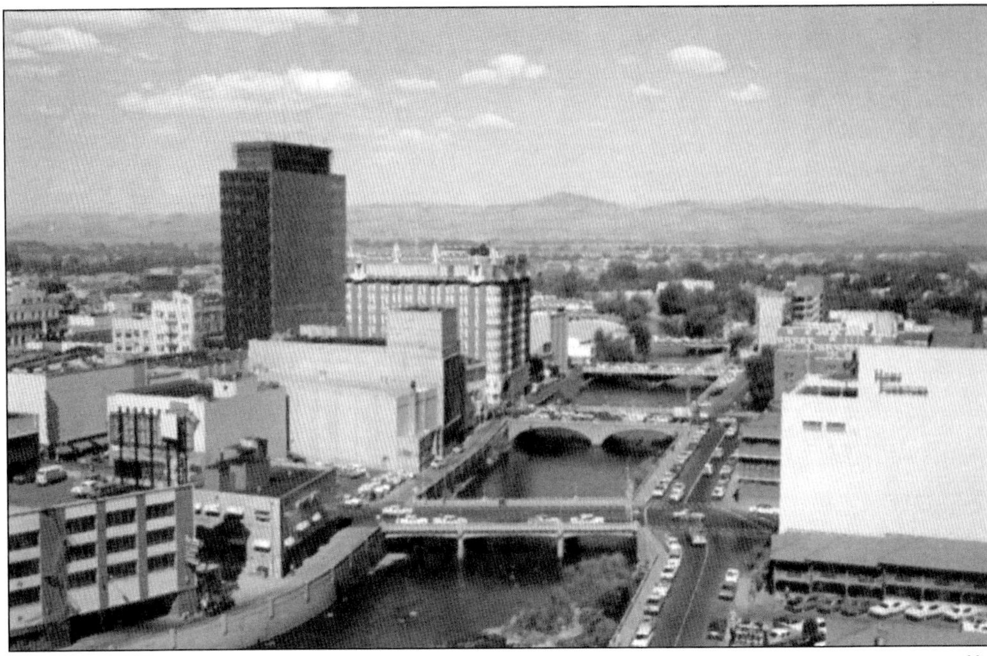

Downtown Reno's Riverwalk consists of three main bridges that allow for continuous traffic flow over the Truckee River into downtown Reno. The Lake Bridge is toward the east, where the original Reno arch now resides, along with the National Automobile Museum. The second (and most-used) bridge is the Virginia Street Bridge, near the Riverside Hotel, and the third is on Sierra Street, next to modern day Wingfield Park. Within the park there are two smaller footbridges, the more popular of which connects the park to the West Street Plaza on First Street. The photograph above is a view of all three main bridges, and the image below shows the Sierra Street Bridge. (UNRS-P1999-12-4, WA-10685.)

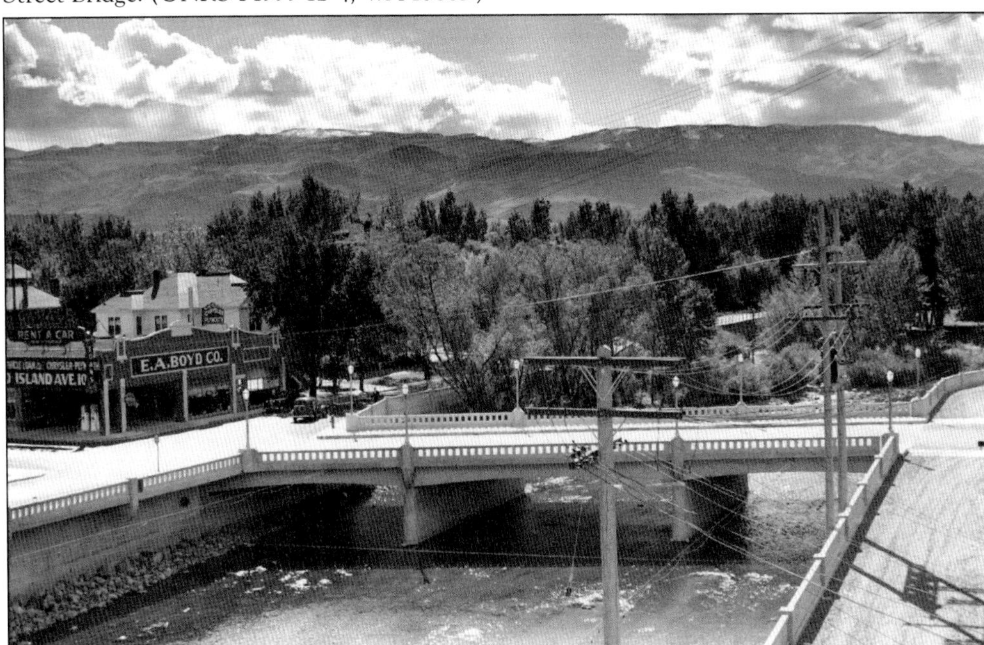

Two

FAITH, EDUCATION, AND CLUBS

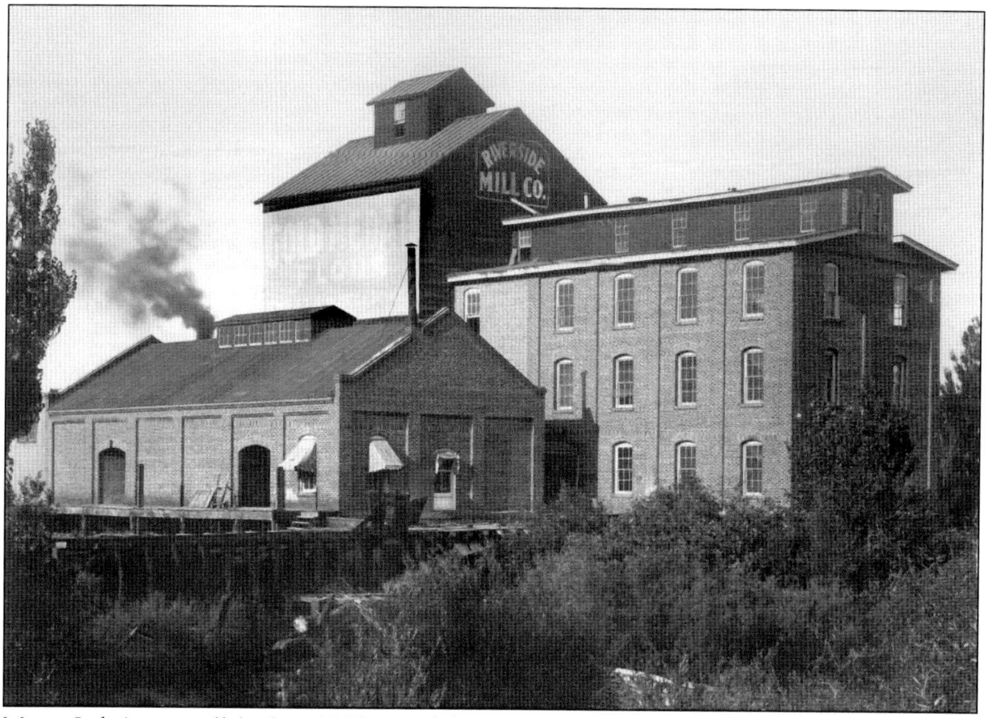

Myron Lake's gristmill, built in 1865, served the community as a multipurpose building, providing additional lodging for the community and a barroom operated by W.B. Whittemore. Located on the corner of First and Virginia Streets, the facility's basement served as the temporary site for Reno's first school, called the Alhambra. (WA-1719.)

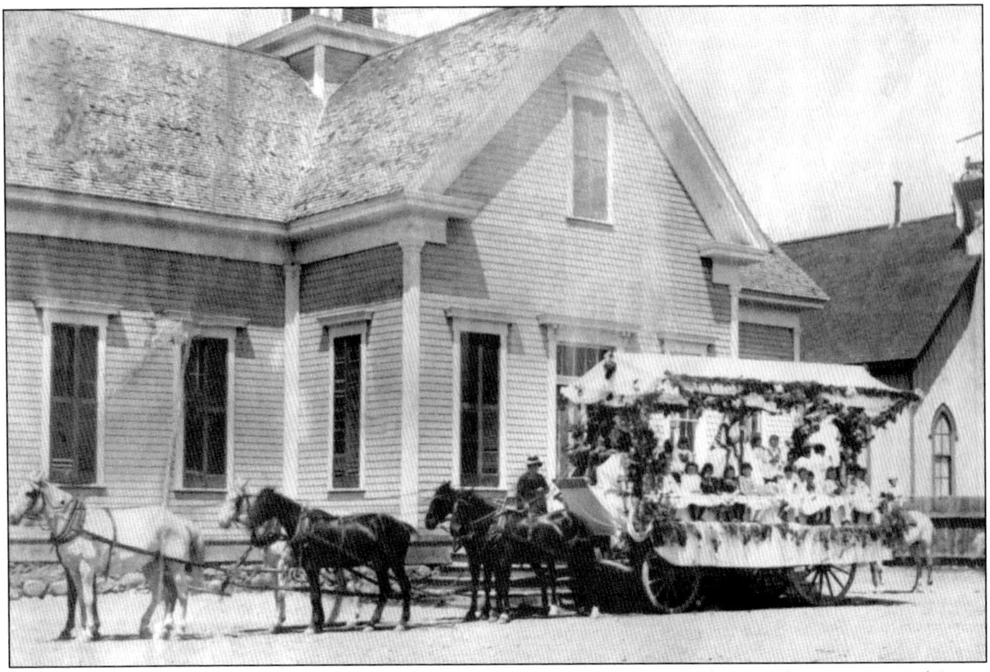

The Alhambra School was run by Mary Kirwan, and the cost of a basic education was $5 per student, with additional fees for French lessons. In 1869, a proper schoolhouse (the Riverside School) was erected on First and Sierra Streets. The building also served as a temporary church for some of the religious organizations in the area. The school grew so rapidly that an addition was constructed in 1877, and another in 1878. Due to Reno's growing population, a larger school, called Central School, was built near Arlington Avenue and Fourth Street. (Both, Nevada Historical Society.)

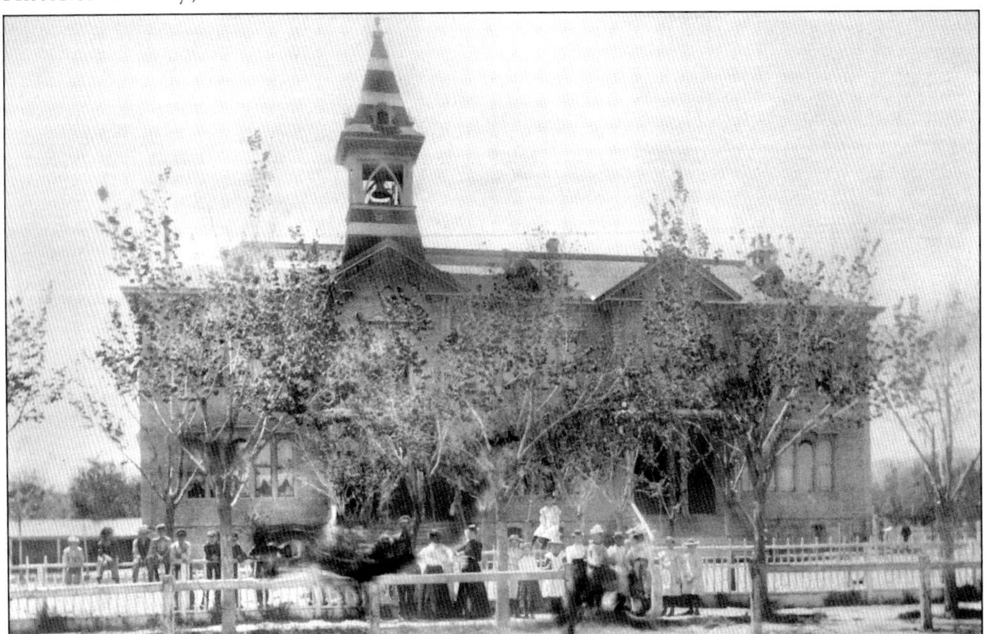

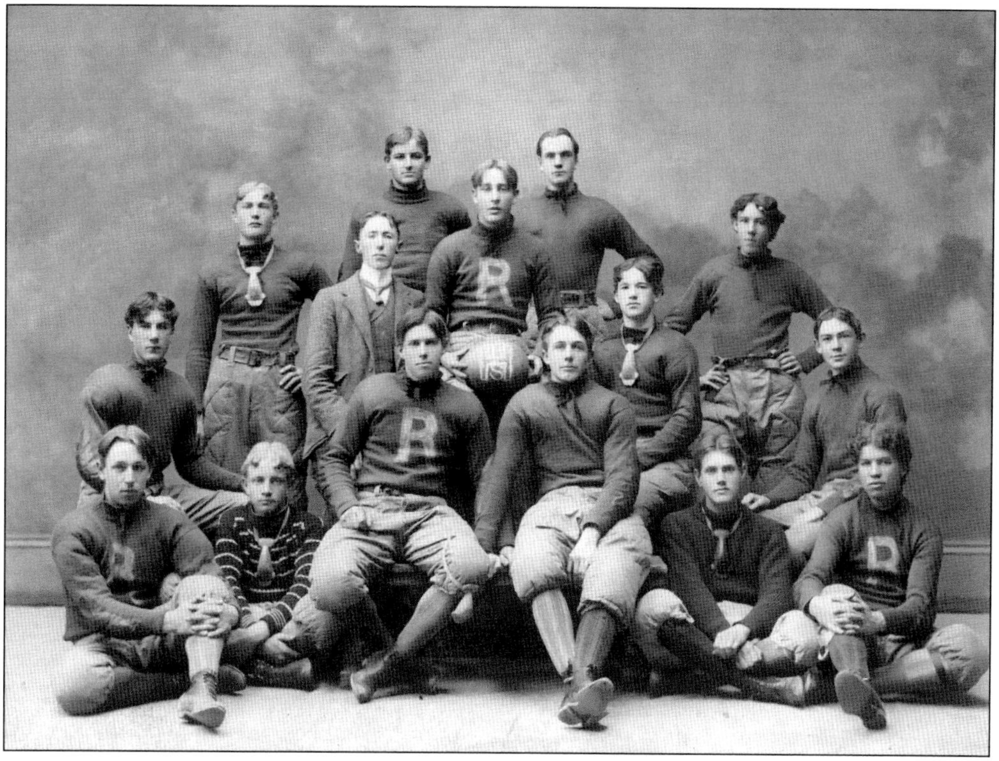

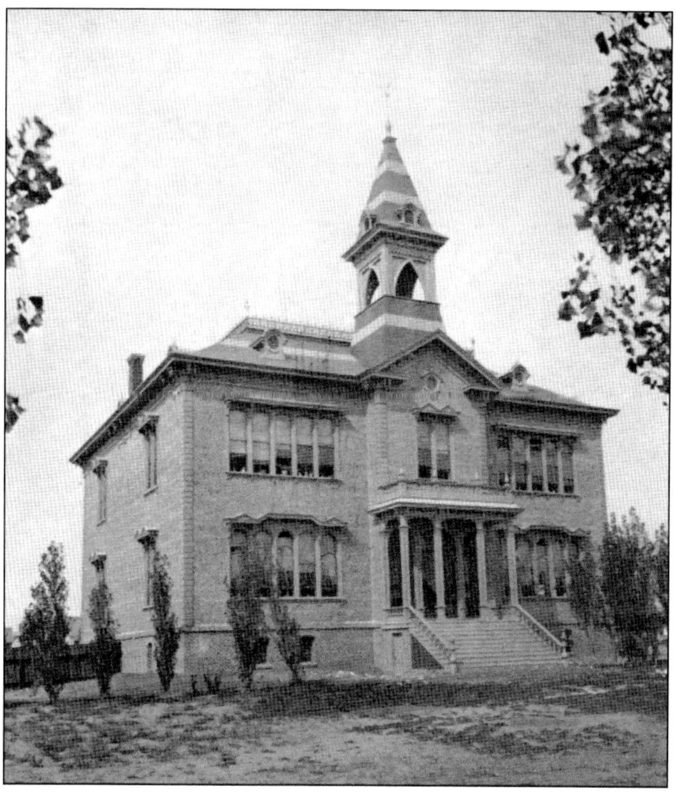

In 1879, the Central School was renamed Reno High School. In 1910, its main building was destroyed by a fire in the chemistry lab. The school was rebuilt in 1912 in downtown Reno, at the site now occupied by the Belvedere. The architecture of the 1912 construction closely resembles that of other schools in the area, such as McKinley Park School on Riverside Drive. In 1951, Reno High moved to its current location on Booth and Foster Streets, south of the Truckee River and Idlewild Park. The present-day campus is less than 200 yards from the Truckee River. (ED-314, ED-321.)

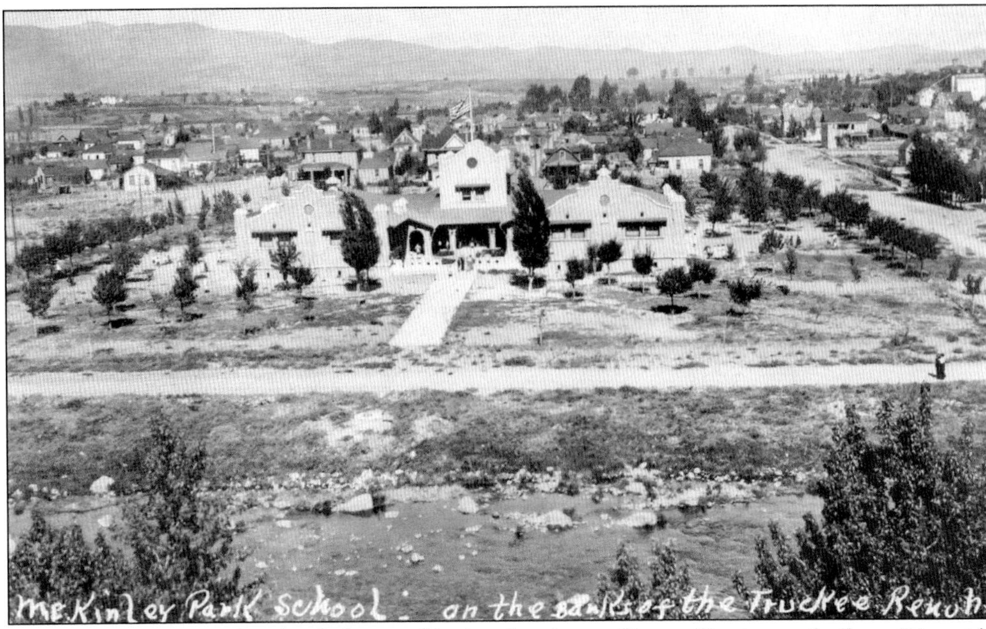

In 1909, McKinley Park School, designed by local architect George Ferris, was built on Riverside Drive overlooking the Truckee River. It was one of four different, single-story Mission Revival–style schools, known as the "Spanish Quartet," that were designed by Ferris. The building has undergone some rehabilitation and now serves as the City of Reno's Arts and Culture Center. (WA-1976.)

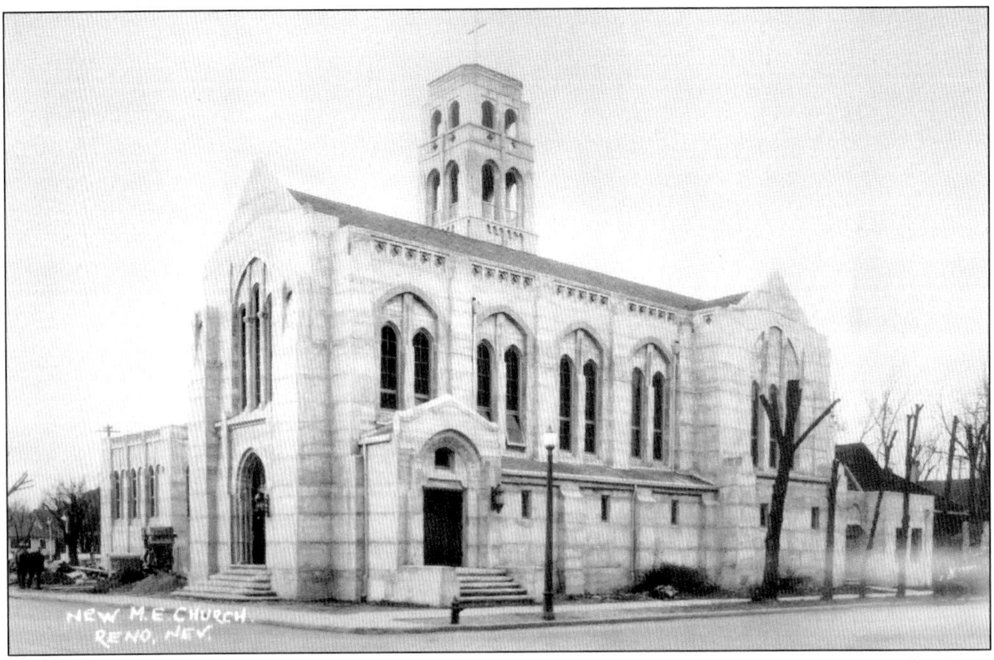

Methodist missionaries were among the first trailblazers in the Reno area. In 1870, the First Congregational Church of Reno was organized by Rev. A.F. Hitchcock inside the Riverside School on Sierra Street. Services were held there for two years until the congregation and the fraternal group the Odd Fellows built a new church on First and Second Streets, where the present-day Reno First United Methodist Church still stands. (WA-2805.)

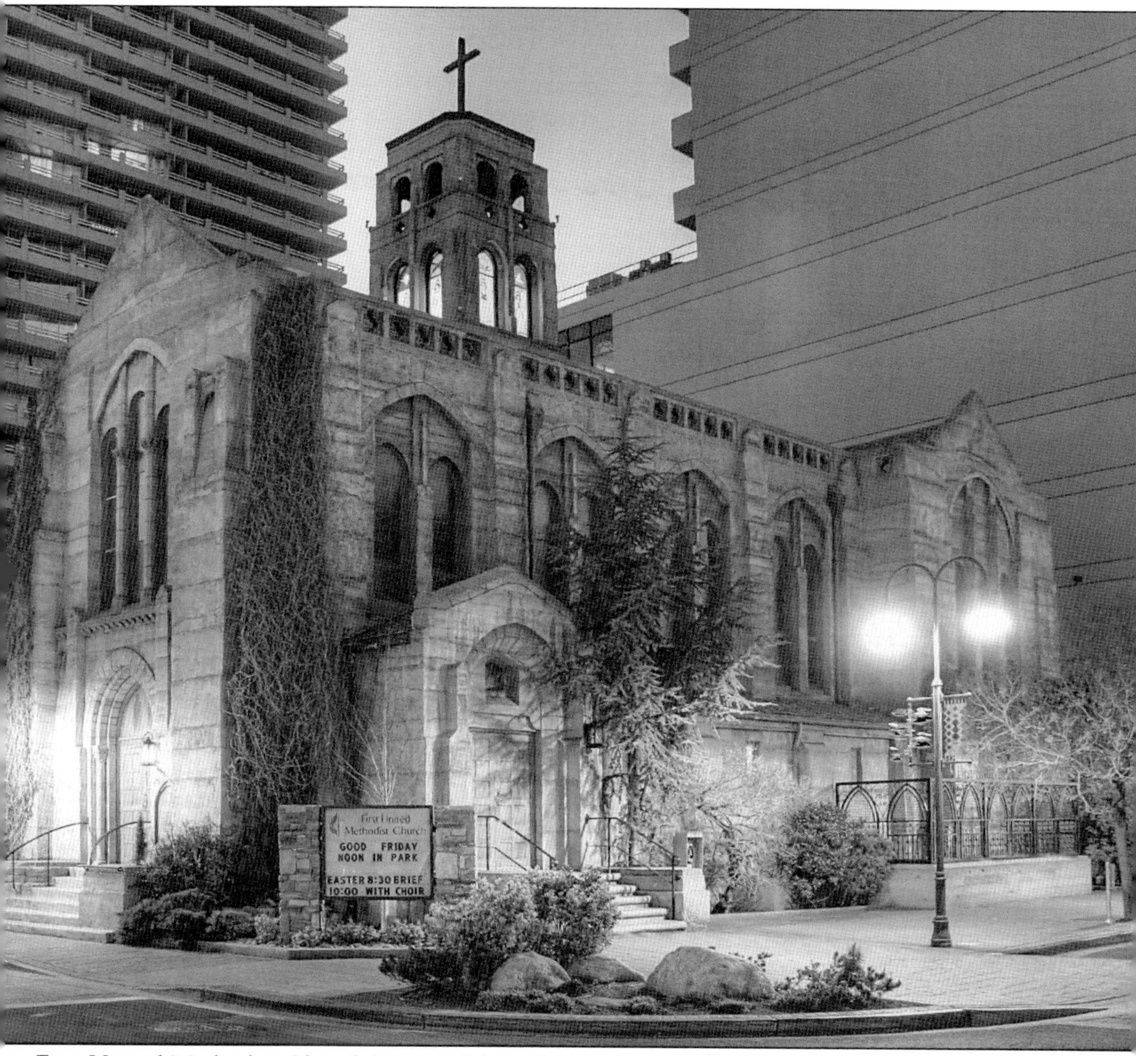

First United Methodist Church is one of the oldest remaining churches in Reno. In 1871, the first church was erected and dedicated between First and Second Streets. In the early 1900s, the original wood-framed church was moved to the back of the lot, and a new brick building was added. In 1925, plans for a new church were created, and the church was dedicated in December of the following year. The sanctuary and parish house were remodeled in 1943, according to the designs of prominent local architect Edward Parsons. (Courtesy of the First United Methodist Church.)

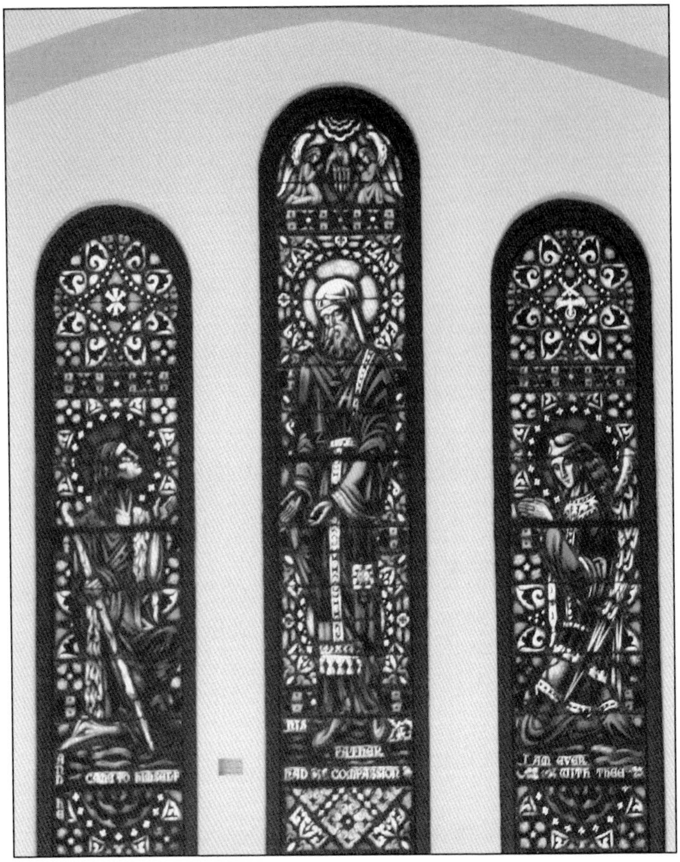

On July 15, 1942, Harold Cummings, of the Cummings Architectural Glass and Interior Design Studios in Sacramento, California, was contacted by Rev. Fredric Hewes Busher regarding the creation of stained glass window for the First United Methodist Church of Reno. The initial sketches were composed by Hilda Sach, a well-known designer of stained glass. The windows were hand blown and designed in traditional Gothic stone tracery. The most prominent of the three windows pictured here features the Holy Trinity. The others depict the Christian graces and the Gospel writers. Also pictured is the Holy Family window, located at the front of the church. (Courtesy of the First United Methodist Church.)

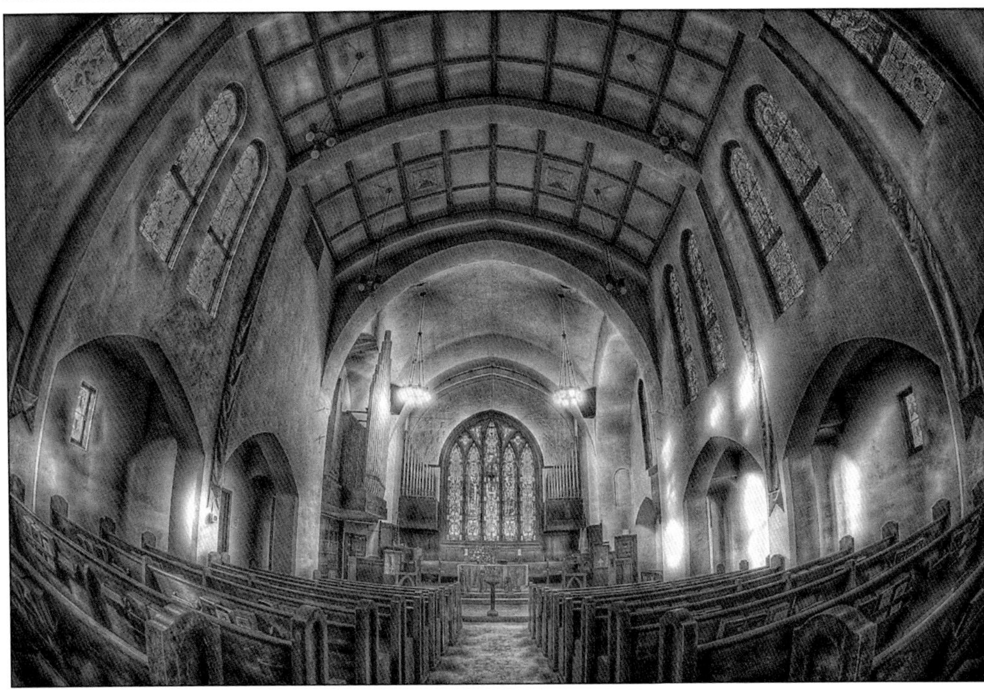

On October 16, 1870, Trinity Episcopal held its first service inside a small school on First Street. In 1873, Bishop Whitaker organized the Trinity Church Mission and called for construction of a new building. (Whitaker was also well known for the 1876 establishment of the Whitaker School for Girls, which offered classes in art, music, and science.) The congregation would temporarily hold services inside the Hall of Justice, originally located at the corner of Sierra and Second Streets in downtown Reno. The church was opened in August 1875 and narrowly escaped a devastating fire in 1879. In 1923, Trinity Church moved to the south bank of the Truckee River, along Island Avenue. The initial design of the church included a bell tower and cathedral, but the plans were soon abandoned. (Right, courtesy of Trinity Episcopal Church; below, LC-DIG-GGBAIN-05652)

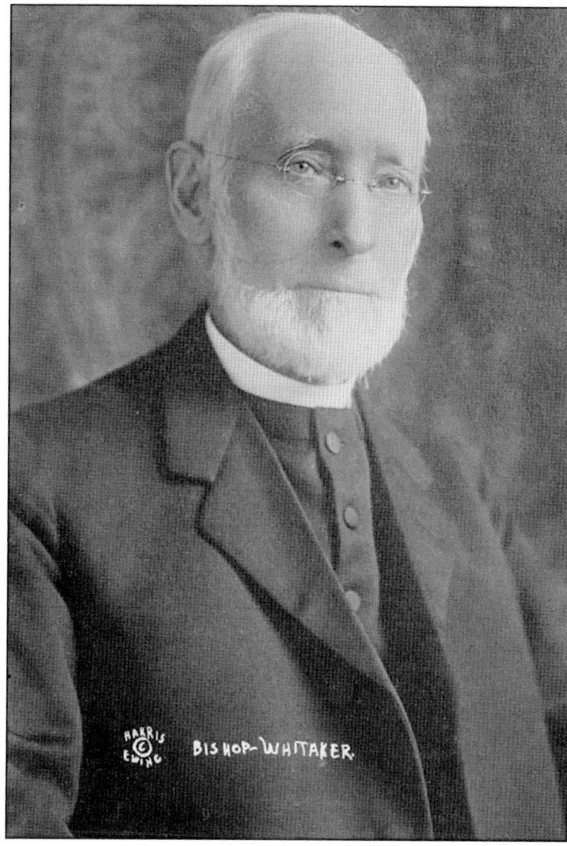

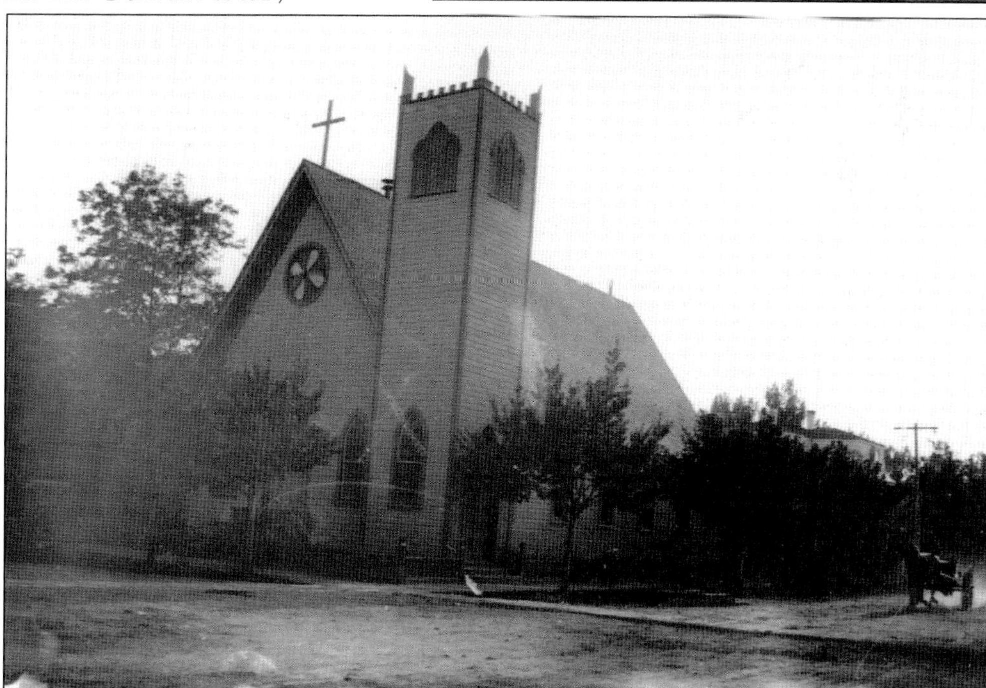

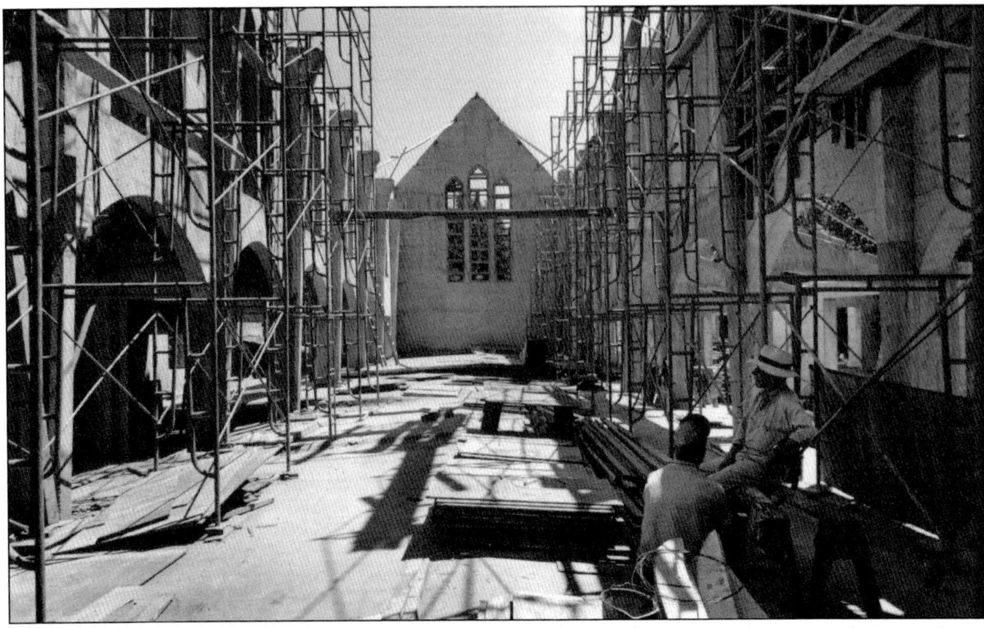

The current church building was constructed in 1948, over the preexisting crypt (often referred to as the "Potato Cellar." The upper church is designed in a modified English Gothic architecture. It was common practice in the early 1920s to excavate and worship in the basement of a building until enough funds could be raised to move the church aboveground. The building's design was one of four different architectural plans by Frederic J. DeLongchamps. By 1859, when Trinity Episcopal Church completed construction, it housed 686 communicants and 384 Sunday school pupils. After a devastating flood in 1955, the parish had to rebuild; Trinity Episcopal Church is currently located on Island Avenue in downtown Reno. (Courtesy of Trinity Episcopal Church.)

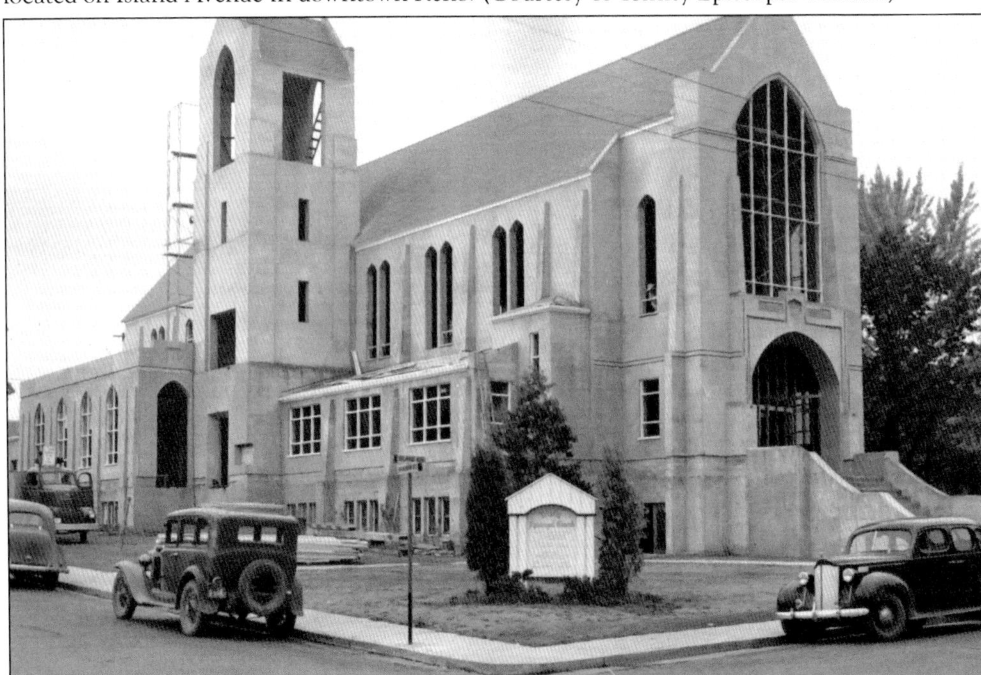

In 1875, Rev. C.L. Fisher was chosen as the missionary pastor to organize the first Reno Baptist Church. For a short time, services were held inside the old Opera House, located on Virginia Street in downtown Reno. At the time the Opera House was owned by the McGintley family. The church soon secured land on Second Street, between Sierra and West Streets. (WA-01763.)

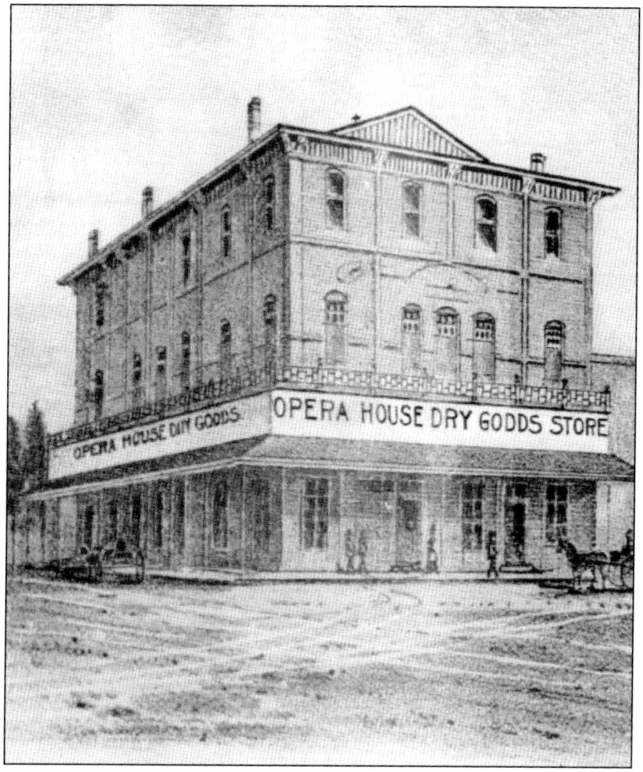

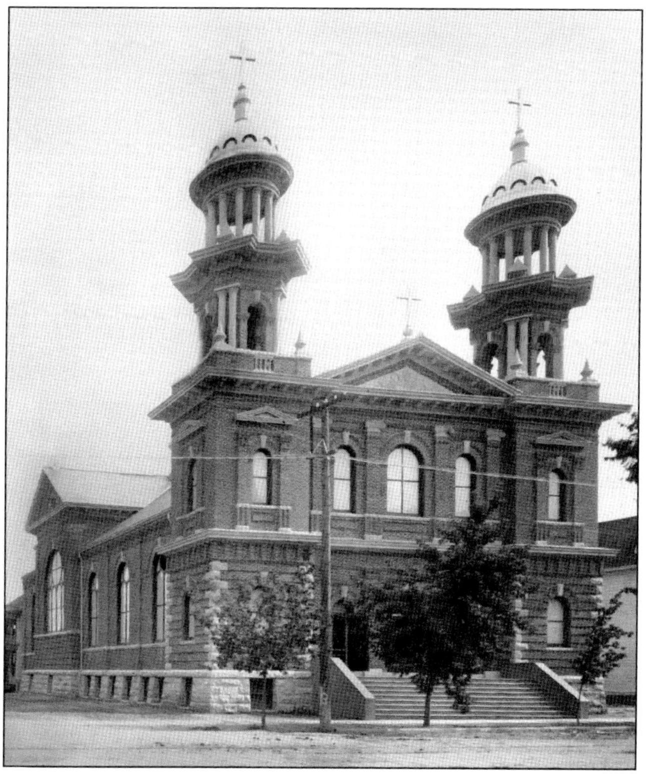

In June 1881, the Reverend Winfield Scott, DD, became pastor, and the new church was completed under his leadership. The building was destroyed by fire in July 1889, and both the courthouse and the Episcopal church building temporarily housed services. The cornerstone of the new Baptist church, which still stands today, was laid in 1926. (WA-09757.)

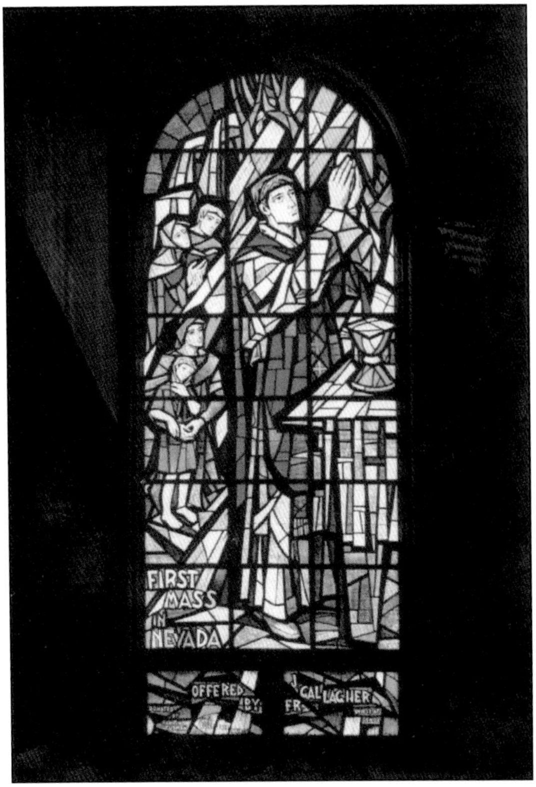

A rise in Reno's Catholic population created a need for a larger church. The diocese purchased the Sol Levy home at the corner of Second and Chestnut Streets (Arlington Avenue) for $10,000. On May 21, 1906, the Cathedral for Saint Thomas Aquinas laid its cornerstone; it was officially dedicated in 1908. (WA-07575.)

Pictured below, the First Church of Christ Scientist, located on Riverside Drive, overlooks the Truckee River in downtown Reno. In 1938, Anna Frandsen Loomis, a wealthy local Christian Scientist, hired Paul Revere Williams (the first African American member of the American Institute of Architects) to construct the historic Neoclassical Revival–style building. (LC-19661R.)

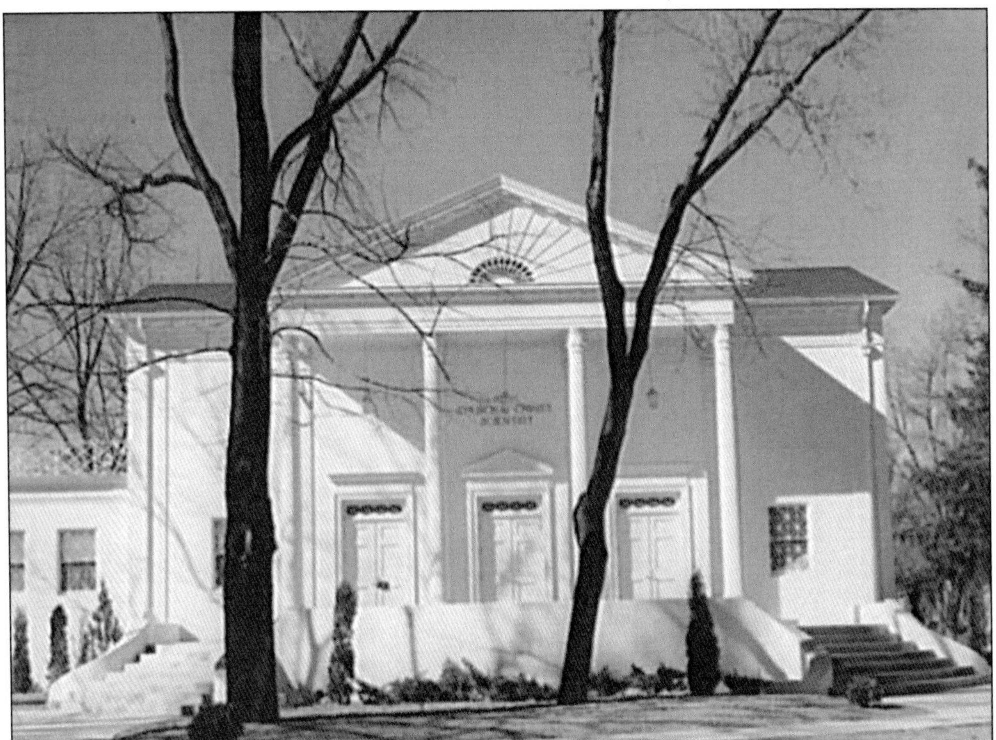

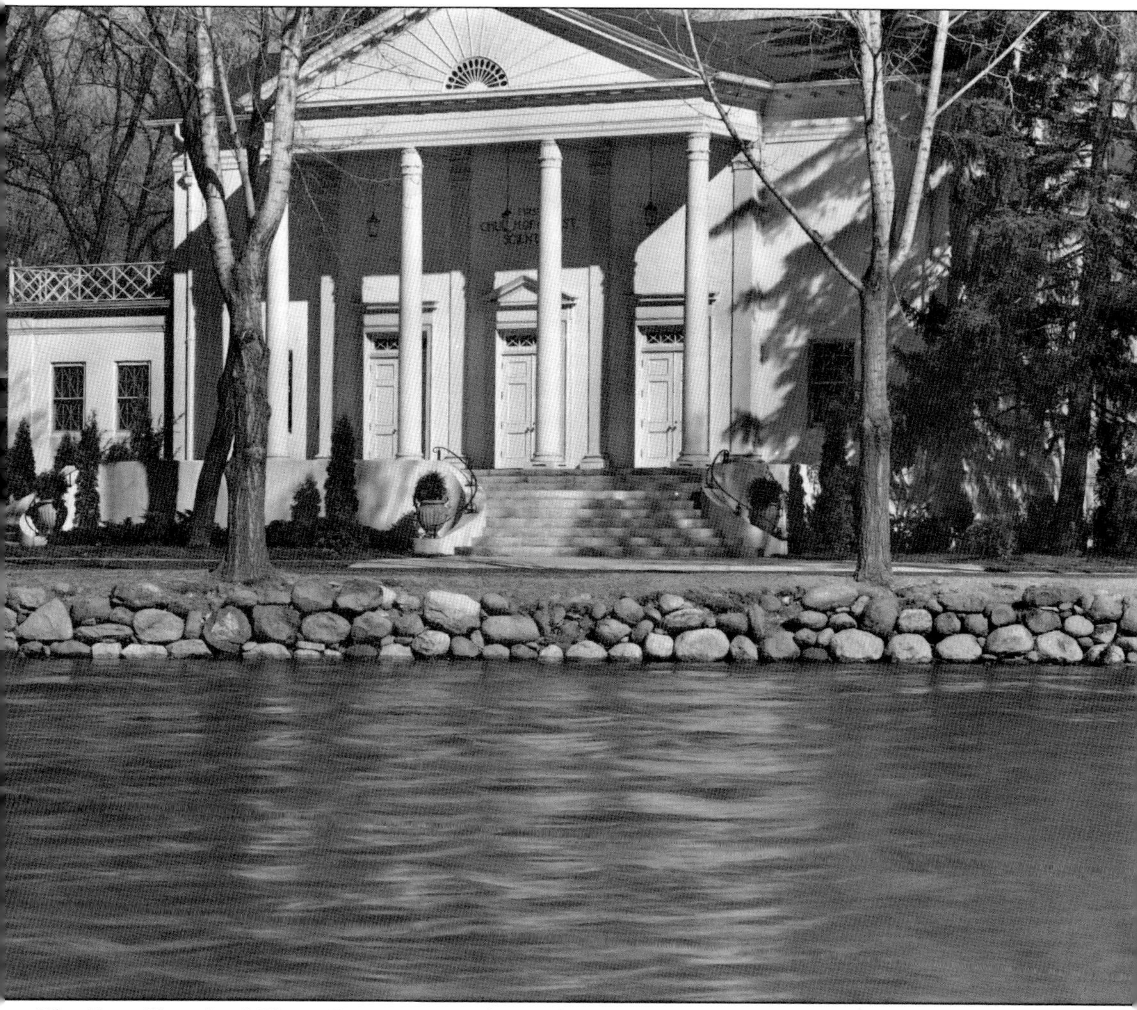

The First Church of Christ Scientist served as a church for 60 years before being sold, in 1997, to the Reno-Sparks Theater Coalition. The funds acquired from the sale were used to construct a new church at West Peckham Lane. In 1998, local theater patron Moya Lear donated $1.1 million to the Reno-Sparks Theater Community Coalition, and the structure was renamed the Lear Theater. Moya Lear, the daughter of Vaudeville comedian John "Ole" Olsen, was the widow of aviation entrepreneur Bill Lear Jr. She was an active member in the community and was eager to preserve the building in its original form and to encourage the further development of arts in Reno. The building is under renovation, having faced several structural problems, including a partially flooded basement. (WA-4136.)

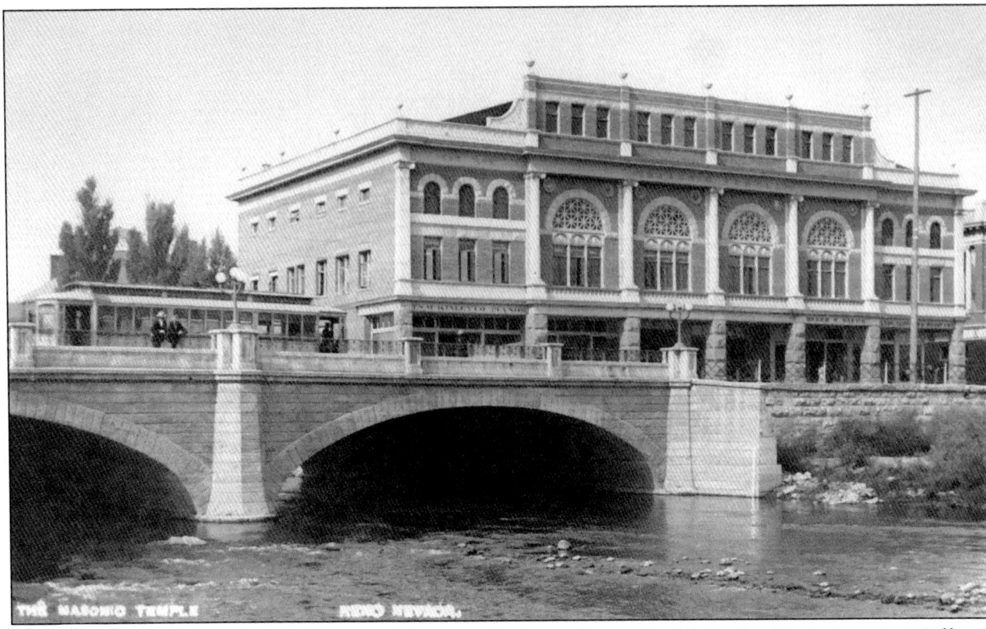

In January 1869, plans began for a new Masonic lodge in Reno. In 1872, the first Masonic Hall was erected; Masons would meet on the second floor of the building, while the first floor was occupied by the Reno Mercantile Company. Located on the southeast corner of West Commercial Row and North Sierra Street, it is one of the oldest commercial buildings in Reno. (WA-3320.)

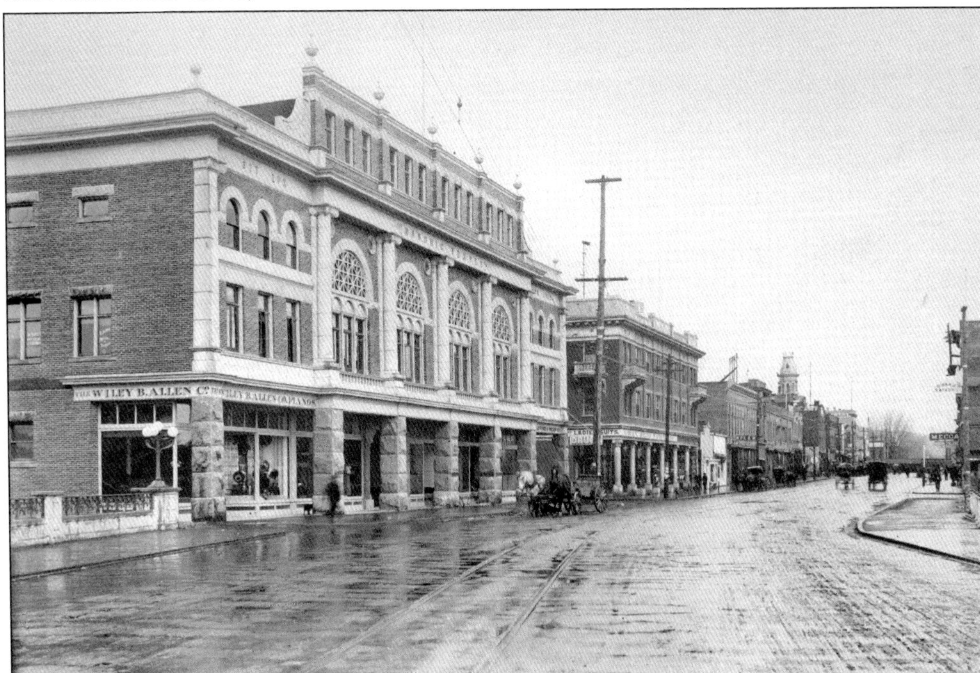

In 1905, the Masons discontinued use of the property on Commercial Row. On September 16, 1905, the Grand Lodge placed the cornerstone for its new building, located along the Truckee River on First and Virginia Streets. Part of the structure was destroyed in a fire on August 15, 1955. In 1967, the current three-story building was erected. (WA-205.)

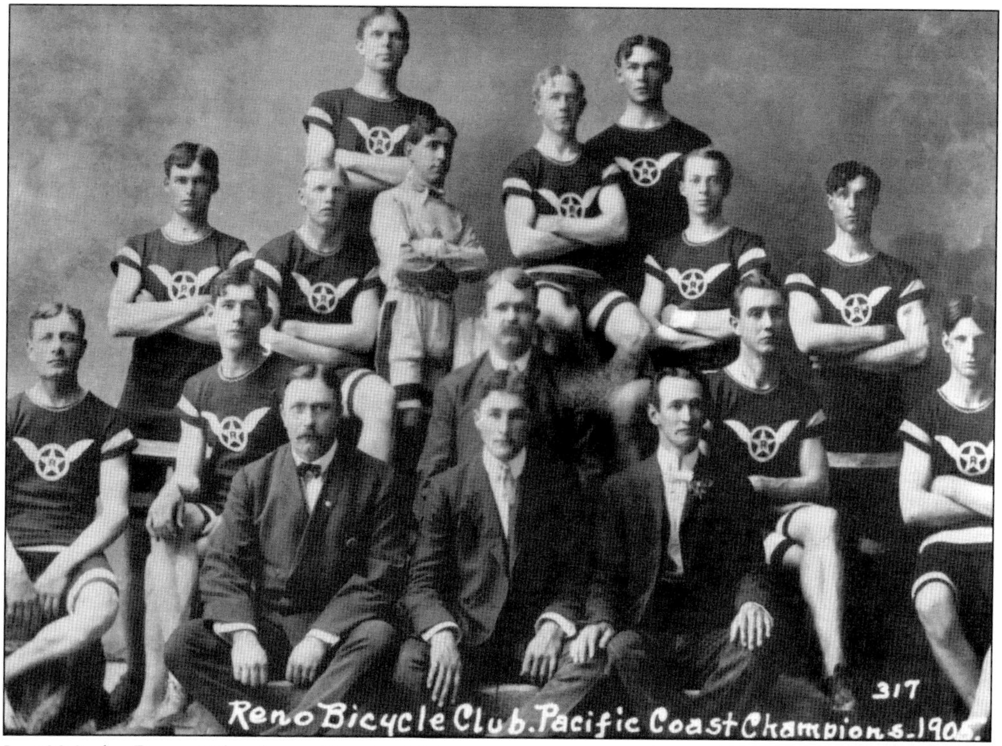

In 1896, the Reno Wheelmen Bicycle Club was conceived in the back room of Charlie Becker's cigar store on Commercial Row. Becker's shop served as the primary headquarters for the group; when they outgrew it, they moved to a new meeting area on the corner of Second and Sierra Streets. The Wheelmen entered numerous races, generating tremendous revenue in winnings, which they would put toward their other endeavors. Race crowds would bring an estimated 1,000 to 3,500 paying spectators. The Wheelmen were the social center of the community, hosting dances, concerts, and, on occasion, plays. (WA-03373.)

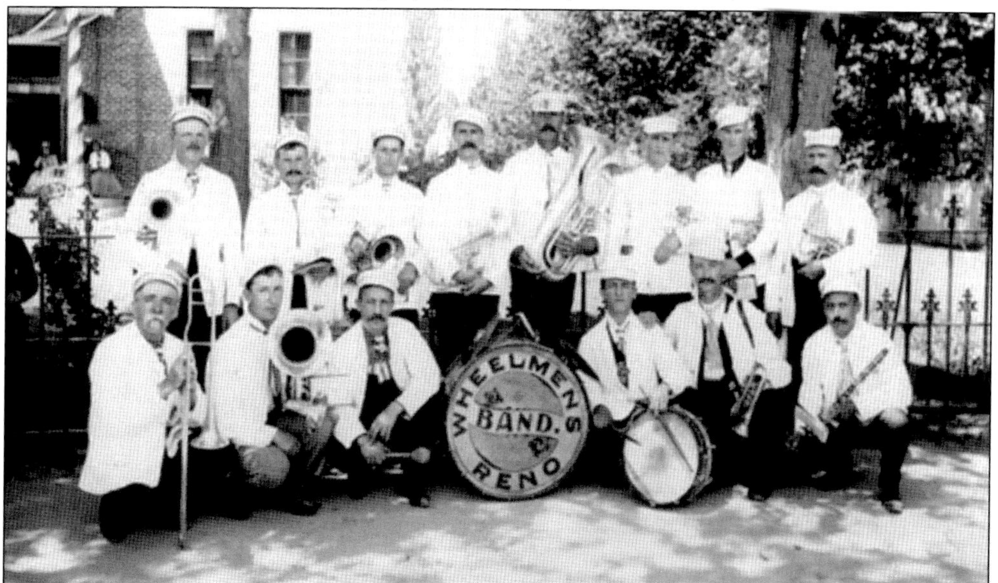

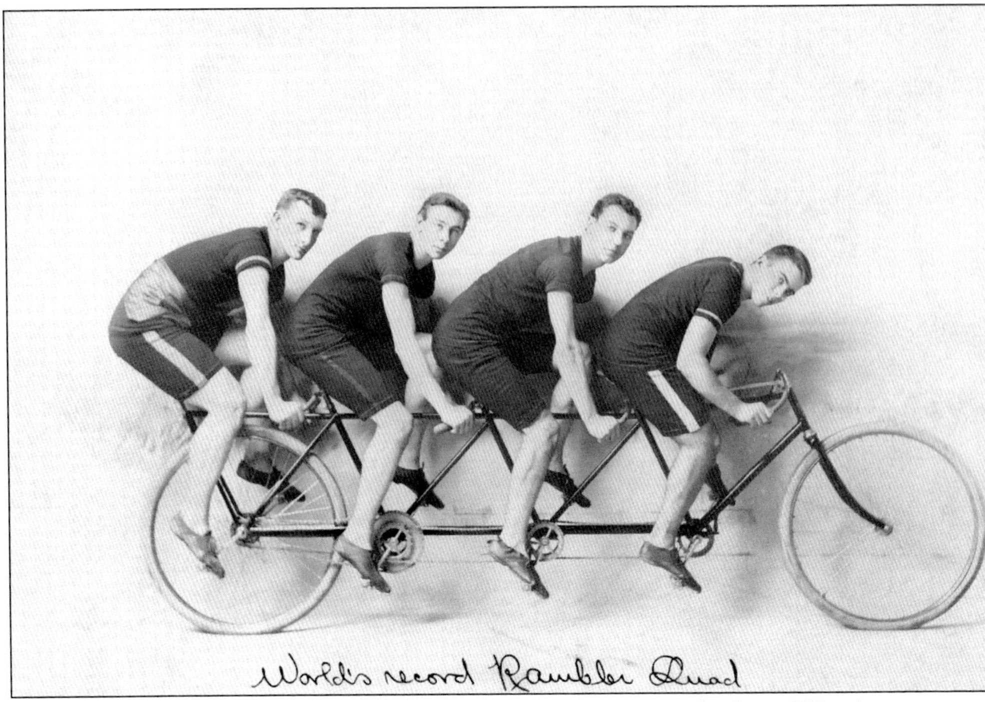

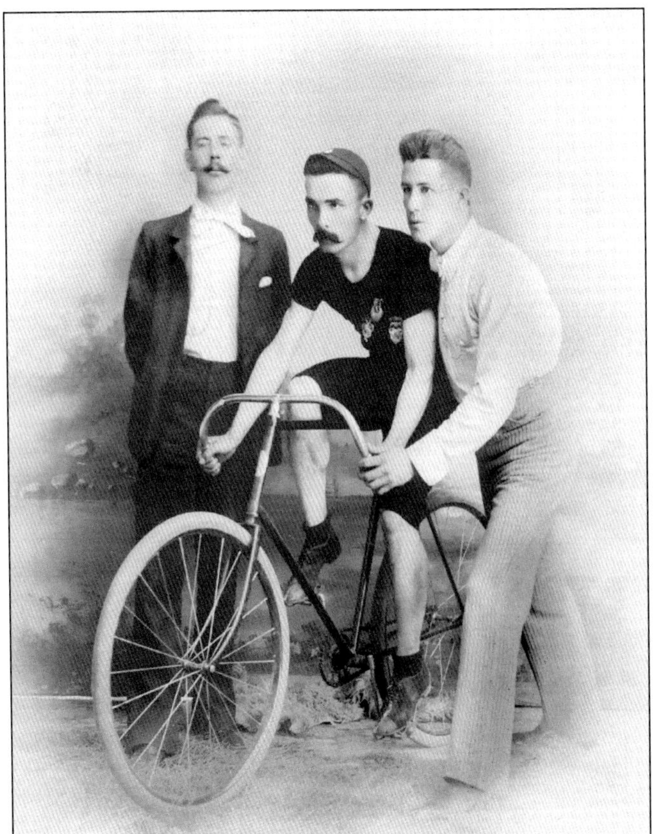

The Reno Wheelmen were incredibly well known and, in their prime, boasted over 400 members. In the early 1900s, they had erected their own clubhouse, Wheelmen Hall, complete with a weight room, swimming pool, social hall, tennis court, football team, private band, and more. The clubhouse was located along the Truckee River, near the present day Twentieth Century Building. The earliest members of the group came from many walks of life; they were doctors, lawyers, politicians, and common gentlemen with a shared passion for cycling. In 1909, the hall burned down, never to be rebuilt. The Wheelmen's organization is still a popular club, and bicycling remains a part of downtown Reno's rich culture. (WA-3382, WA-3402.)

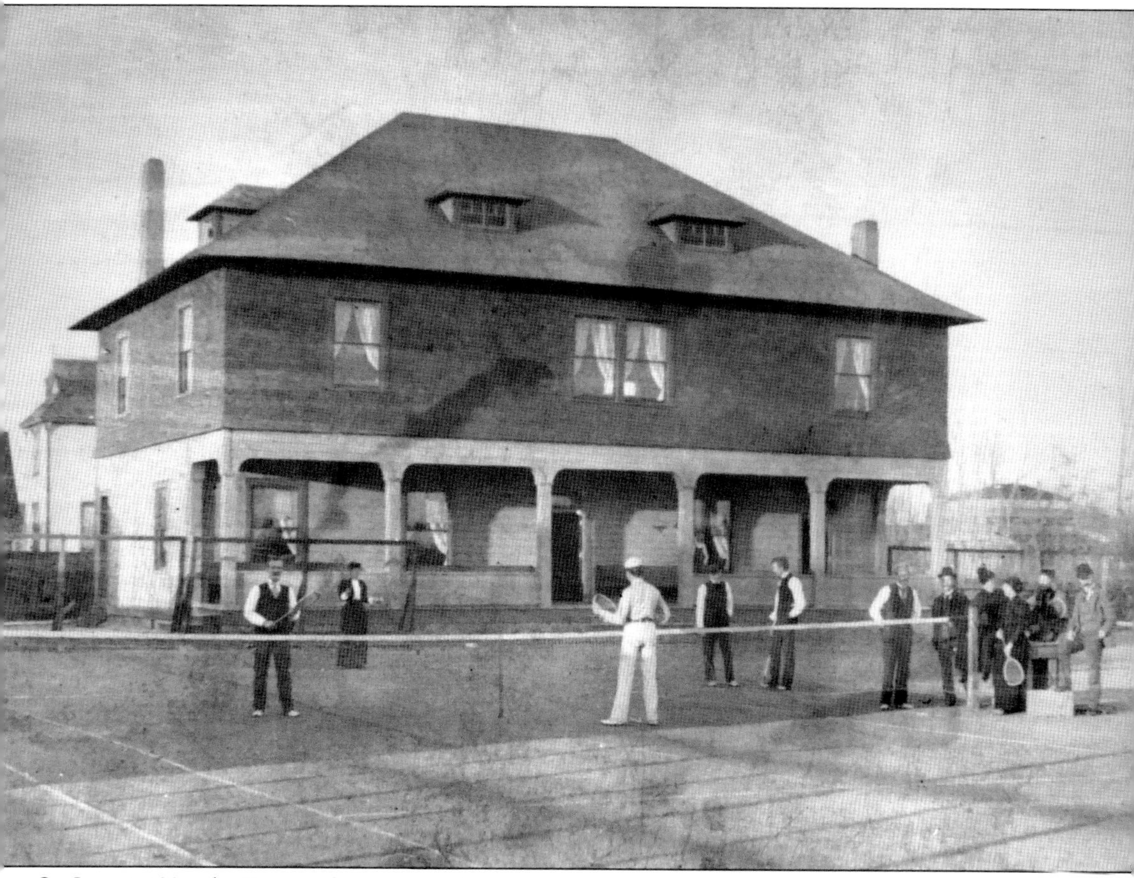

On June 4, 1894, the Twentieth Century Club was organized with the goal of providing a supportive association for the women of Reno while promoting the welfare of the public. The first officers of the club were Walter Mc N. Miller (president), J.N. Evans (vice president), H. Elizabeth Webster (treasurer), and John Michael (secretary). In the fall of 1908, the Twentieth Century Club of Reno issued a convention with all of the women's clubs of the state with the intention of forming a state federation. The growth of the Nevada Federation was slow, as chapters were few, and each had little time or money to devote to the cause. However, the group persevered, soon increasing from five chapters to nine, with active departments in education, civics, art, legislation, and conservation, as well as a library extension. In this photograph, members of the club are visible to the far right. (UNRS-P2000-06-0179.)

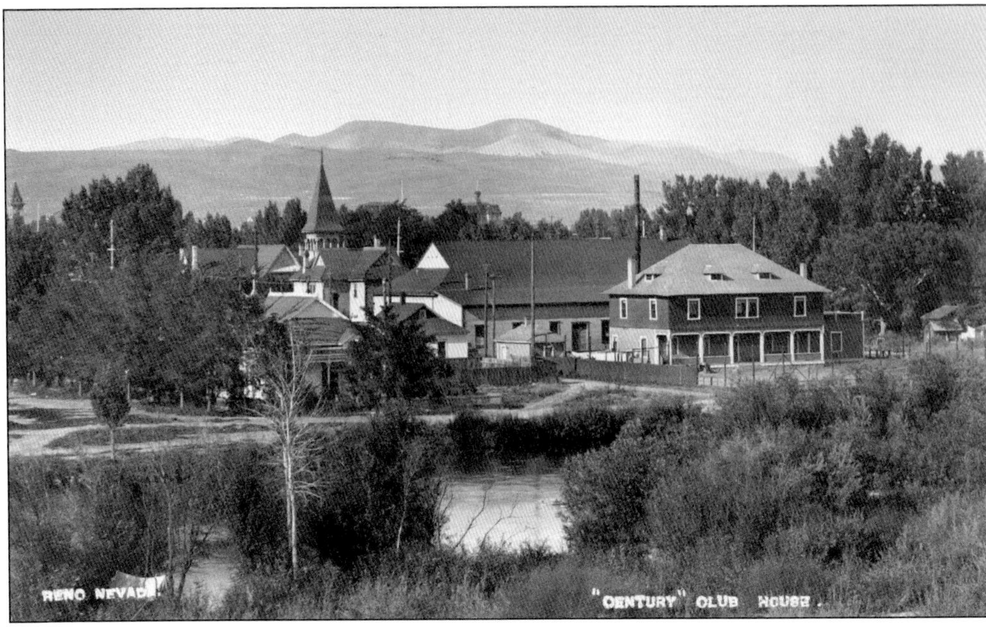

The Twentieth Century Club was open to all women of good reputation and included the most prominent women of the community. Members were involved in a variety of causes, ranging from supporting laws prohibiting spitting on sidewalks to education and social issues. Additionally, the group served as a forum of discussion regarding current issues and events. Membership in the club at one time peaked at approximately 1,000. In 1925, Fred M. Schadler, a prominent Reno architect, designed the new building near the Reno Wheelmen's clubhouse, situated on the western limits of the downtown core near the Truckee River. (WA-2025, WA-7133.)

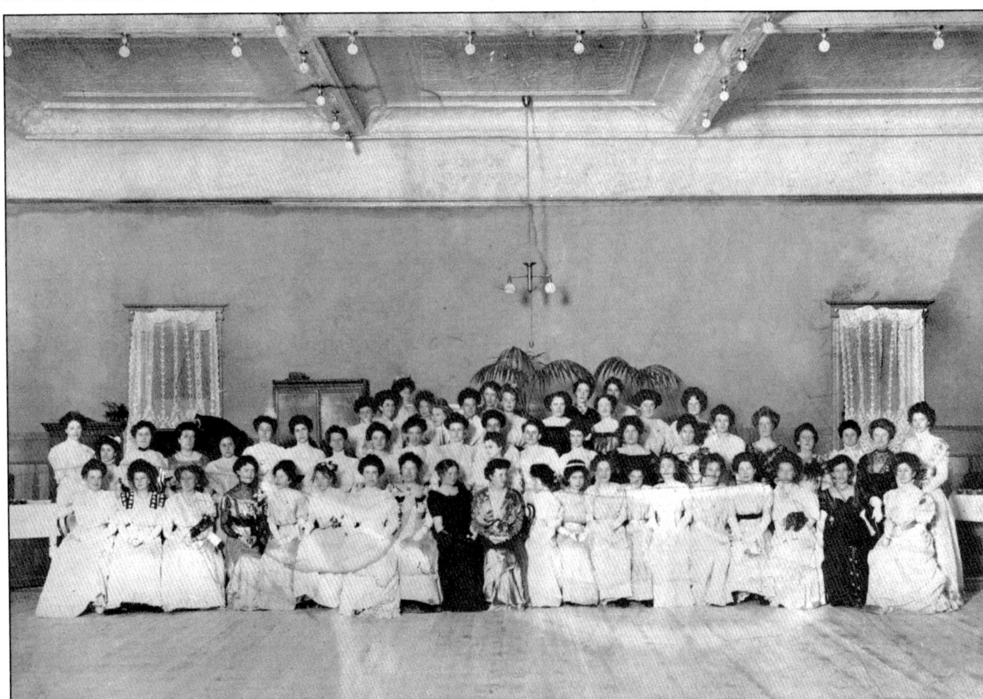

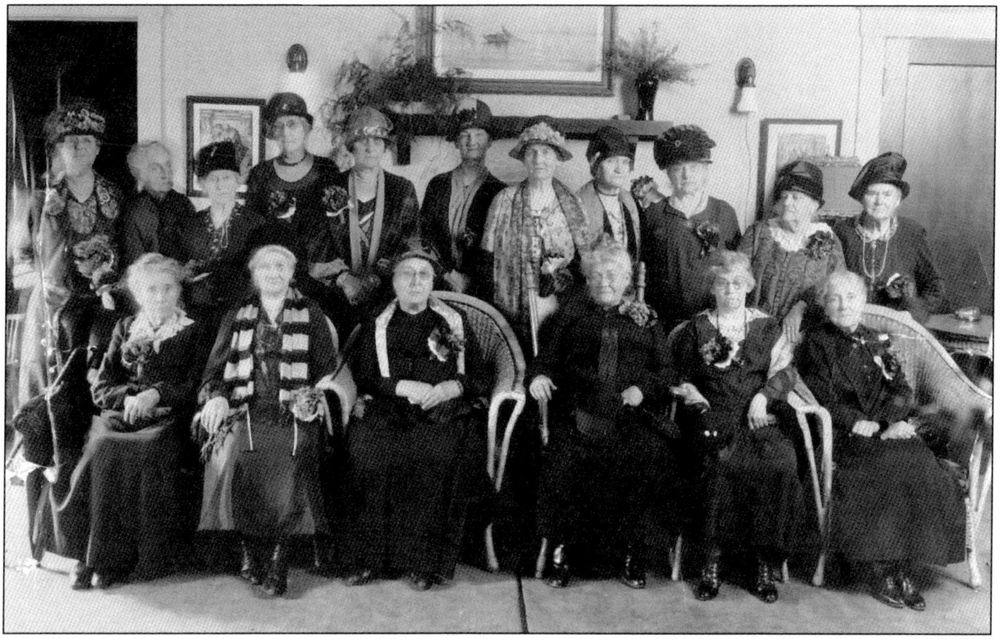

This photograph, which appeared in the *Reno Evening Gazette* on Friday, April 8, 1927, shows 17 pioneer women of Reno at a luncheon given by the Twentieth Century Club. The event, attended by over 100 women, was held in honor of the pioneers. (UNRS-P0528-1.)

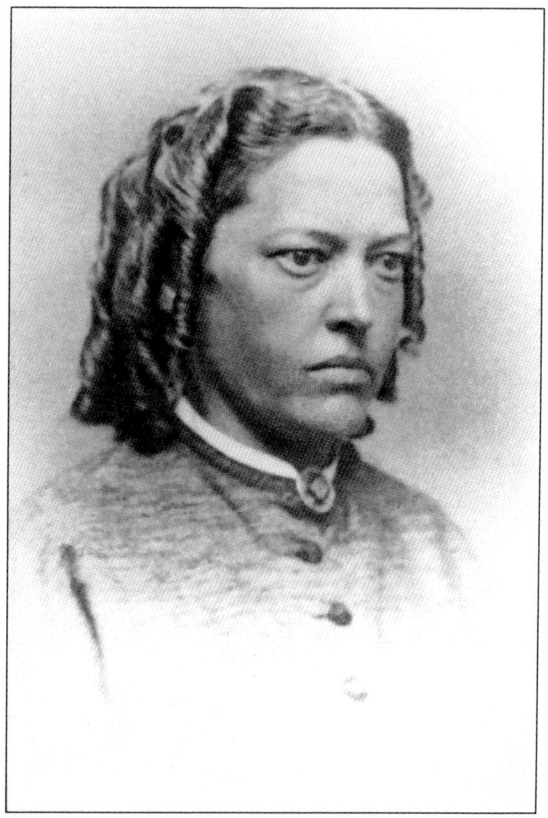

Hannah Keziah Clapp, born in 1842 in upstate New York, established a private school in the Carson area. The institution was frequently visited by Mark Twain, and some of Clapp's teaching methods were used as a basis for scenes in *The Adventures of Tom Sawyer*. Clapp was one of the prominent founding members of the Twentieth Century Club and worked with the other women to plant the many trees along Riverside Drive. (BIO-0368.)

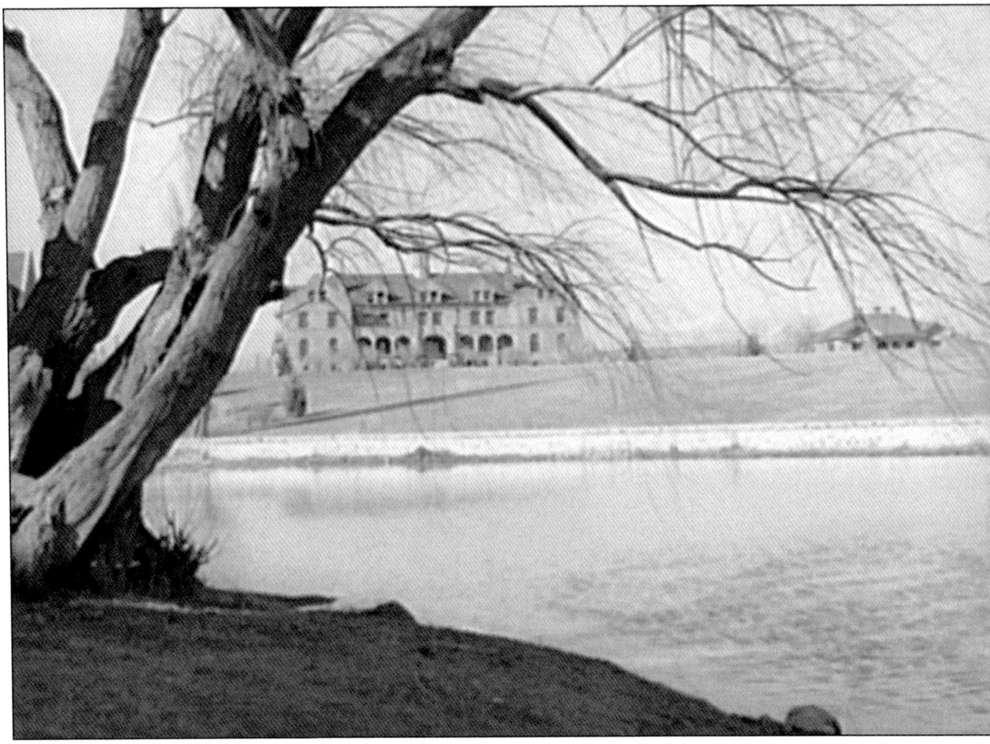

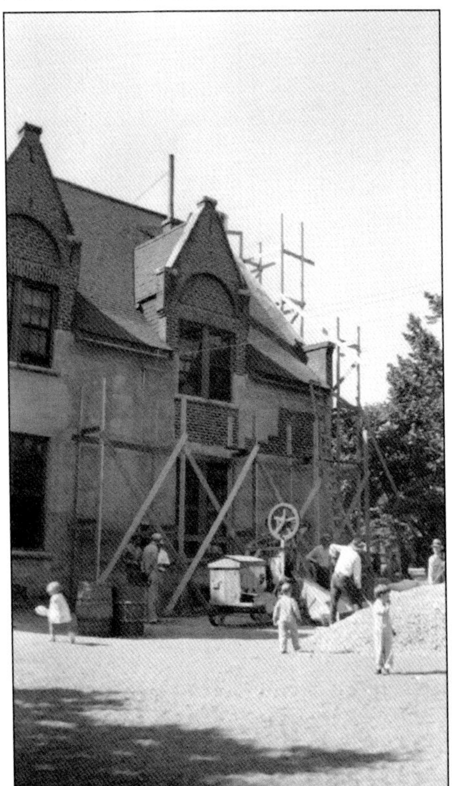

In 1877, Hannah Clapp and coworker Eliza Babcock opened Nevada's first kindergarten. In 1887, when the new University of Nevada was transferred from Elko to Reno, Pres. Leroy Brown hired Clapp as the university's first female faculty member. She was appointed professor of history and English, in addition to overseeing the university library in newly constructed Morrill Hall. These images feature the 1937 improvements to the Babcock Kindergarten (left) and an early view of the University of Nevada, Reno (above). (UNRS-P1999-12-29, LC-USF34-029798-D.)

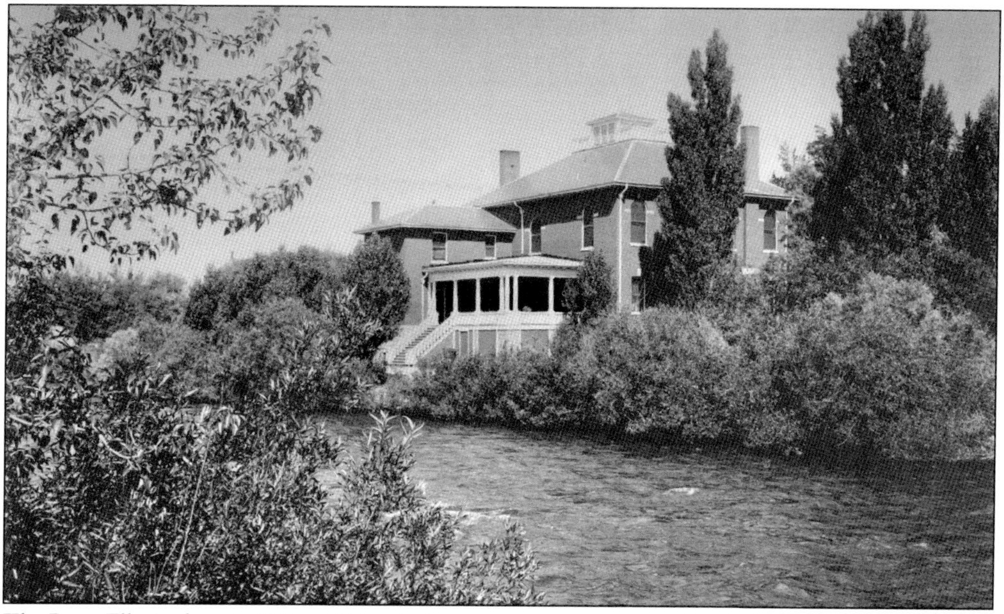

The Reno Elks Lodge No. 597, at 50 North Sierra Street (now occupied by the Palladio condominiums) was chartered on June 30, 1900. It remained in that location for 53 years and, during the early 1900s, was Nevada's only Elks lodge. Among its members were men from the mining camps of Tonopah and Goldfield. (WA-3351.)

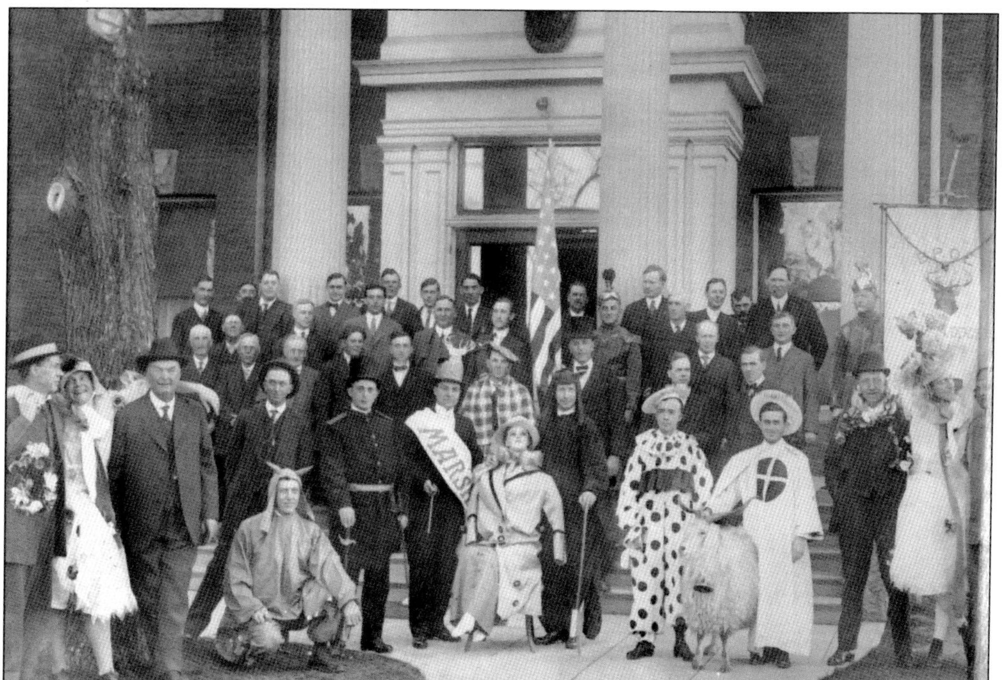

From March 1957 until the completion of the current lodge in 1961, the members of the Reno Elks Lodge met in downtown Reno inside both the historic Mapes Hotel and the old Holiday Hotel Casino (present-day Siena Hotel). The organization continues to be a social center of the community and performs many charitable events in and around the Reno area. (WA-8043.)

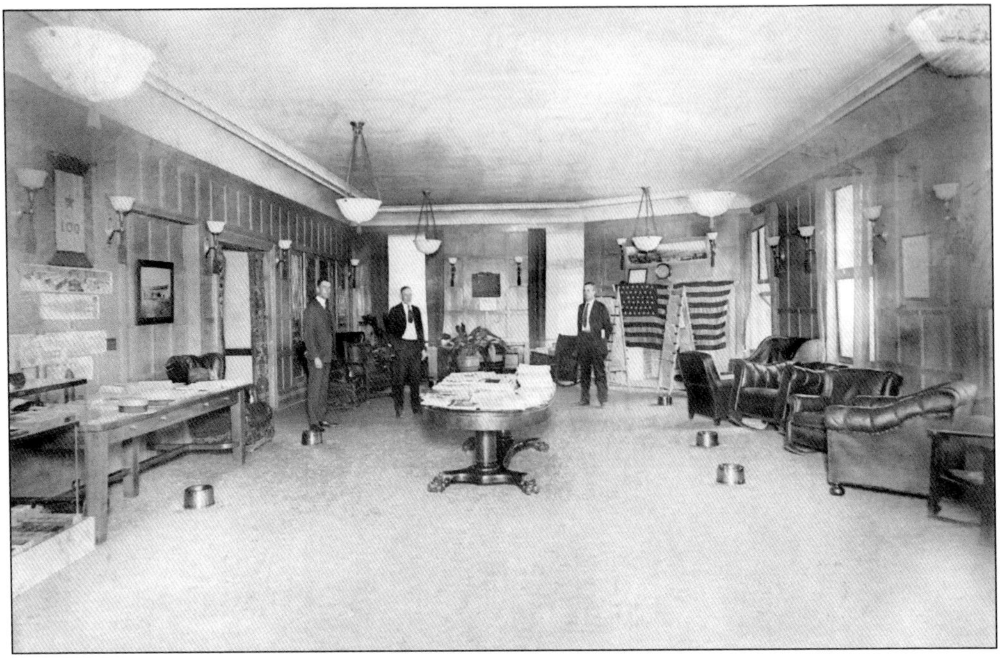

Following the destruction of much of the Elks Lodge on 50 North Sierra Street (below) in a devastating explosion and fire, not to mention a flood, the Reno Elks built a new facility at 597 Kumle Lane. The newest building was erected on five acres of property donated by Raymond I. "Pappy" Smith. At the time of its completion, it was considered one of the finest buildings of its type in the west. The lodge, a ranch-style building that encourages family participation in Elks affairs, was dedicated on February 5, 1961. The Elks celebrated 112 years in Reno on June 30, 2012. (WA-3353, WA-3344.)

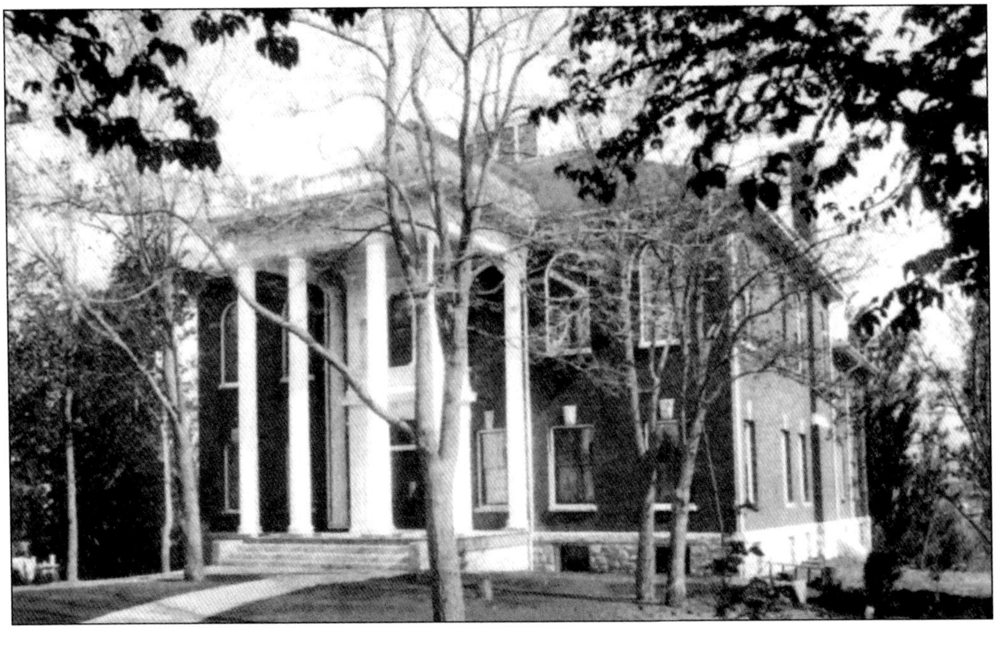

Three

Building a Residence

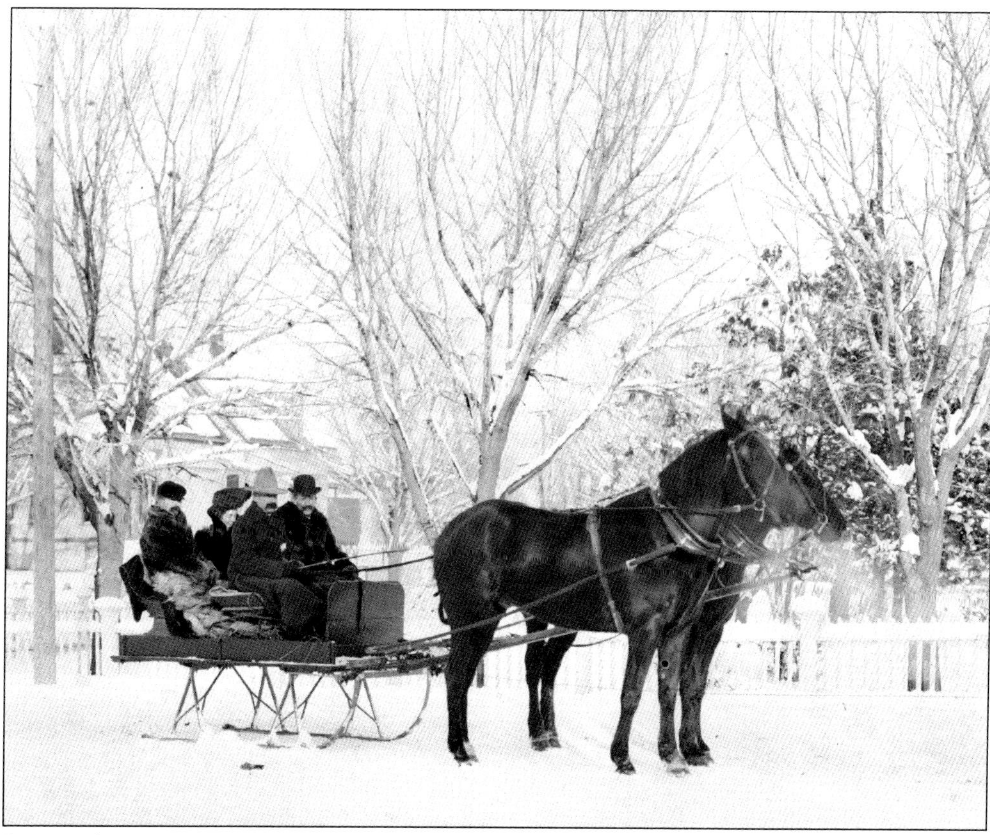

During the 1900s, thousands of individuals flocked to Reno and the surrounding countryside, searching for a new life. Reno boasted thousands of modest, well-cared-for cottages and mansions and was considered a city in which families with small children would want to come and live in beautiful, inspiring surroundings, offering an abundance of opportunity. The homes and neighborhoods along the river were the most well known residences in Reno. This image shows a family in winter in their carriage along Riverside Drive. (Nevada Historical Society.)

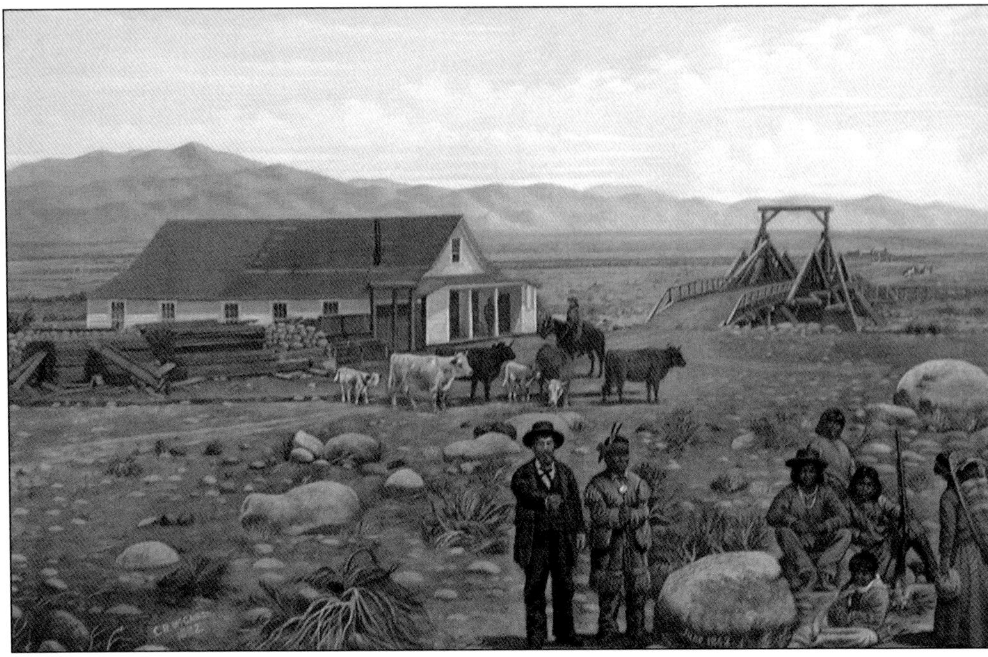

In the early part of 1860, Myron Lake purchased Fuller's crossing from Charles William Fuller, who had built a small bridge and lodge on the banks of the Truckee River. In 1869, Lake rebuilt the small lodge and quickly turned it into a bustling hotel, serving weary travelers as they passed by on their way to strike it rich at the Comstock Lode. After Lake's death in 1884, his daughter and son-in-law operated the hotel, which they renamed the Riverside Hotel. After a devastating fire, the hotel was bought and rebuilt by George Wingfield and was used as a temporary residence for wealthy divorce-seekers. The Riverside offered 60 single rooms and 40 furnished corner suites that included kitchen facilities and connecting rooms for children and servants. (WA-1492, WA-1493.)

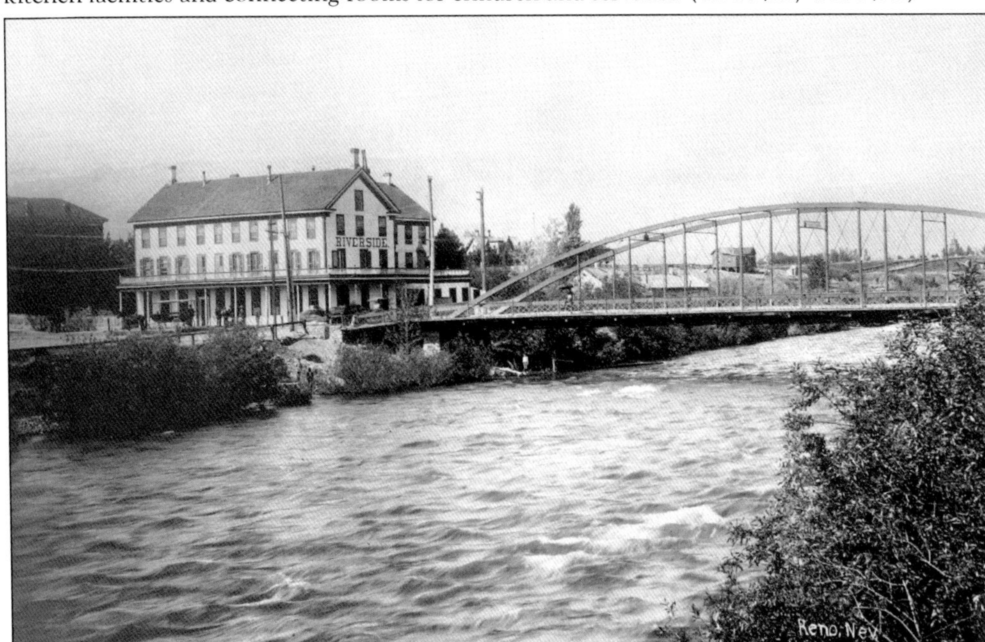

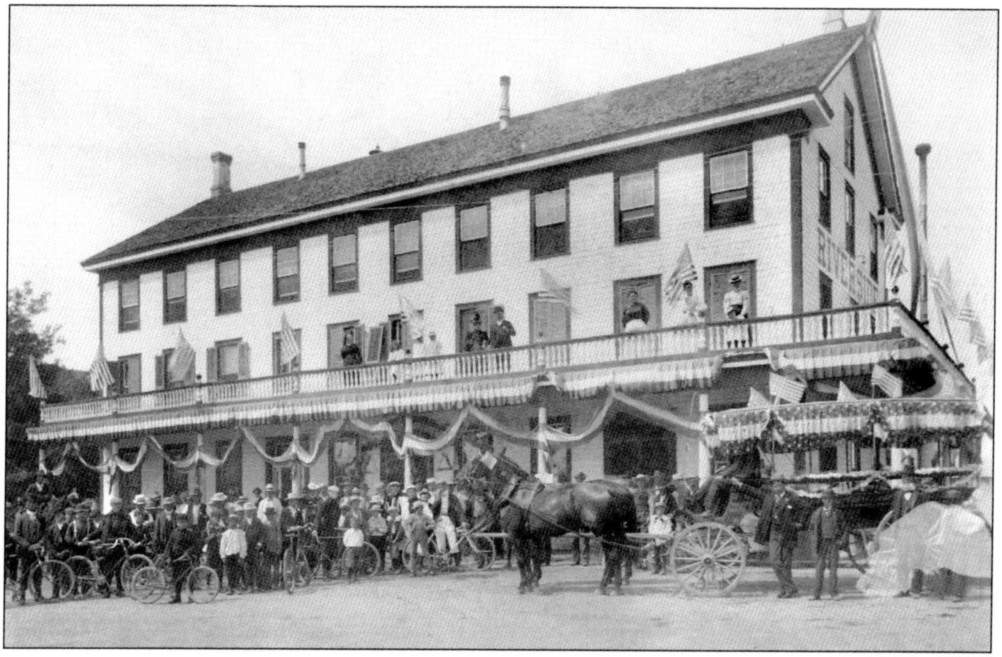

Myron Charles Lake, Reno's first citizen, was considered a hot-tempered and tight-fisted individual. By 1883, between his lodge and his toll bridge, Lake had monopolized most of the city. By 1884, Lake owned half the town's north-side real estate and just about all the land worth owning on the south side, including a 900-acre ranch. In 1864, Lake returned briefly to Honey Lake Valley to marry Jane Conkey Bryant, whose family had been Lake's neighbors prior to his move to Reno. The couple lived at the Lake House until their move to the Lake Ranch in the south of town. Pictured below is the dining room at the Lake House. (Courtesy of VSA arts of Nevada, Lake Mansion Collection.)

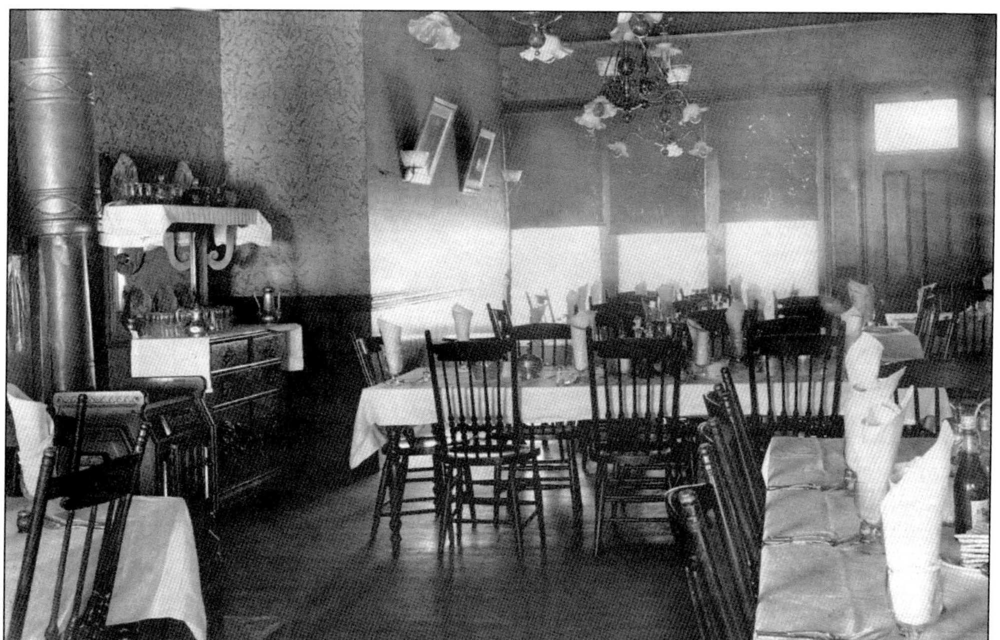

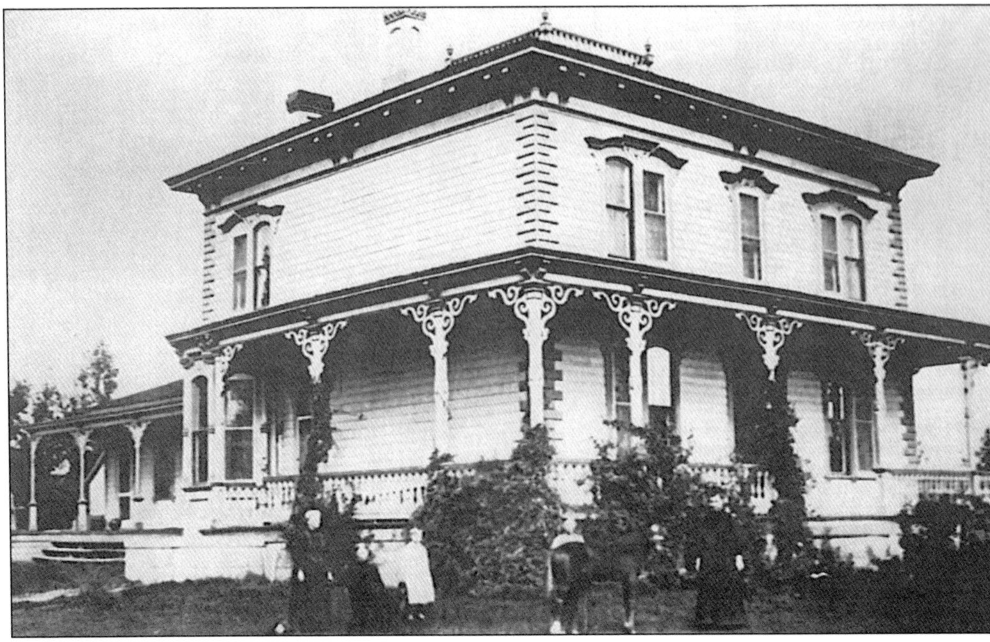

In 1876, Myron Lake sold a portion of land to Washington Jerome Marsh, who used the South Virginia Street and California Avenue site for a Victorian mansion, completed in 1877. The Marsh family lived there for two years. In November 1879, Marsh sold the land (and mansion) back to Lake. Through Lake's estate, in 1888 (following Jane and Myron Lake's 1881 divorce and Myron Lake's death in 1884), the property was acquired by Jane. Throughout the years, many prominent families lived in the mansion. To prevent its demolition in 1971, the mansion was relocated to the corner of South Virginia Street and Kietzke Lane close to the Centennial Coliseum, now the Reno-Sparks Convention Center. In 2004, the mansion was moved for the second time, arriving at its current location near the Truckee River at Court Street and Arlington Avenue. (Courtesy of VSA arts of Nevada, Lake Mansion Collection.)

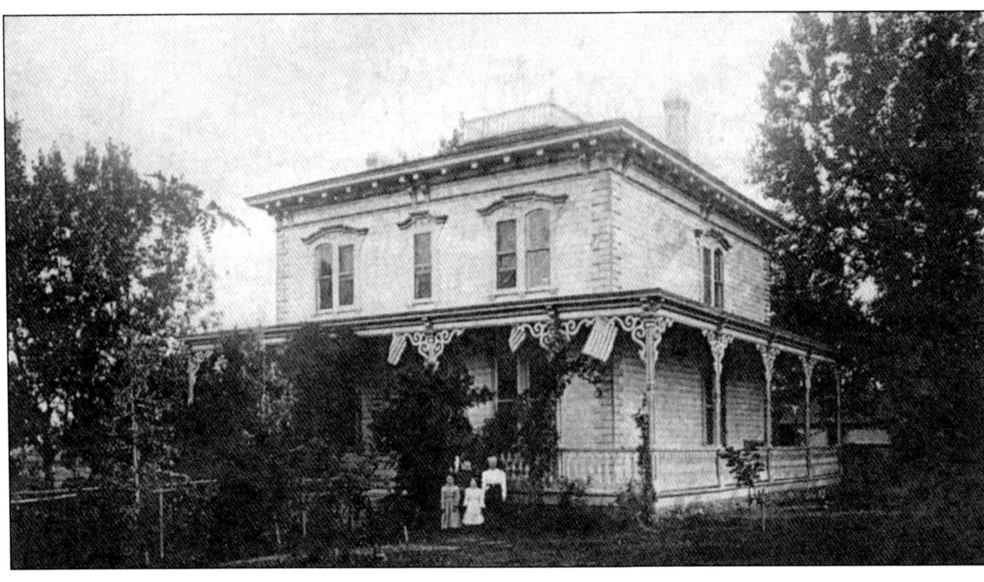

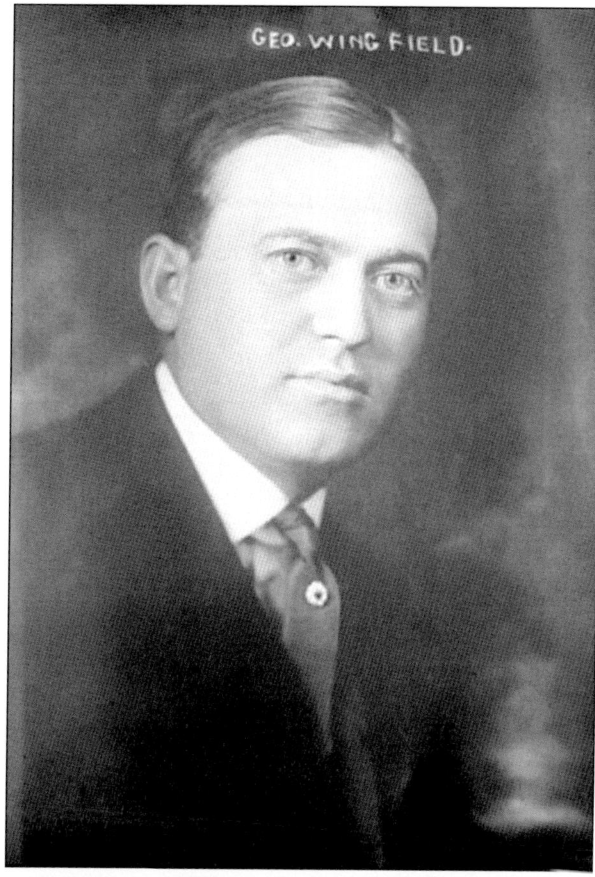

The Wingfield Mansion was built in 1907 by Reno pioneer and business tycoon George Wingfield. The Classical Revival–style home was located adjacent to the Trinity Episcopal Church, along the Truckee River. One of the more prominent features was a one-story porch that encircled three sides of the home. The building unfortunately burned down in 2001, after being listed in the National Register of Historic Places. A great contributor to the growth of Reno, George Wingfield had tremendous political power and served as a leading figure in mining, banking, and industrial and commercial development during the early 20th century. At one point, Wingfield was owner of every bank in Nevada; he is also known for contributing to the reconstruction of both the impressive Riverside Hotel and the Hotel Golden in downtown Reno. (LC-B2- 2588-13, UNRS-P1992-03-1321.)

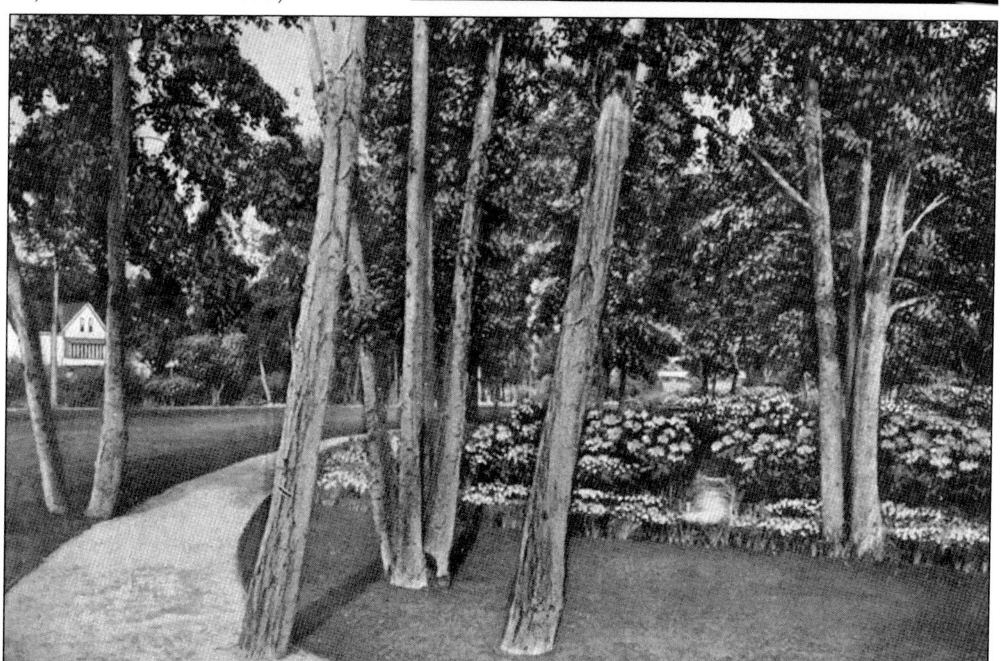

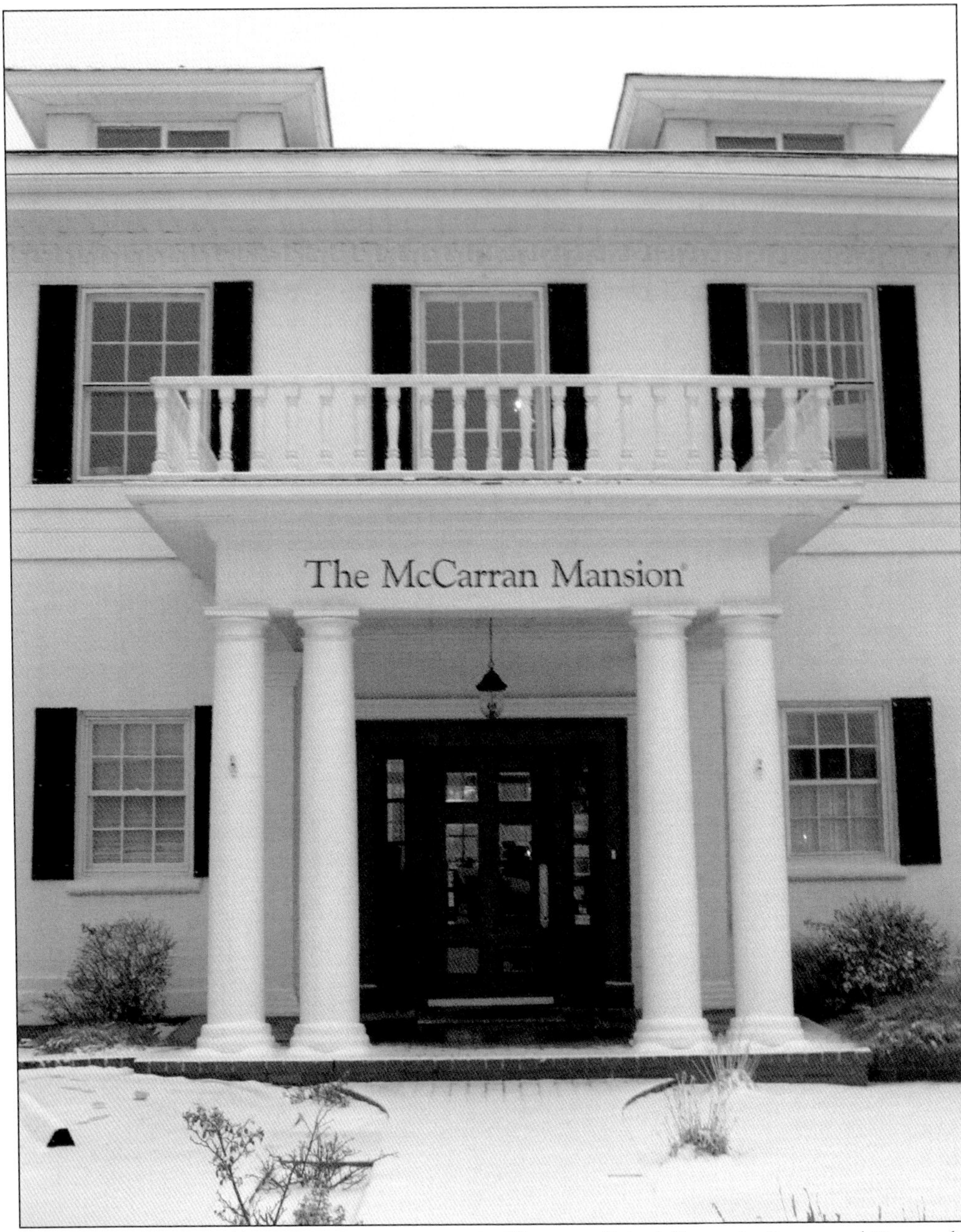

In 1913, Lewis A. Gibbons, an important and affluent political figure in Reno and Tonopah, commissioned Frederic J. DeLongchamps to design an elegant Colonial Revival mansion. The house was purchased by Patrick A. McCarran, who served Nevada as a US senator from 1933 to 1954. The McCarran family moved into the mansion in 1921. The rear of the house has a large veranda, which overlooks Barbara Bennett and Wingfield Parks, as well as the Truckee River. McCarran is well known as the judge who secured Mary Pickford's divorce from Owen Moore on March 2, 1920, in Douglas County. The home has since been recognized as the McCarran Mansion. (Photo by Courtney Meredith.)

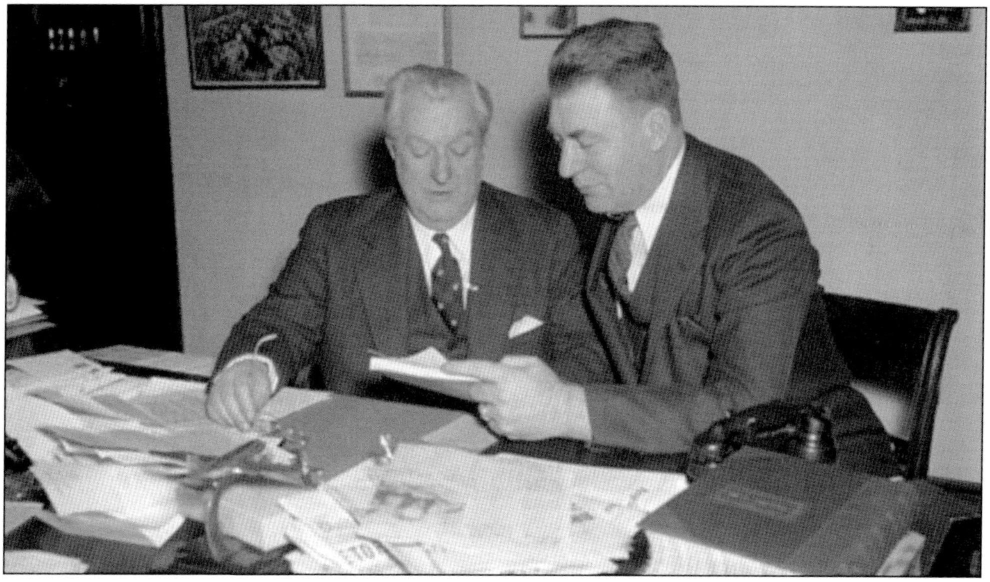

Patrick A. McCarran, born in 1876 in Reno, descended from a strong family of Irish immigrants whose sheep ranch resided 15 miles east of Reno. McCarran was a headstrong individual and was considered by Nevadans to be "saddle educated," referring to the fact that he was a self-made man who learned a great deal while working on his father's ranch. Through the years, McCarran continued to support Nevada's mining, ranching, and gaming industries. (LC-DIG-HEC-22107.)

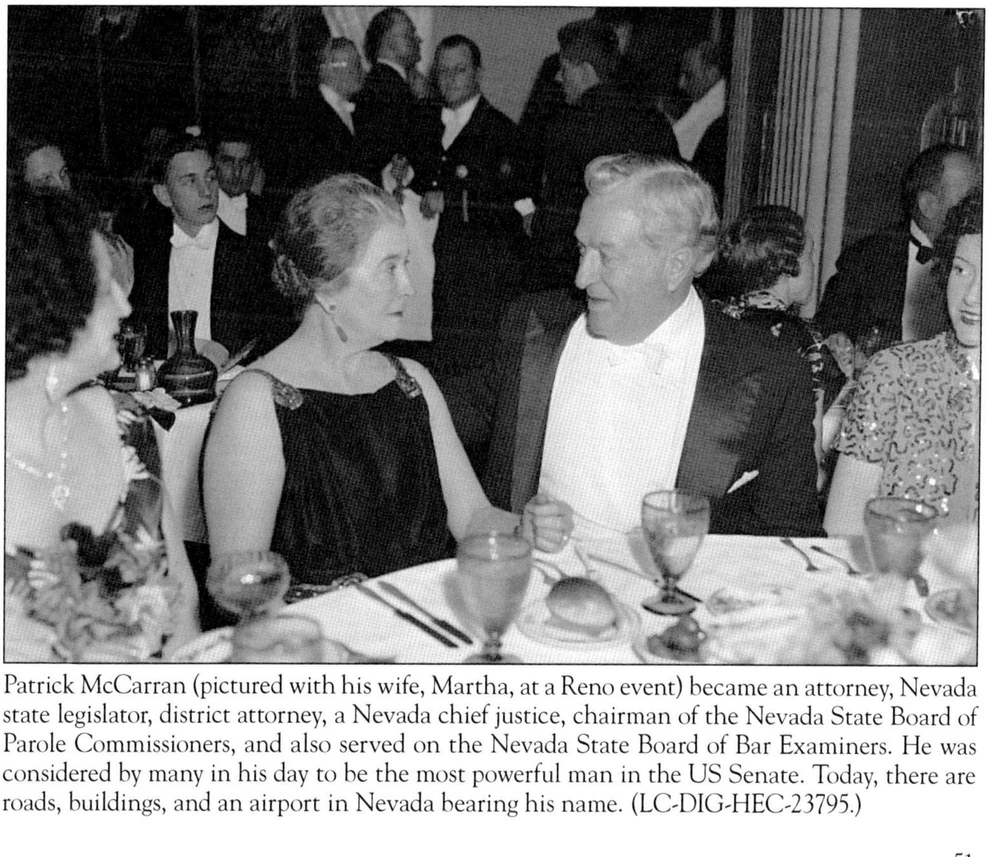

Patrick McCarran (pictured with his wife, Martha, at a Reno event) became an attorney, Nevada state legislator, district attorney, a Nevada chief justice, chairman of the Nevada State Board of Parole Commissioners, and also served on the Nevada State Board of Bar Examiners. He was considered by many in his day to be the most powerful man in the US Senate. Today, there are roads, buildings, and an airport in Nevada bearing his name. (LC-DIG-HEC-23795.)

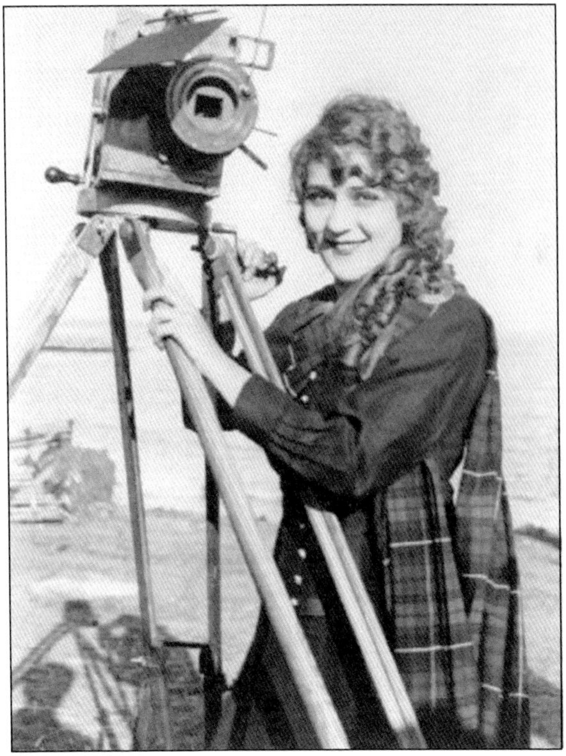

It is often thought that Patrick McCarran purchased the mansion at the corner of the future Newlands Heights area from attorney's fees he collected from the controversial Mary Pickford divorce, secured in March 1920. During a US tour in 1918, Mary Pickford (pictured) began a secret love affair with Douglas Fairbanks while still married to Owen Moore. (LC-DIG-GGBAIN-3C131504.)

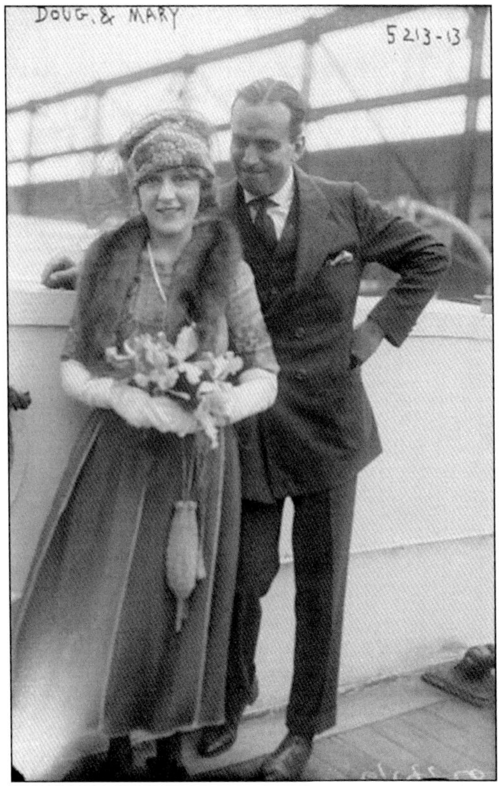

Pickford filed for divorce from Moore and, on March 28 of the same year, married Fairbanks (pictured together). Mary Pickford was a Canadian-born motion picture star and the cofounder of United Artists. She was known as "America's sweetheart," and was the first actress to own a production company. Pickford gained international fame as one of the most important performers and producers in the history of silent film. The American Film Institute named Pickford 24th among the greatest female stars of all time. (LC-DIG-GGBAIN-30611.)

Overlooking downtown Reno, the Nixon Mansion is easily seen from Riverside Drive along the Truckee River. The 15,325 square foot Italian villa–style home was built in 1907 by US senator George S. Nixon. Nixon, who had made most of his fortune in banking, purchased the land in 1906 from business associate and fellow senator Francis G. Newlands, who owned the adjacent property. (LC-DIG-ggbain-03755.)

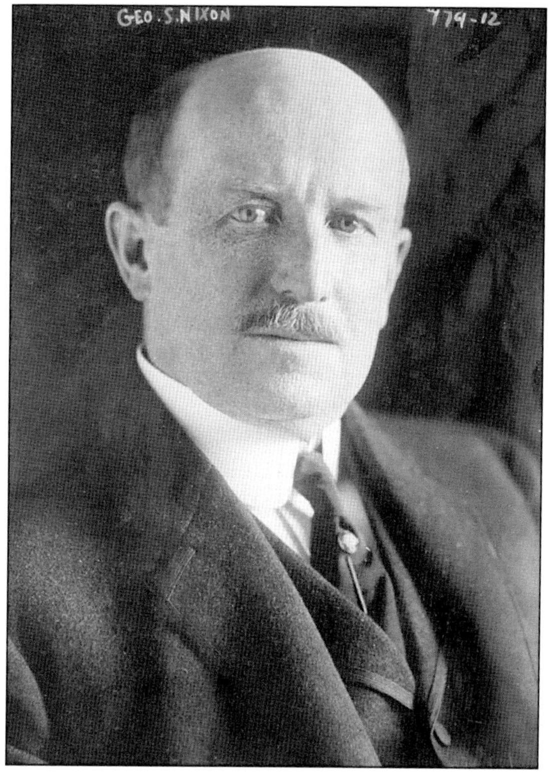

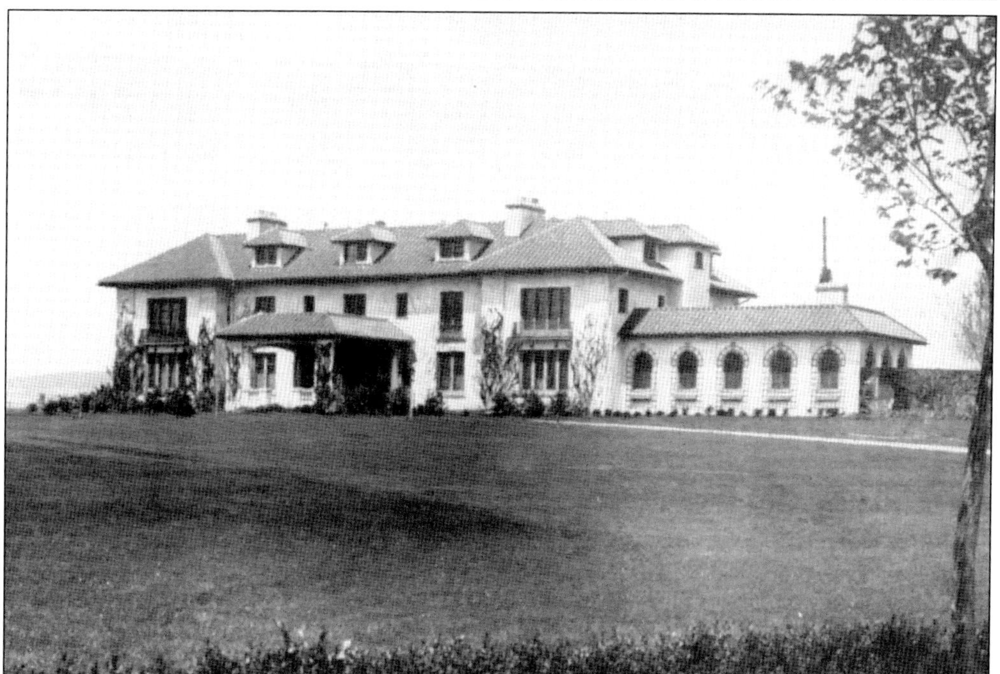

The Nixon Mansion sits on 2.03 acres and was originally built with 33 rooms, including 11 bedrooms, 7.5 baths, and 7 fireplaces. It now holds only eight bedrooms, nine full baths, and four half baths. It was one of the first homes in Reno to house an elevator. (UNRS-862.)

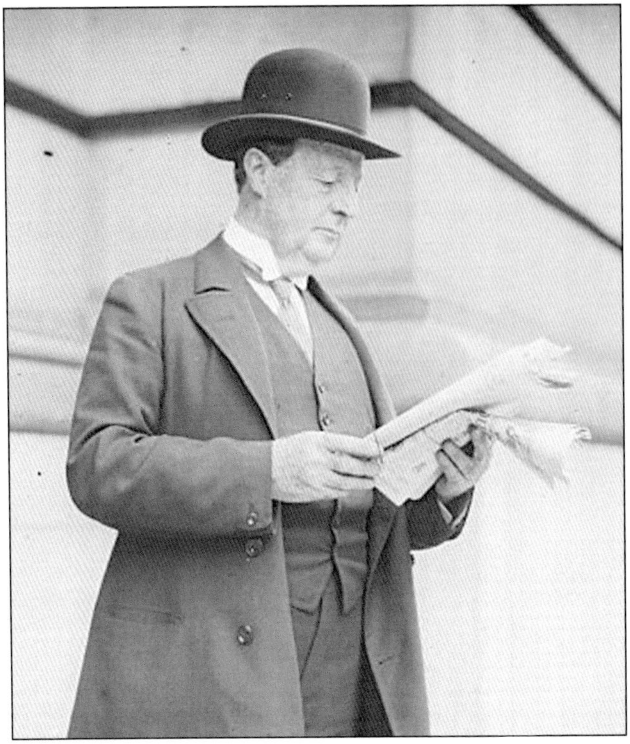

Adjacent to the Nixon Mansion was the residence of Francis G. Newlands (US congressman from 1893 to 1903 and US senator from 1903 to 1917). Newlands traveled to Nevada in 1888 to manage the interests of William Sharon, one of the primary silver barons of the Comstock. Newlands was elected to the House of Representatives in 1892 and to the Senate in 1903. (LC-DIG-ggbain-06963.)

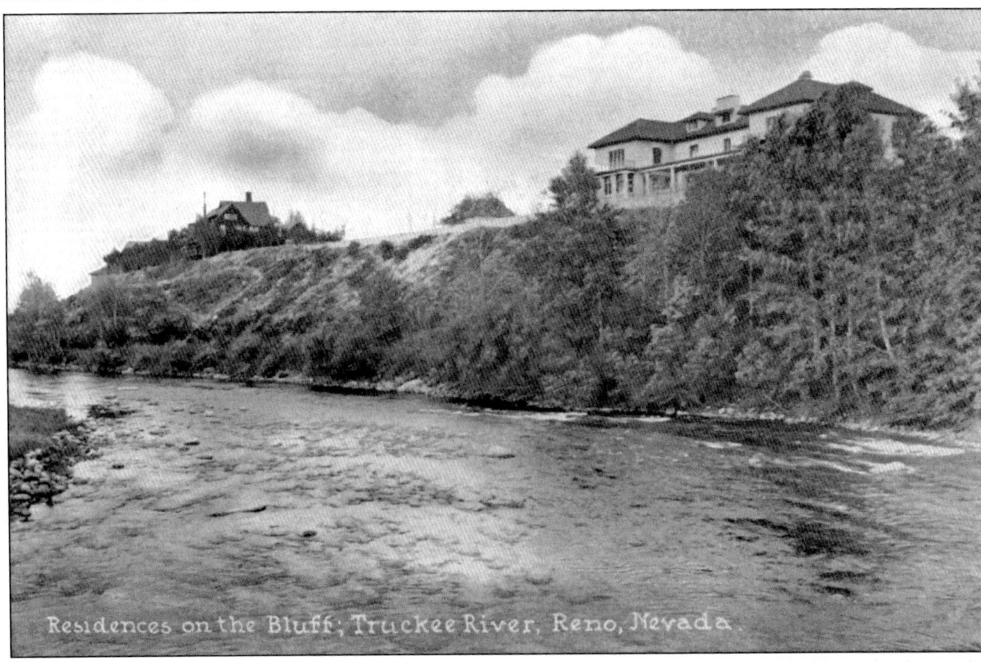

Newlands's mansion, built in 1889, was the first residence built along the bluff overlooking the Truckee River; the area would later grow into a prominent neighborhood known as Newlands Heights. Today, the area is home to many historic mansions and homes. Most were constructed between 1920 and 1940 and feature architectural styles ranging from Colonial Revival and Spanish Colonial Revival to French chateaus and Craftsman bungalows. (WA-06645.)

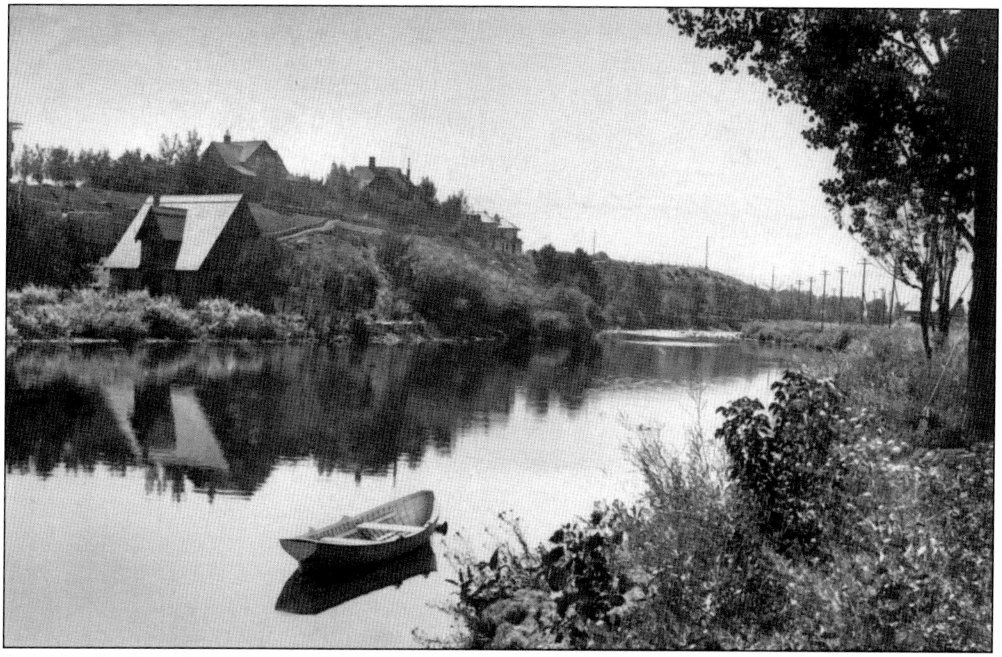

In 1911, the Joseph Grey House was designed by the owner and founder of the Gray Reid Wright department store. The 3,441 square foot Colonial Revival–style home, with a pediment porch supported by a pair of Tuscan columns, is situated in the south bluffs area above the Truckee River. It can be seen from what was once Belle Isle (now Wingfield Park). (WA-06964.)

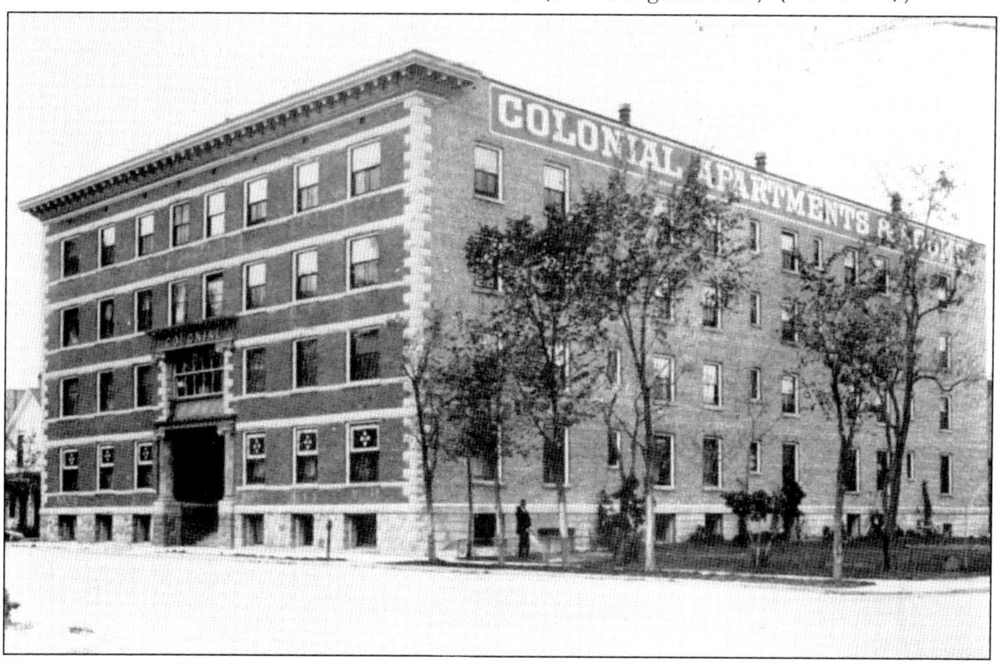

The present-day Ross Manor, located on First Street across from the Truckee River, was Reno's first large apartment building. Originally known as the Colonial Apartments, the structure was built in 1907 by C.E. Clough. Clough was organizer of Reno's first power company, the first water system in the city of Sparks, and the Reno Press Brick Company. (UNRS-862.)

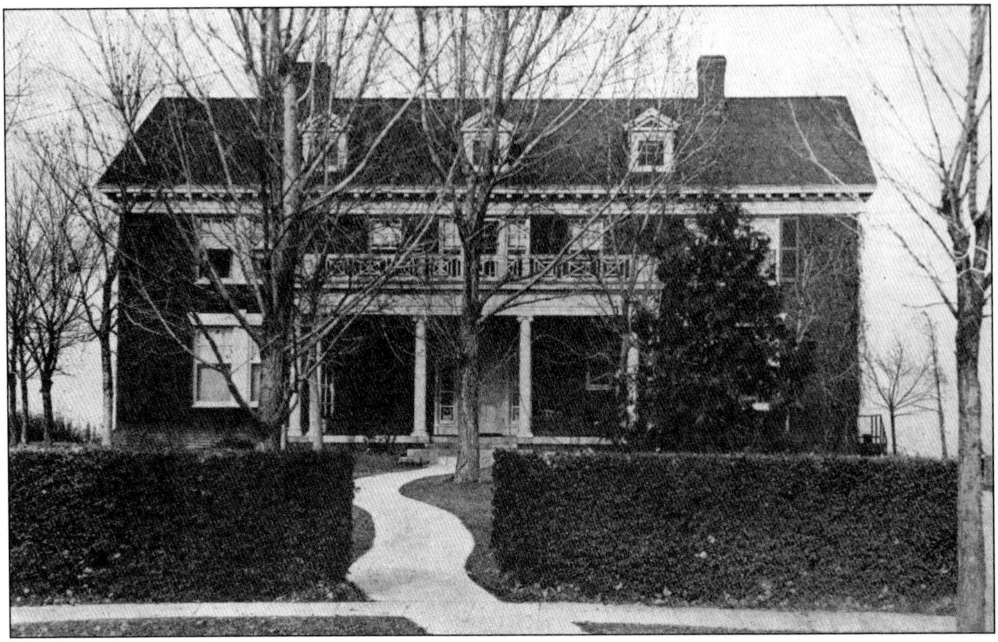

The Hawkins family, considered one of the earliest families of Nevada, was prominent in business and banking circles, and members were recognized for their contributions to art, science, and music. In 1911, Los Angeles architect Elmer Grey was commissioned by Reno attorney Prince A. Hawkins to build a large Colonial Revival home in Newlands Heights. Hawkins owned the property until 1978, when it was purchased by the Sierra Nevada Museum of Art. (WA-6656.)

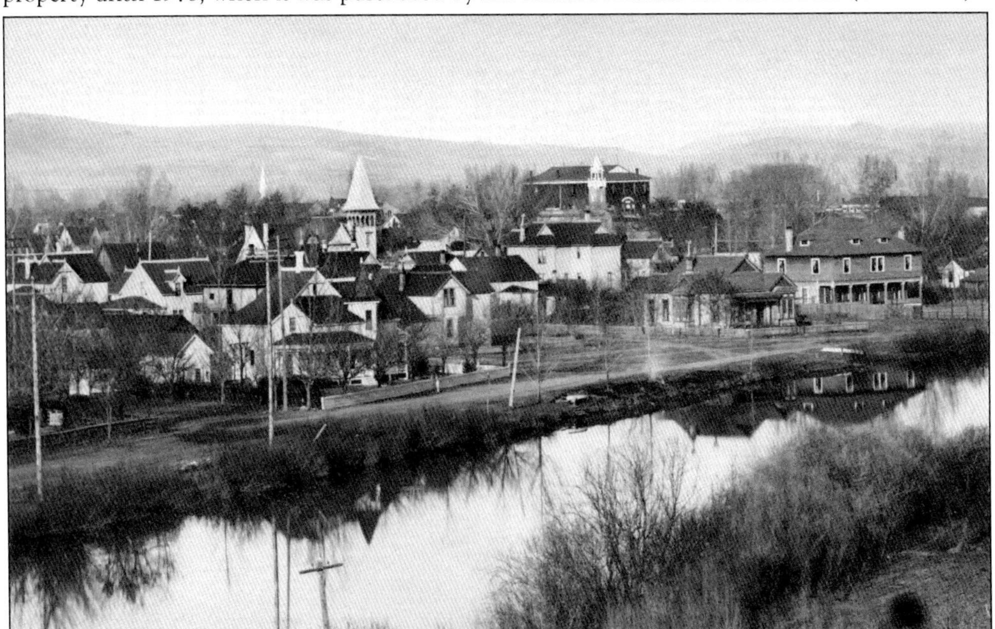

As development of new neighborhoods continued, many of the families of mine owners and laborers began to build residences. The 1888 Powning's Addition west of downtown began populating thanks to its large lots, wide alleys, good sewage, and safe location from fire. Currently, the area is known as the Powning Conservation District. (WA-02000.)

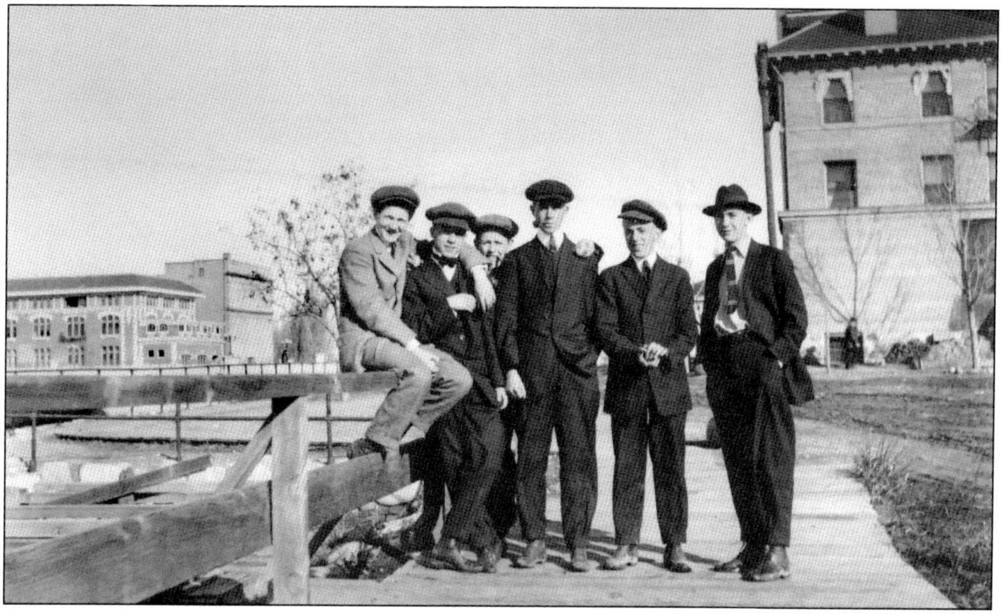

Reno provided new immigrants with good employment, allowing many of them the opportunity to acquire real estate. Soon the western section of the Powning Addition became known as Little Italy because of the increasing number of Italian families moving into the area. Many of the residents had small vineyards where they regularly made wine; these vineyards and gardens reflected economic stability as well as the area's distinct Italian heritage. (WA-02107.)

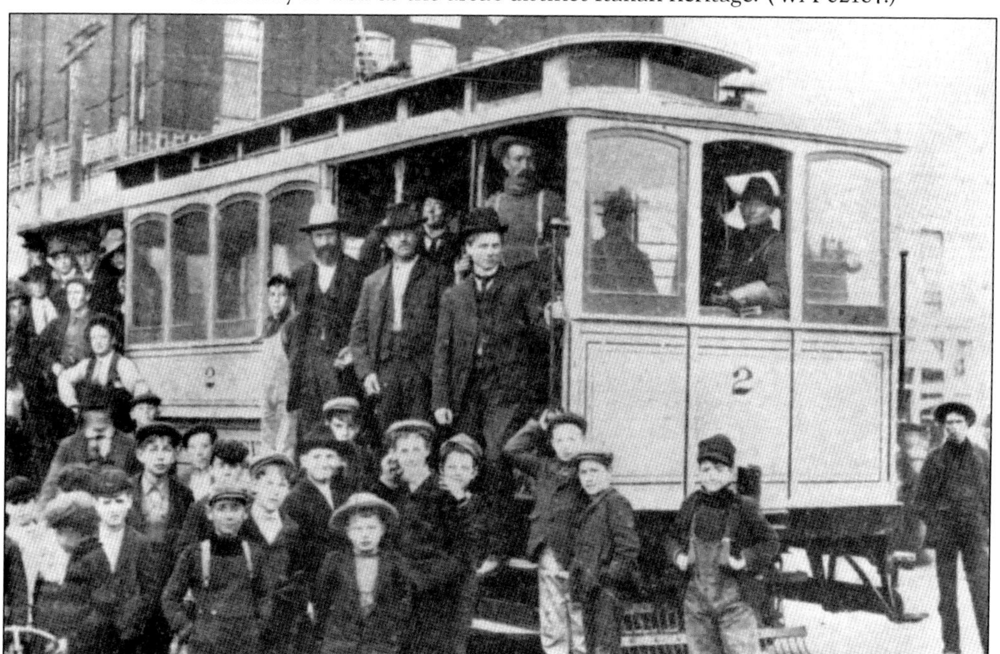

As Reno's population along the Riverwalk and neighboring areas quickly grew, the transportation of goods and people became increasingly important. In November 1904, Reno Nevada Transit Company introduced the first electric car in the state. This image shows one of Reno's earliest trolleys sitting on Virginia Street. (WA-06490.)

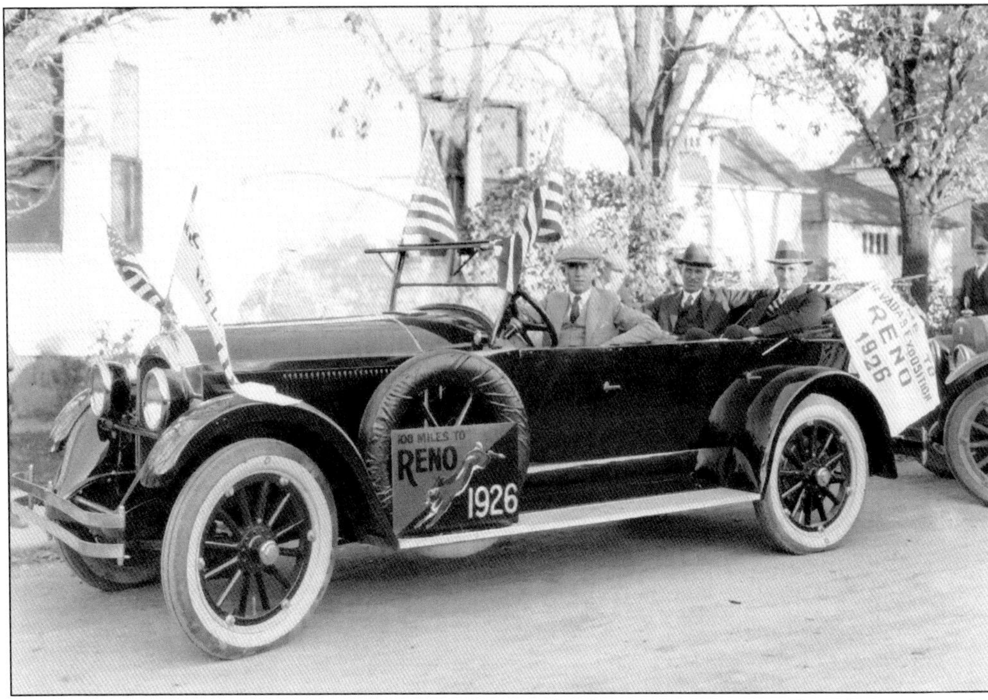

By 1915, the automobile had made it easy for thousands of Americans to visit Reno's most popular neighborhoods. Road construction became increasingly important to the local economy, and the development of the new Lincoln and Victory Highways would bring new visitors to the area. (UNRS-P1992-01-2203.)

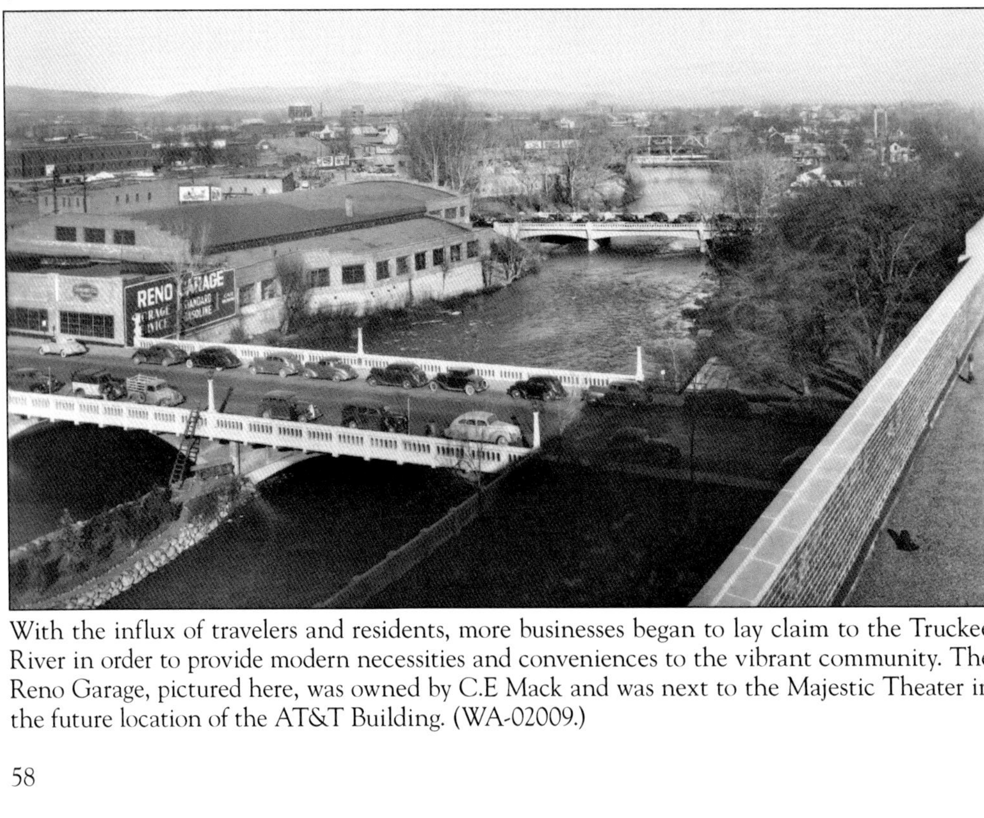

With the influx of travelers and residents, more businesses began to lay claim to the Truckee River in order to provide modern necessities and conveniences to the vibrant community. The Reno Garage, pictured here, was owned by C.E Mack and was next to the Majestic Theater in the future location of the AT&T Building. (WA-02009.)

Four

STRUCTURES OF THE AGES

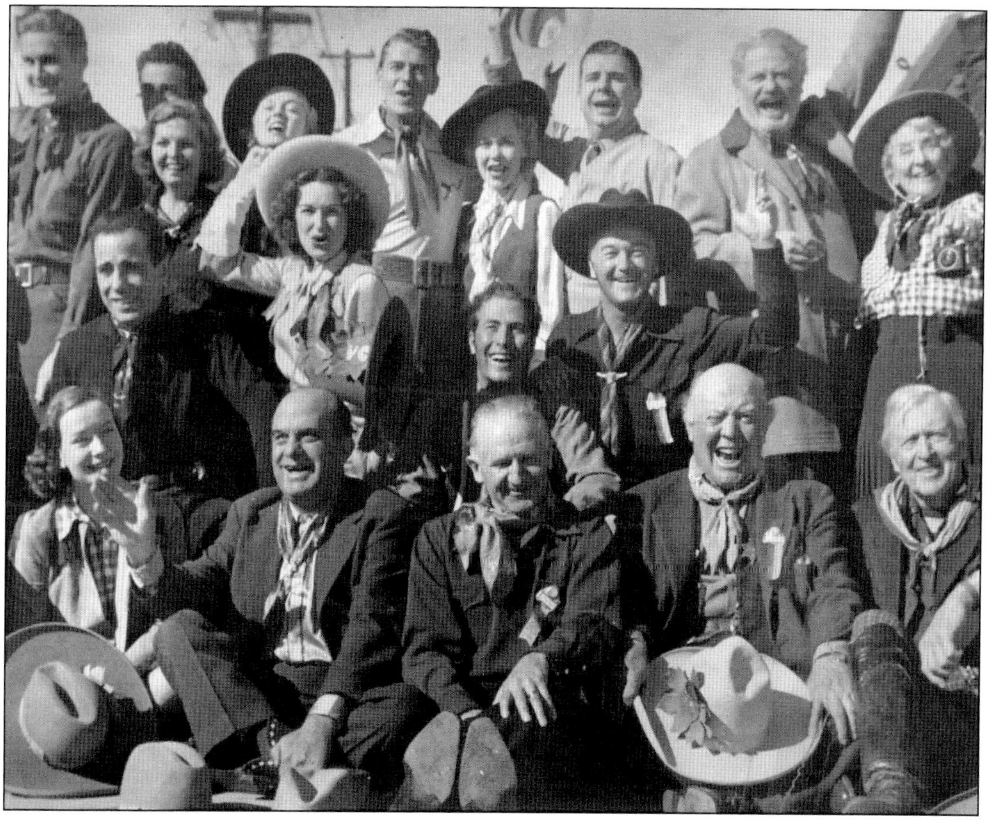

Reno is known for some of the most memorable and historic structures in Nevada, including the National Automobile Museum, the Majestic and Granada Theaters, the Mapes Hotel, and the original Riverside Casino, all of which have hosted a variety of entertainers and movie legends who traveled to Reno during the late 1940s and well into the 1950s. In this 1940 image, actors (including Ronald Reagan, Humphrey Bogart, and Errol Flynn) gather at a movie premier in downtown Reno. (BIO-B0555.)

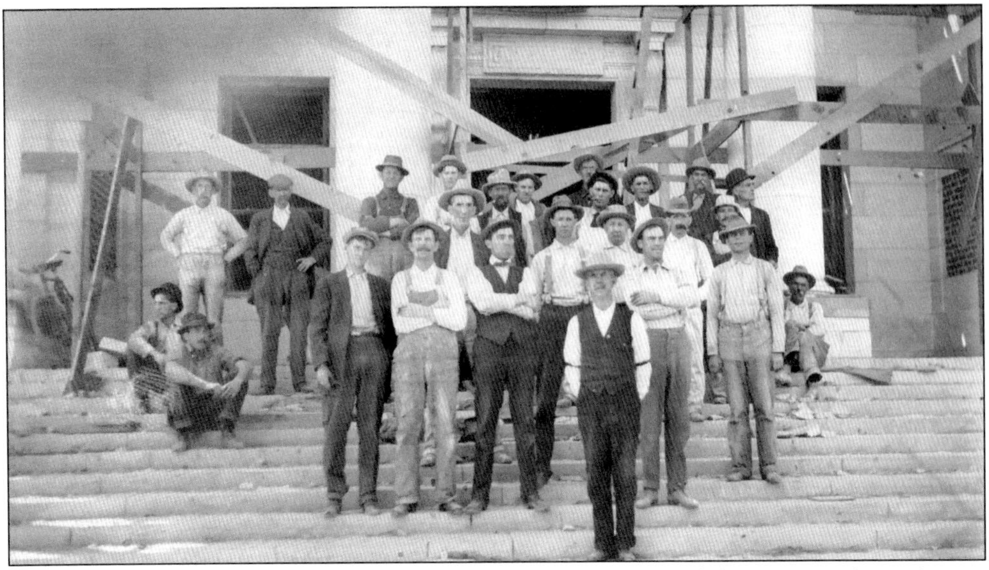

When the county seat was moved to Reno in 1871, construction of the city courthouse began. The initial red brick construction was completed in 1873 and still exists as an internal component of the building. In 1909, the courthouse was replaced by a new structure, designed by Frederic DeLongchamps. DeLongchamps won the project, which would be the first of his solo career, during a design competition. The building is Classical Revival style with a Beaux Arts influence, featuring a very recognizable copper dome. Over the years, new wings were added to the sides and back of the building. Pictured above are workers hired to construct the current courthouse.

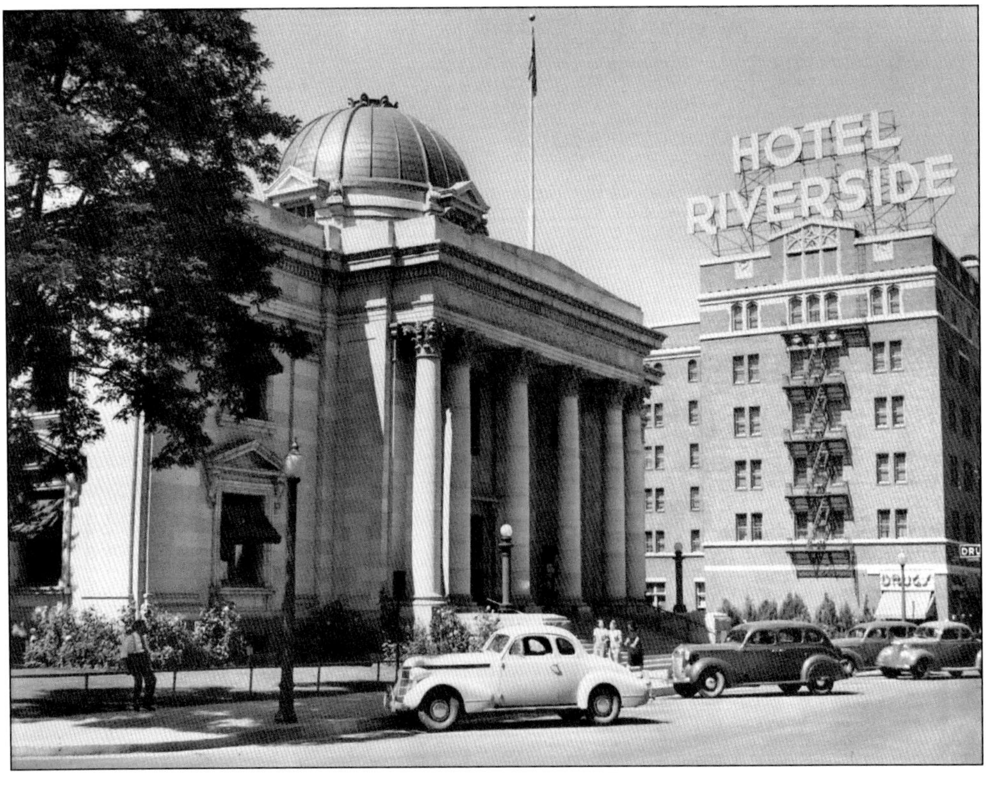

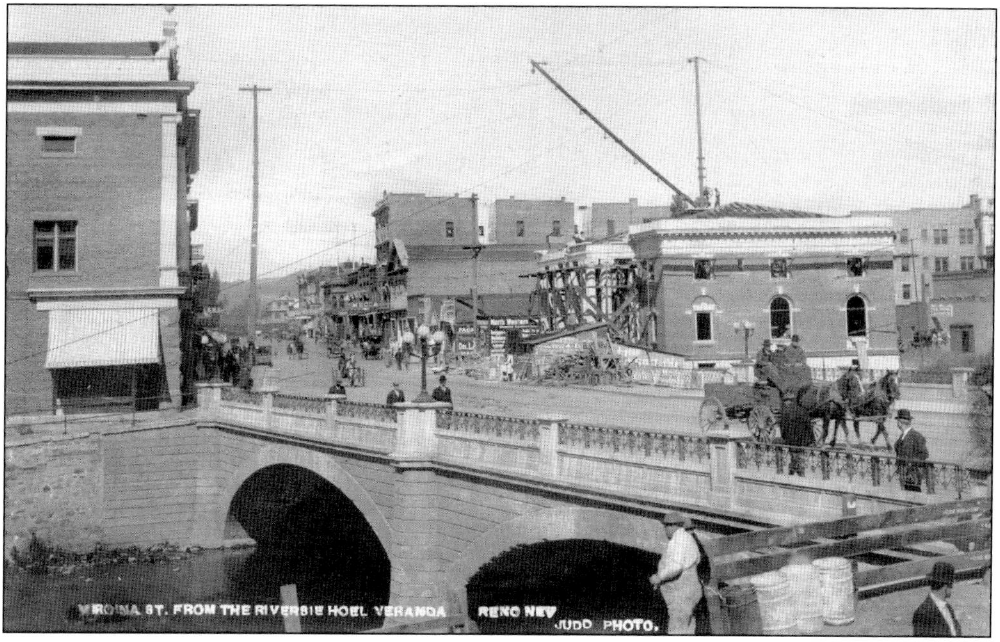

In 1904, Reno's Carnegie Free Public Library was constructed at the corner of South Virginia Street, where it provided services to the residents of Washoe County. In 1930, the Carnegie Library moved to a larger space in the old State Building in Powning Park across Mill Street. (WA-01688.)

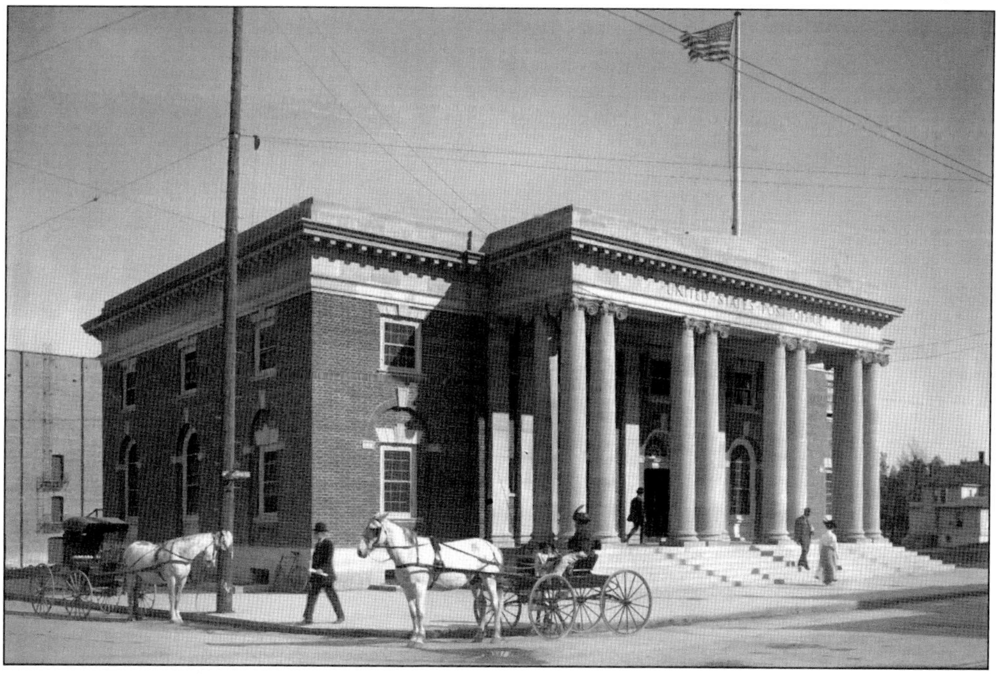

In 1931, a portion of the land occupied by Reno's Carnegie Free Public Library was sold by Katherine Kincart Coughlin of the Riverside Realty Company. The structure was soon demolished to make way for the city's new post office. In 1932, the new post office was designed by prominent Reno architect Frederic DeLongchamps. In the winter of 2013, the post office was relocated to Sierra Street. (WA-01468.)

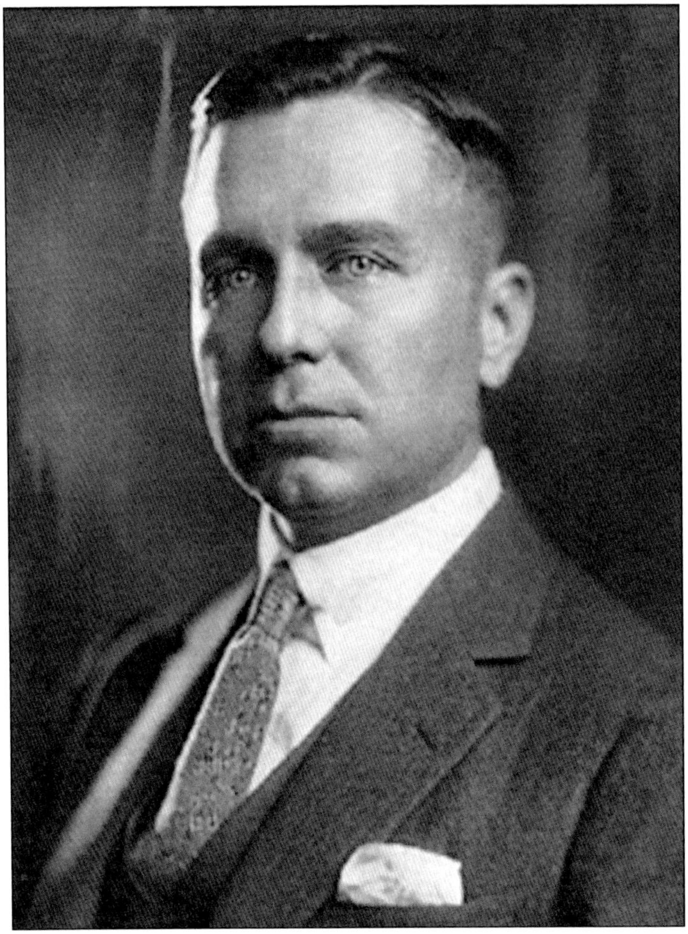

For over 50 years, Frederic DeLongchamps dominated the region as Nevada's most prolific architect. DeLongchamps, who had no extensive training in architecture, designed over 500 buildings and homes. His works included the Washoe County Courthouse, the Reno Main Post Office, the Riverside Hotel (pictured below), the First Federal Savings and Loan Association, and nine courthouses. In 1919, DeLongchamps was the only person in Nevada to hold the title of official state architect. A plaque dedicated to his memory is viewable along Virginia Street. (BIO-D-211, UNRS-P1989-55-3158.)

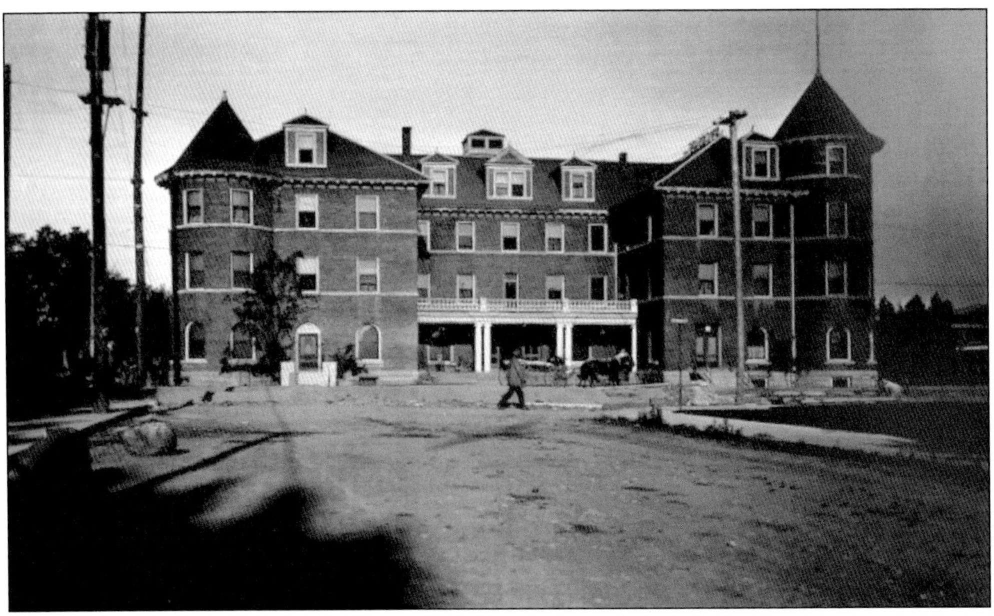

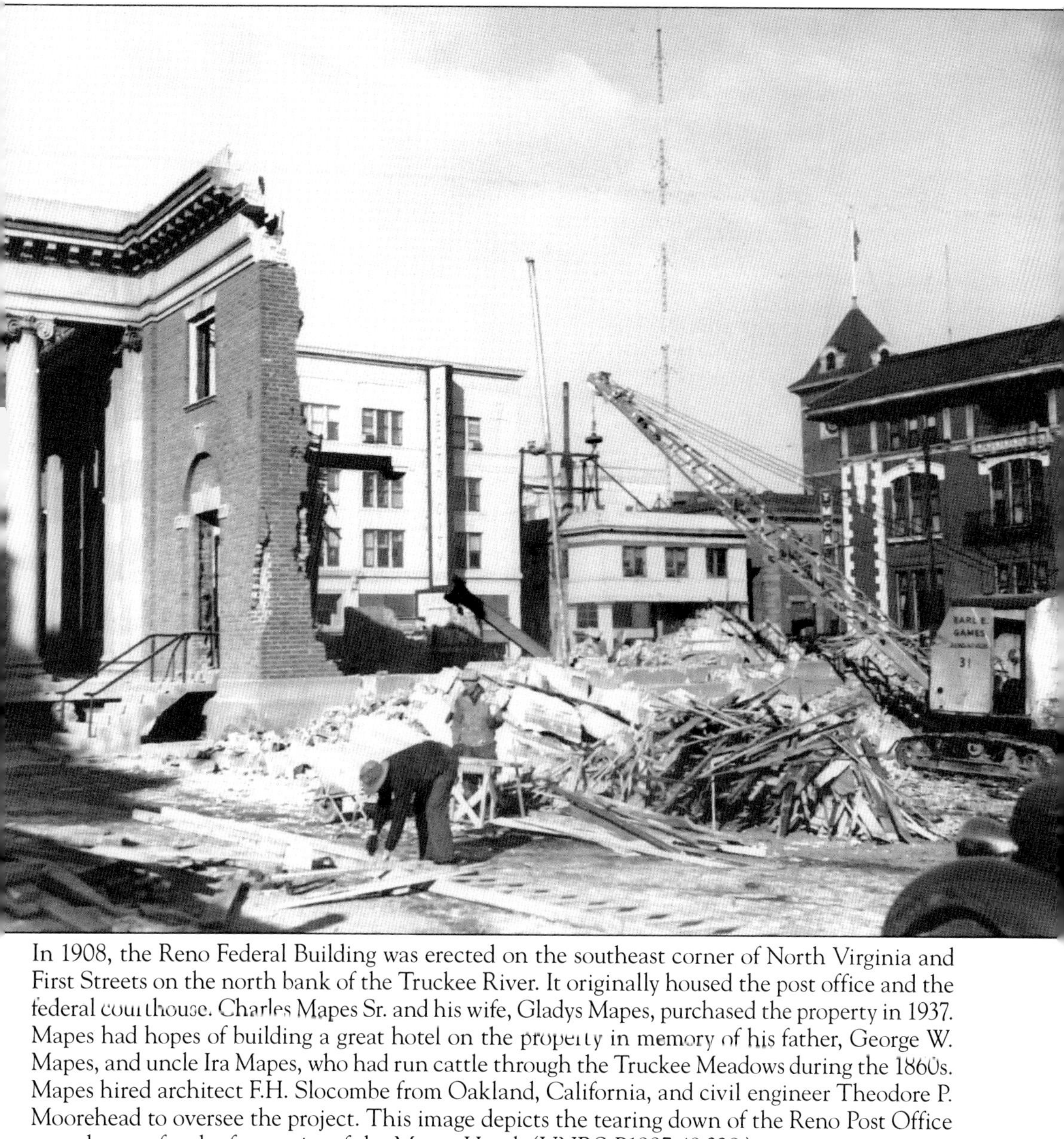

In 1908, the Reno Federal Building was erected on the southeast corner of North Virginia and First Streets on the north bank of the Truckee River. It originally housed the post office and the federal courthouse. Charles Mapes Sr. and his wife, Gladys Mapes, purchased the property in 1937. Mapes had hopes of building a great hotel on the property in memory of his father, George W. Mapes, and uncle Ira Mapes, who had run cattle through the Truckee Meadows during the 1860s. Mapes hired architect F.H. Slocombe from Oakland, California, and civil engineer Theodore P. Moorehead to oversee the project. This image depicts the tearing down of the Reno Post Office to make way for the future site of the Mapes Hotel. (UNRS-P1997-49-328.)

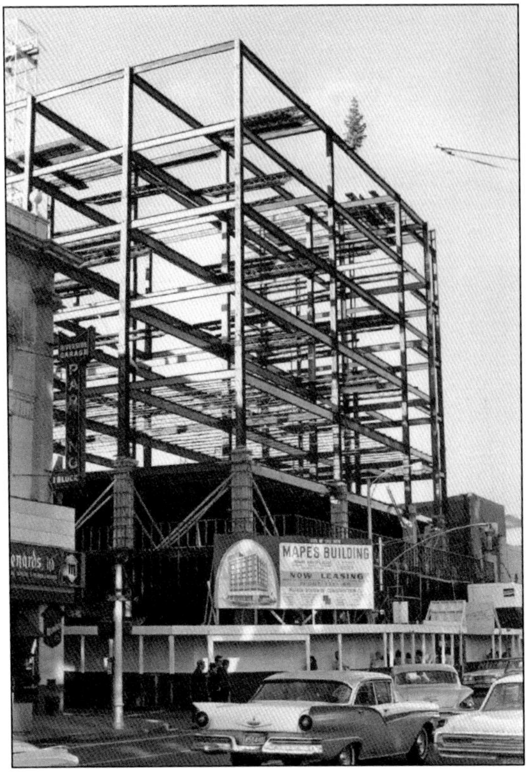

George W. Mapes began construction in January 1946; plans for the building were inspired by New York City's Art Deco–style Chrysler Building as well as the Empire State Building. The Mapes officially opened its doors on December 17, 1947, and was the first skyscraper built in the western United States since the start of World War II. The hotel contained 300 rooms as well as 40 suites—each with a living room, dining room, kitchen, bedroom, and tiled bathroom. Three corner suites were especially distinctive because the main corridor could be closed off, allowing up to five additional bedrooms to be added to the suites. (WA-04352, WA-01616.)

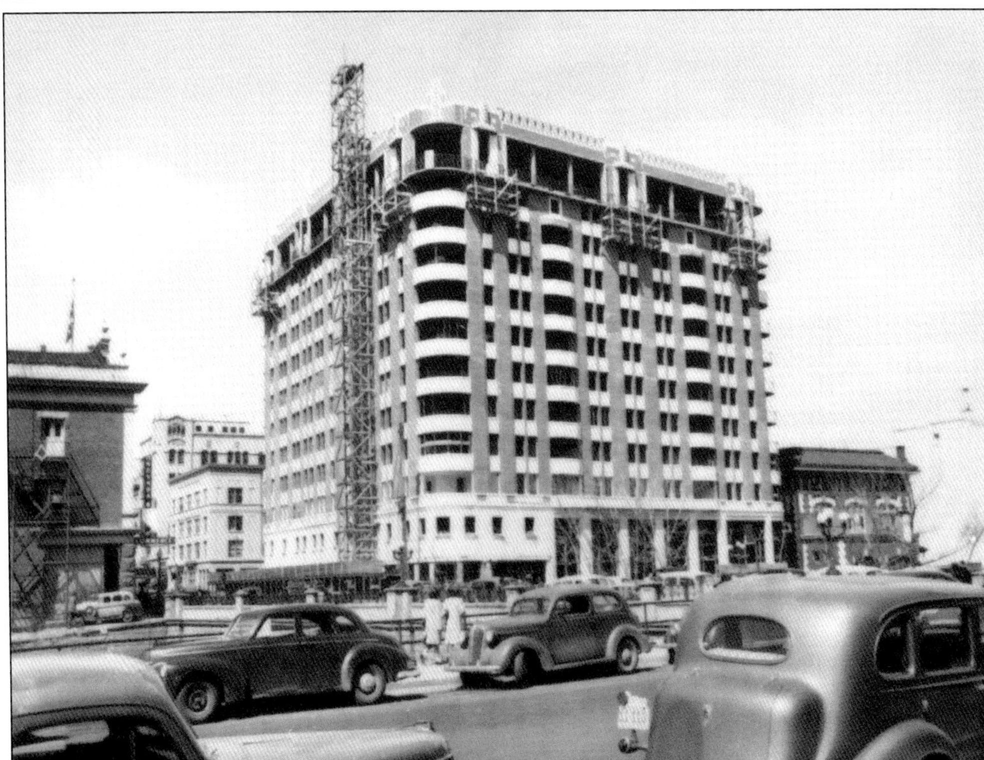

During the majority of the 1950s and 1960s, the Mapes was the premier hotel in Reno. It was popular among many celebrities of the era, including Marilyn Monroe, Montgomery Clift, and Clark Gable, who stayed in the corner suites during the filming of *The Misfits*. Other guests included Sen. Joseph McCarthy and Pres. Harry Truman. (WA-01633.)

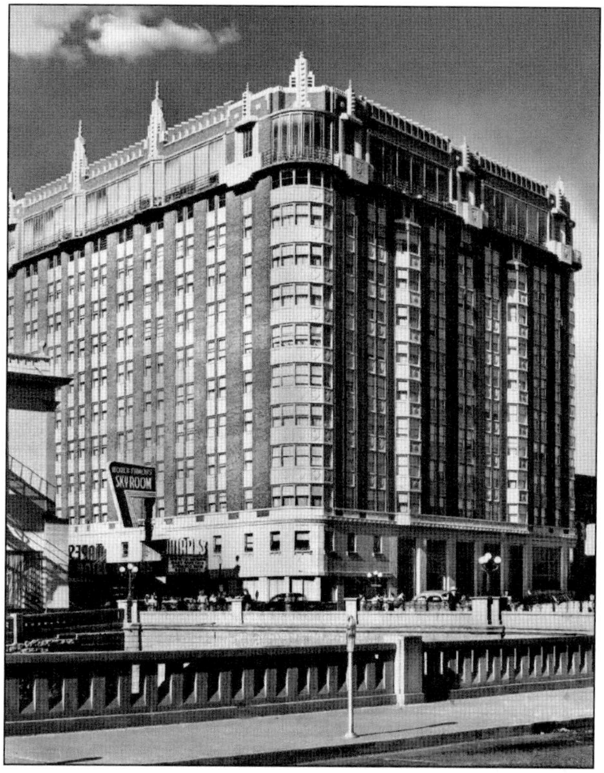

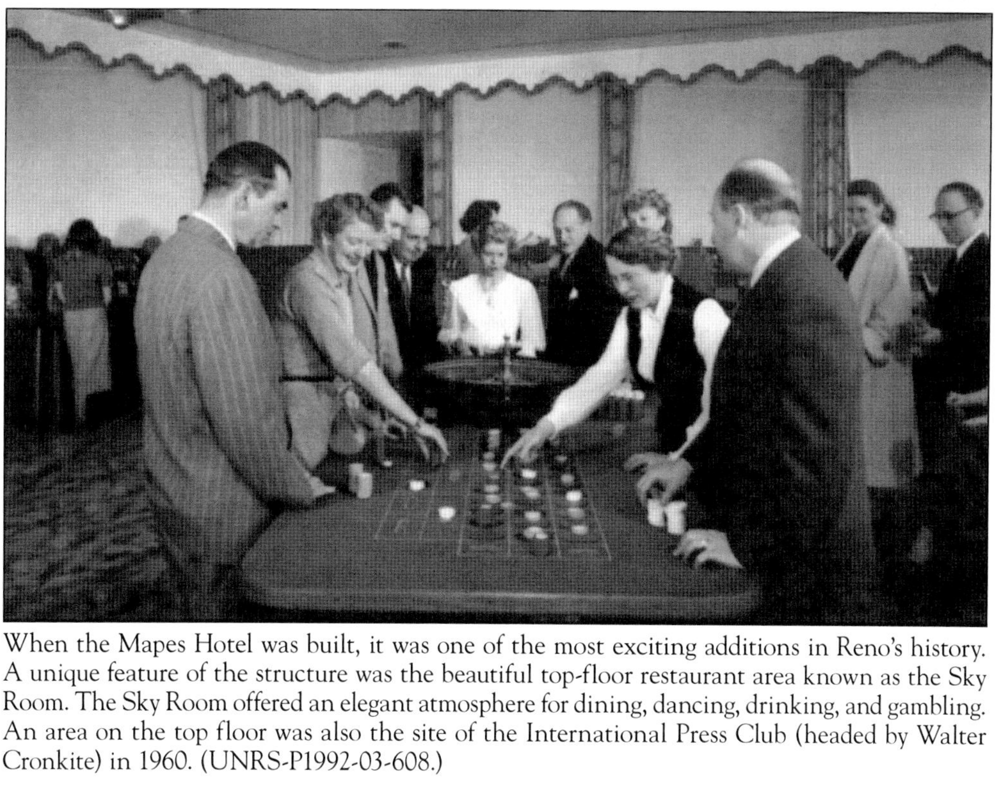

When the Mapes Hotel was built, it was one of the most exciting additions in Reno's history. A unique feature of the structure was the beautiful top-floor restaurant area known as the Sky Room. The Sky Room offered an elegant atmosphere for dining, dancing, drinking, and gambling. An area on the top floor was also the site of the International Press Club (headed by Walter Cronkite) in 1960. (UNRS-P1992-03-608.)

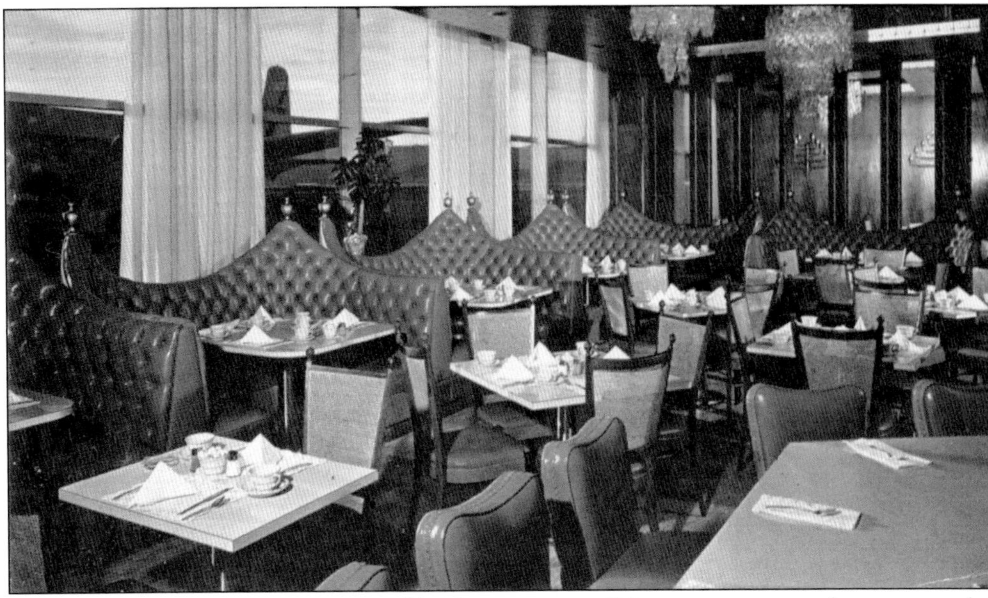

The Mapes Ambassador Room was capable of serving up to 400 guests at a time and was surrounded by large windows providing unrivaled views of the Washoe Valley and Truckee River. The Hotel was a popular venue for famous entertainers of the time, including pianist Liberace, burlesque dancer Gypsy Rose Lee, Sammy Davis Jr., Mae West, Judy Garland, and the Marx Brothers. (UNRS-P1992-03-592.)

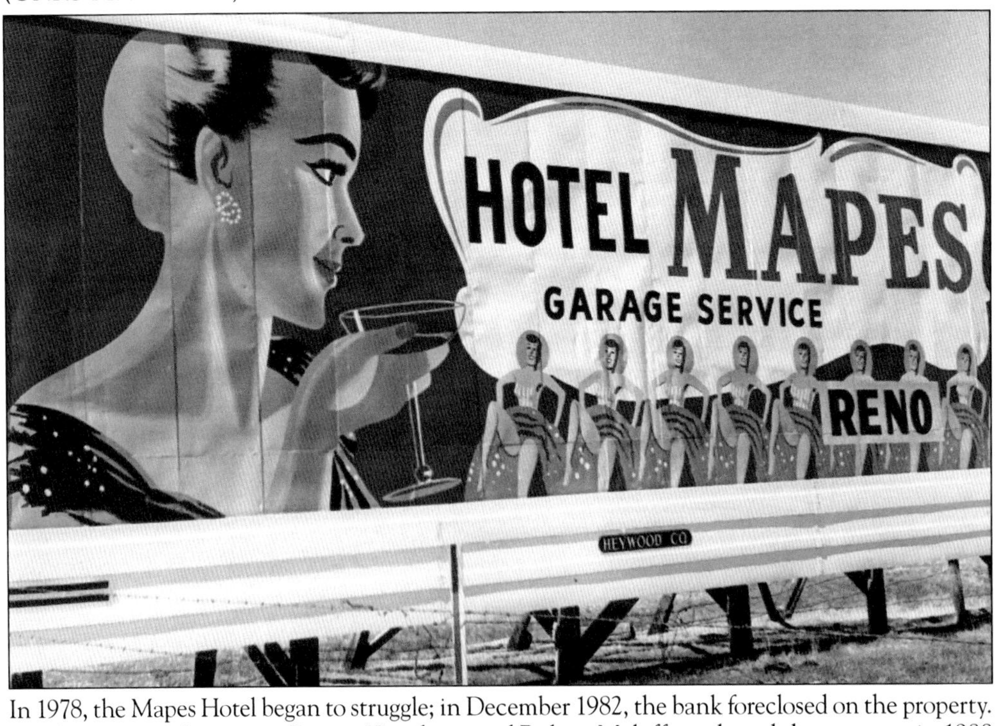

In 1978, the Mapes Hotel began to struggle; in December 1982, the bank foreclosed on the property. Sundowner Hotel partners George Karadanis and Robert Maloff purchased the property in 1988 but never reopened it. In 1996, they sold the property to the Reno Redevelopment Agency. The Reno City Council demolished the hotel on January 30, 2000. (UNRS-P1985-08-14095.)

Located on East First Street, immediately to the east of the Mapes Hotel, the Majestic Theater was built by Sen. George Nixon in 1910. The theater offered dramatic productions, vaudeville performances, and, in later years, movies. During the first two seasons of the theater's existence, legendary performer Sarah Bernhardt (below) one of the pioneer silent movie actresses of the era, appeared in a production of *Camille*. The theater was purchased in 1974 by the Mapes family, who replaced the building with a parking structure for hotel guests. (WA-1812, LC-3C04487C.)

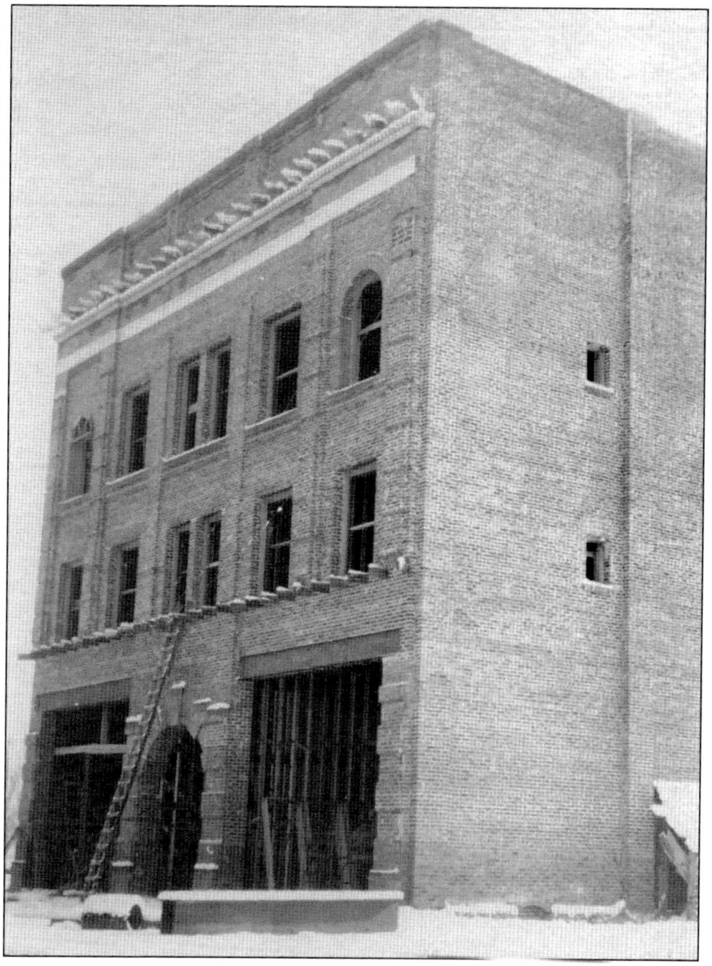

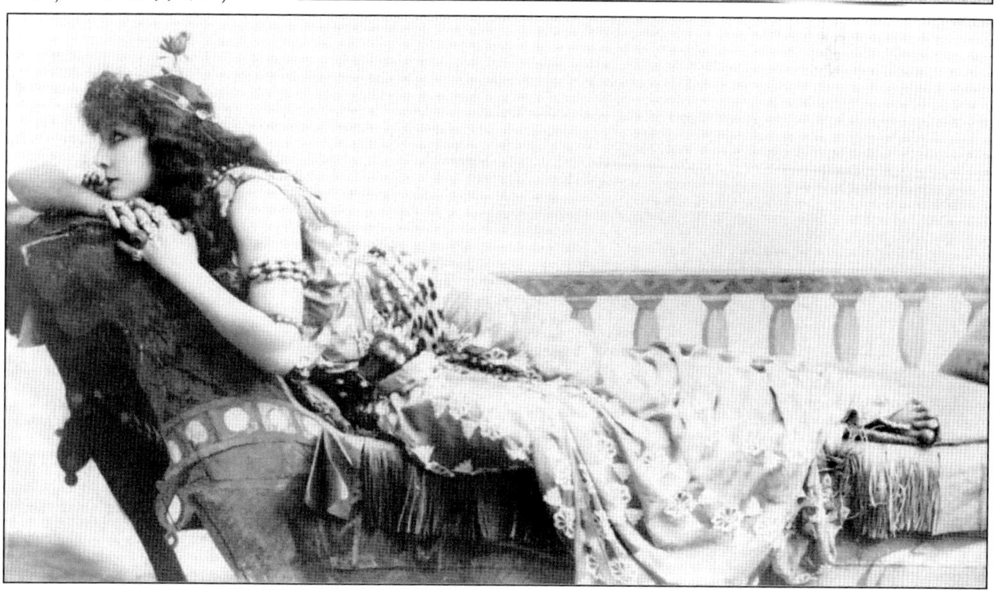

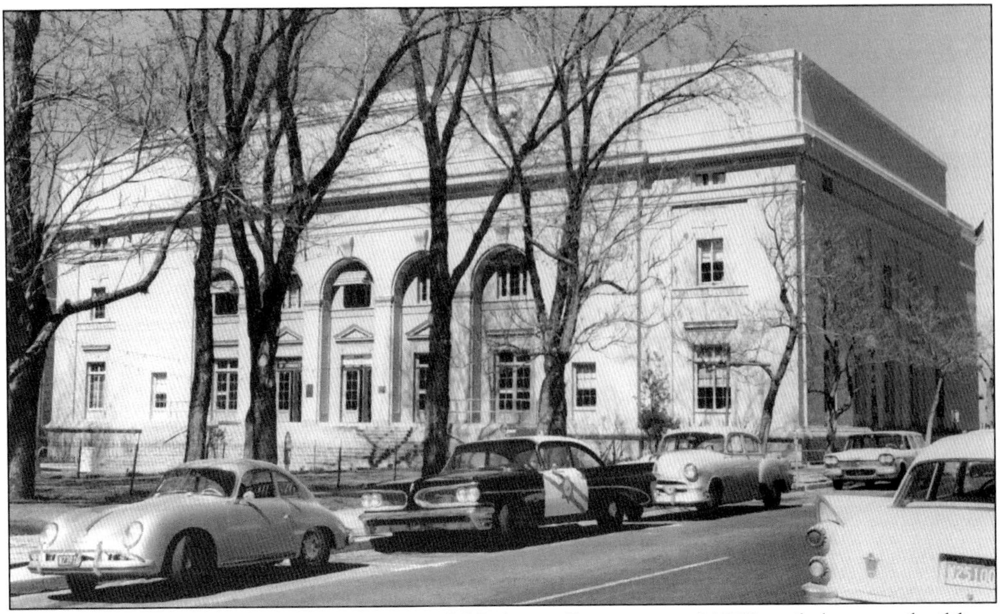

The headquarters for the Transcontinental Highway Exposition of 1927 and the state building were built in 1926 on the southeast corner of Mill and Virginia Streets; this location later became the home of the Pioneer Center for Performing Arts, and the building was used by the community for over four decades. (WA-001383.)

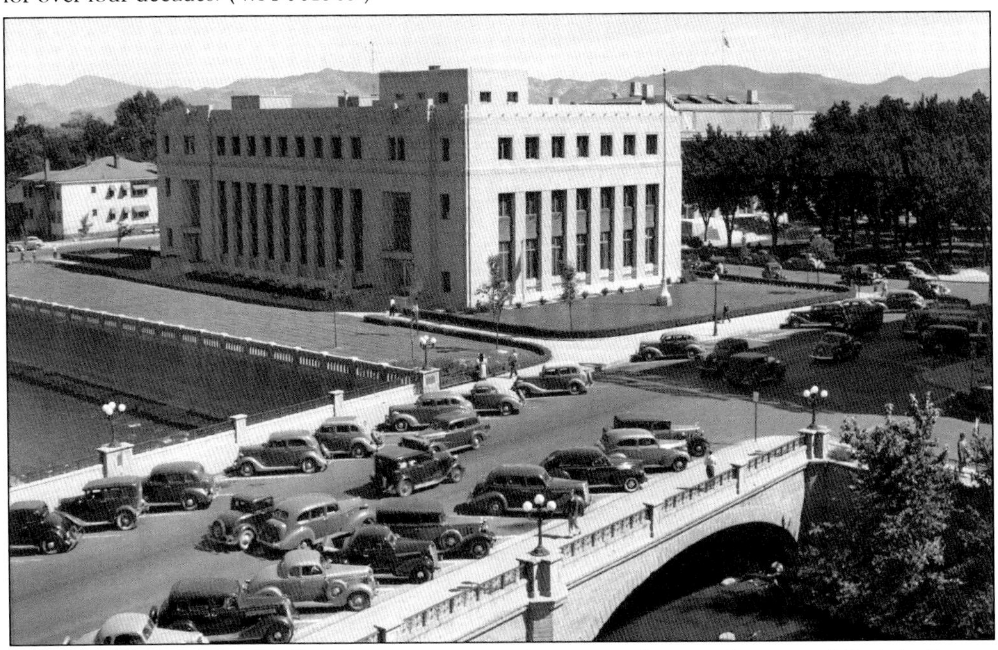

On August 16, 1906, a small park was constructed opposite the courthouse on Virginia Street. Simply called City Park, it was Reno's first public square. In 1911, the space was renamed in honor of Christopher Columbus Powning, one of the most influential citizens of Washoe County. On the east side of Powning Square stood the new State Building, where the Pioneer Theater for the Performing Arts currently stands. Powning Square can be seen to the right of the building. (WA-1481.)

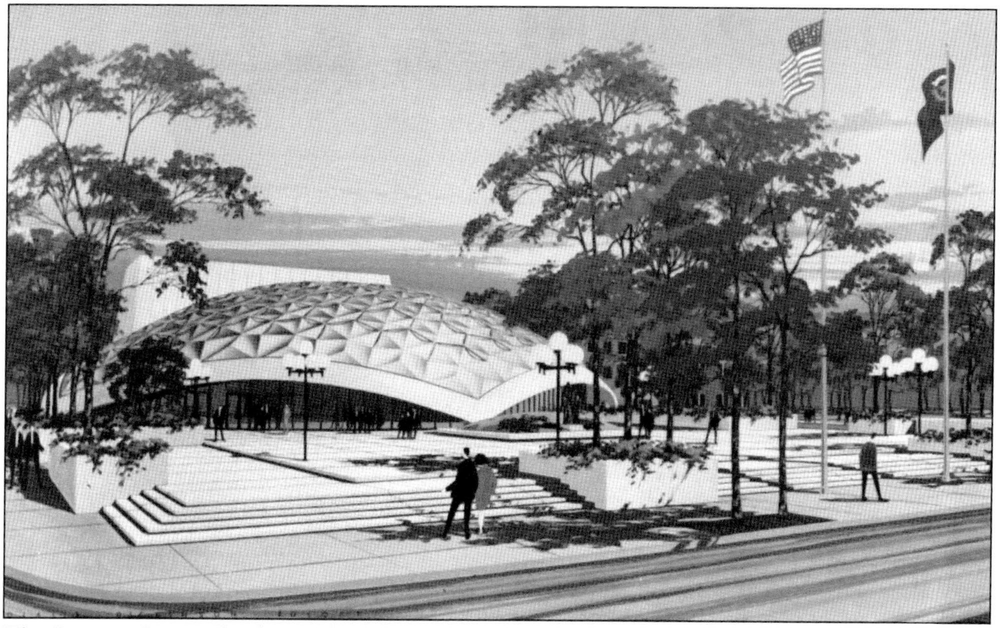

The Pioneer Center for the Performing Arts (originally the Pioneer Theater-Auditorium) was at various times home to the Nevada Historical Society, Nevada Department of Motor Vehicles, the National Guard, the Justice of the Peace, and the Washoe County Library. The current building was inspired by architect R. Buckminster Fuller and opened to the public in 1968, becoming the prime venue for performance art and culture in Reno. (WA-01370.)

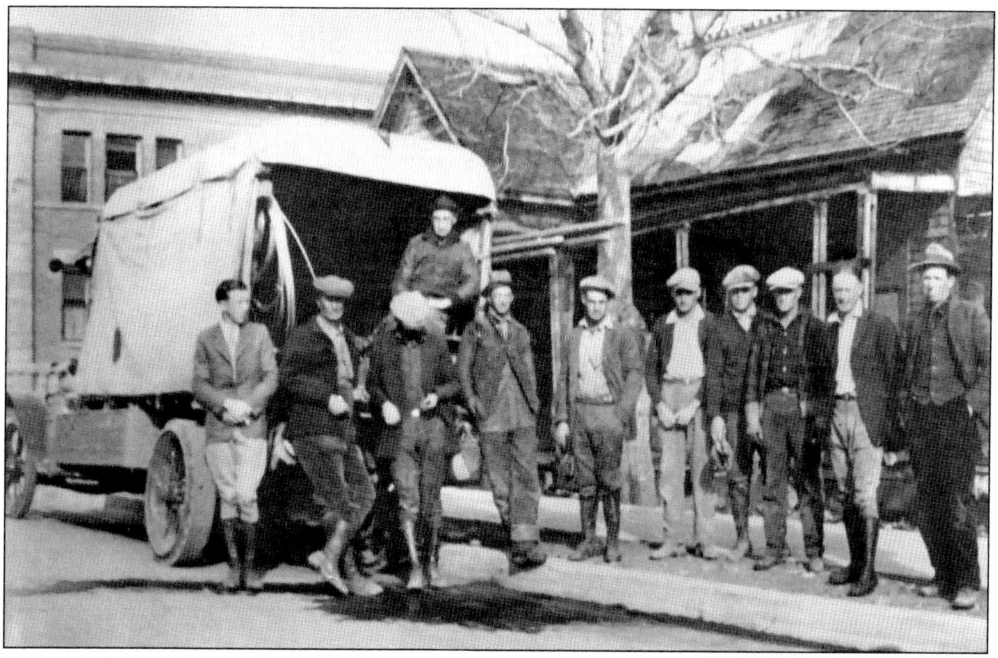

In 1880, the innovation of the telephone made its mark in the county clerk's office in Reno. Shortly after that, the Nevada Bell Company was built on First and Center Streets. In 1996, the building was replaced by the Cal Neva parking garage. This image shows early workers of the telephone company in downtown Reno. (WA-1764.)

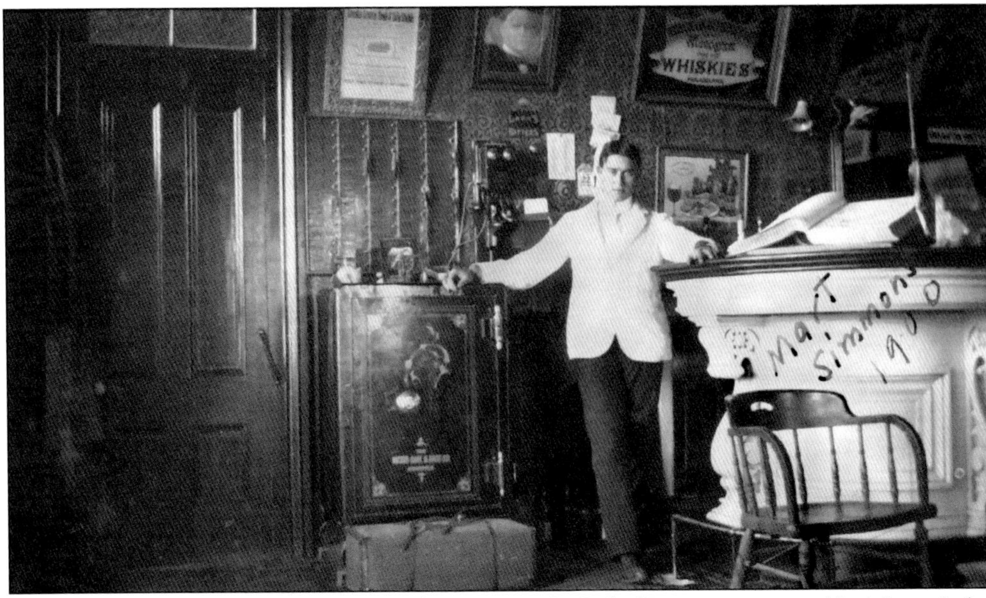

In 1880, William Thompson purchased the very popular Lake House once owned by Myron Lake. Thomas operated the hotel until 1896, when he sold it to Harry Gosse. By 1907, Gosse had built what was described by one *Nevada State Journal* reporter as being "by far the most pretentious hotel in the [state] of Nevada." This photograph was taken from the bar inside the Lake House in 1900. (WA-10691.)

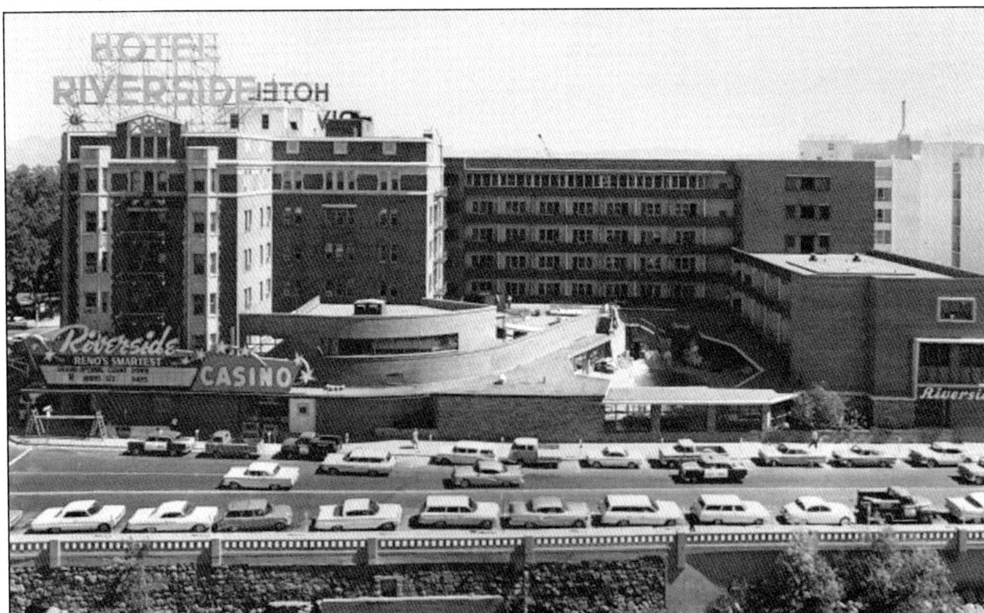

Harry Gosse had rebuilt the property to include a three-story, 110-room brick structure, which featured some of the finest accommodations in Reno. After the property was destroyed in a devastating fire in 1922, Gosse sold the property to local banker George Wingfield. Wingfield commissioned well-known local architect Frederic DeLongchamps, who designed the hotel as a six-story brick building with arched windows, traceried parapets, and terra-cotta trim. (Courtesy of Wild River Grille.)

The Riverside Hotel thrived for the next three decades under the management of George Wingfield and his various partners. The popular hotel attracted a variety of famous guests, such as Ted Lewis, Frank Sinatra, Gloria Vanderbilt, and Clare Boothe, some of whom had come to Reno for quick divorces. This image is of Sunny Ainsworth Manville taking residence prior to her divorce from wealthy asbestos heir Tommy Manville. (BIO-A-133.)

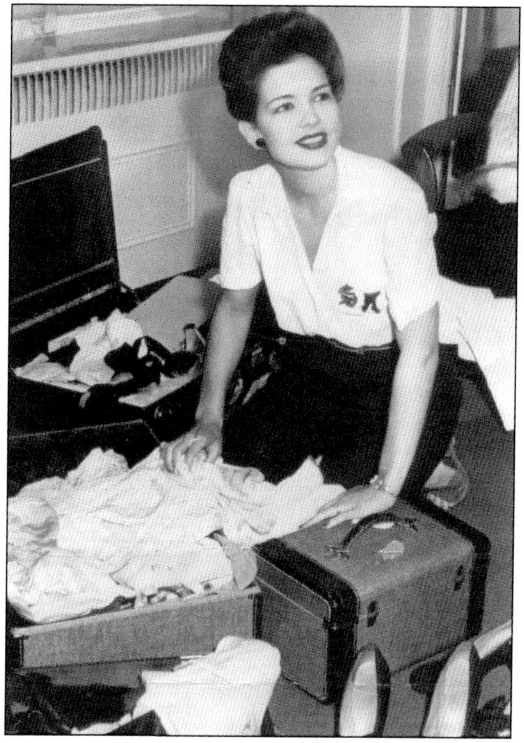

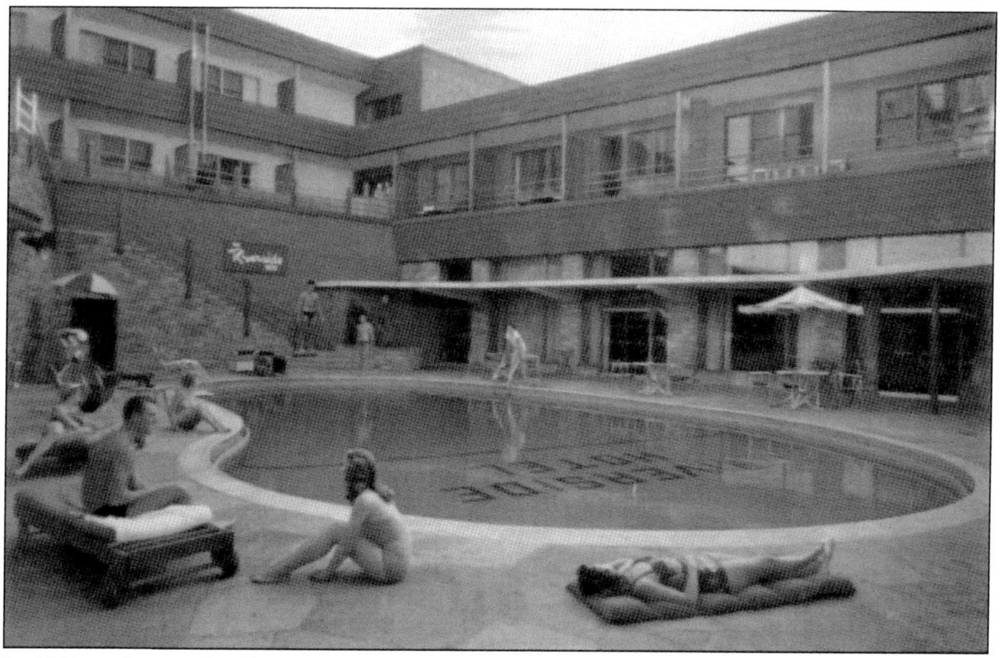

In 1949, architects Frank Green and Frederic DeLongchamps designed an addition on the west side of the Riverside Hotel. The new section featured an additional casino, theater, restaurant, and extra hotel space, as well as Reno's first hotel swimming pool. The $1 million expansion, which faced the Truckee River and spanned from Virginia to Sierra Streets, quickly distinguished the Riverside as one of the most modern hotels in the western United States. (WA-08121.)

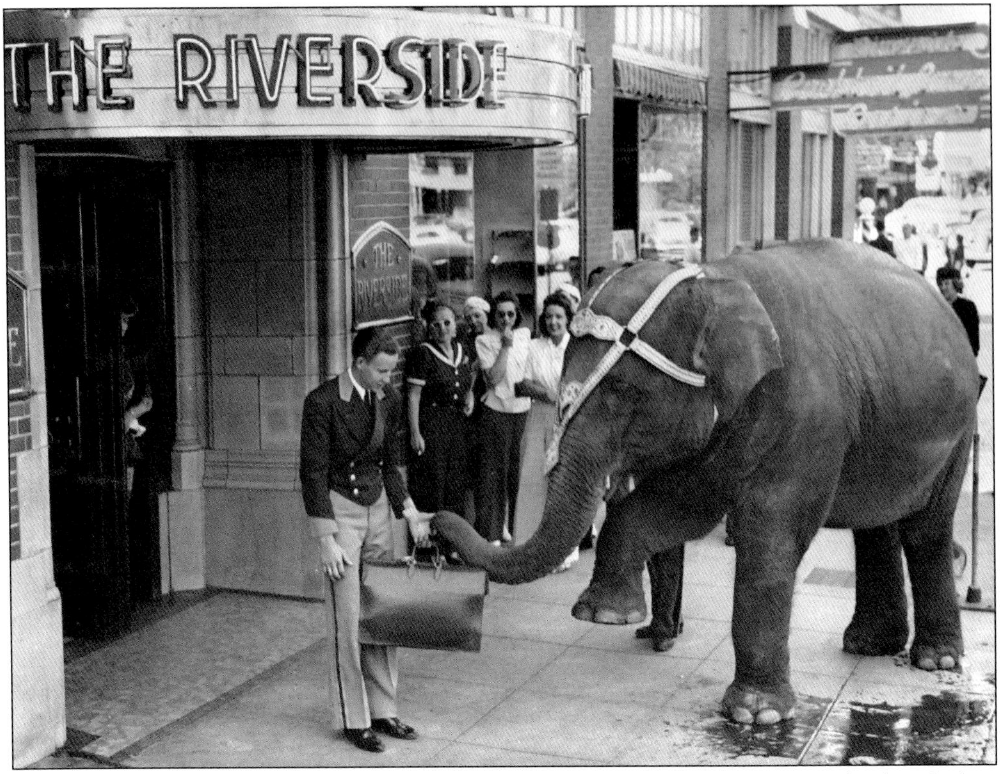

George Wingfield sold the Riverside to a group of businessmen in 1955, beginning the slow decline of the property, which underwent several changes in ownership over the next three decades. During the 1960s, the Riverside was forced to close four separate times because of bankruptcy, tax delinquency, and crooked gambling practices. In 1971, Jessie Beck purchased the property and opened her own casino. (WA-3310.)

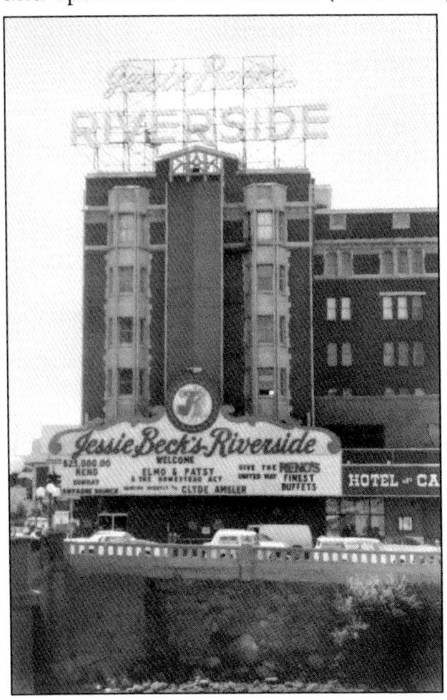

Jessie Beck ran the hotel until 1978, when she sold the Riverside property to Harrah's Entertainment, which then sold it to "Pick" Hobson. Pick oversaw the hotel and casino until its closure in 1986. In 1989, Canadian businessman Peter Ng purchased the property, which stood empty for the next eight years. In 2000, Artspace, a Minneapolis-based developer, converted the hotel into 35 artist lofts and developed the ground floor into retail space. (WA-01555.)

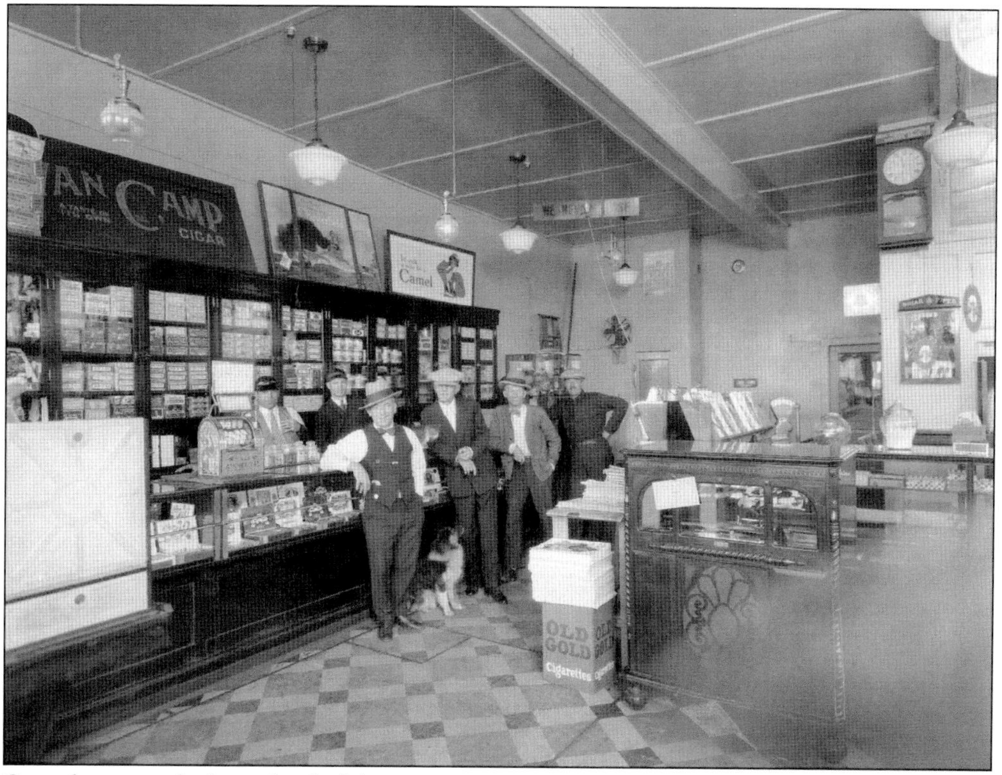

Over the years, the lower level of the Riverside was home to a variety of retailers, restaurants, and bars. The 1927 image above, taken by the Nevada Photo Service, shows the Riverside Cigar Store operated by Mr. Goldwater. The photograph to the right shows a man with his bike in front of the Pettis Riverside Pharmacy around 1950. The Riverside was also host to a daily newspaper stand, retail shops, and restaurants; there was also a small airline service in the main lobby for making travel reservations. Today, the Riverside is home to elegant dining establishments and artist studios. (RS-P1992-01-8942, Dave Stafford Collection.)

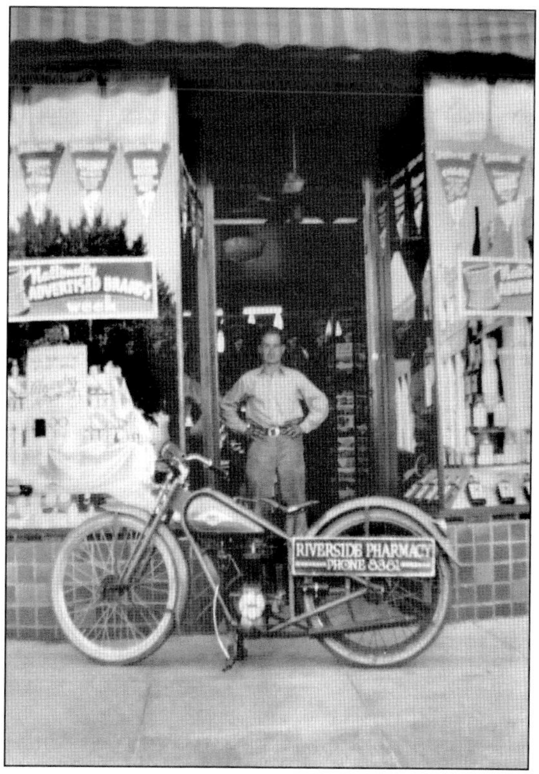

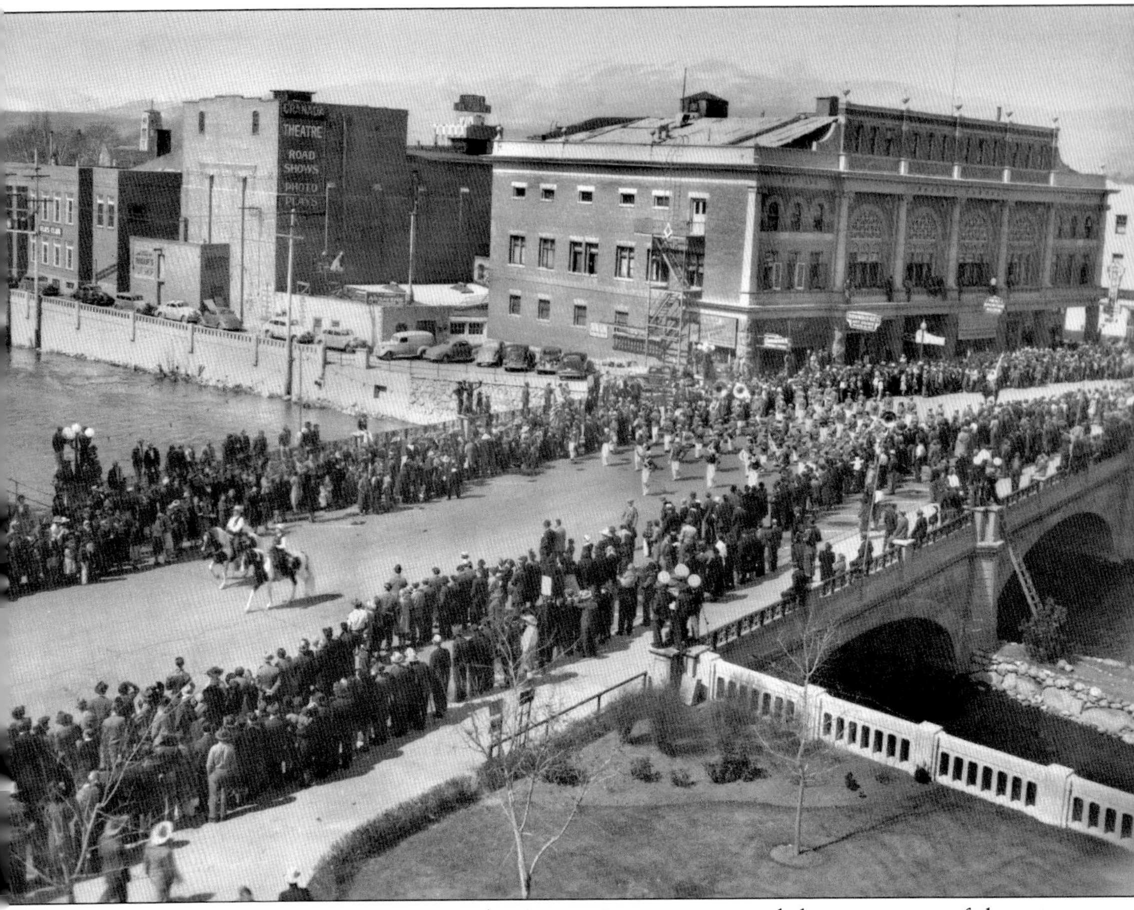

Upon its opening in 1890, McKissick's Opera House entertained the city as one of the primary theaters in the community. In 1910, US senator George S. Nixon constructed a second theater, called the Majestic Theater, on East First Street. Only five years later, the Rialto (Reno's third theater) was constructed on the corner of West First and Sierra Streets, where the Century Riverside Theaters now reside. The Rialto, which had a beautiful neon blue sign above the front entrance, was much larger than the Majestic Theater. It was later renamed the Granada and was considered the most popular theater between New York and San Francisco. The theater can be seen to the left of the bridge in this photograph taken during a parade down South Virginia Street. (WA-3140)

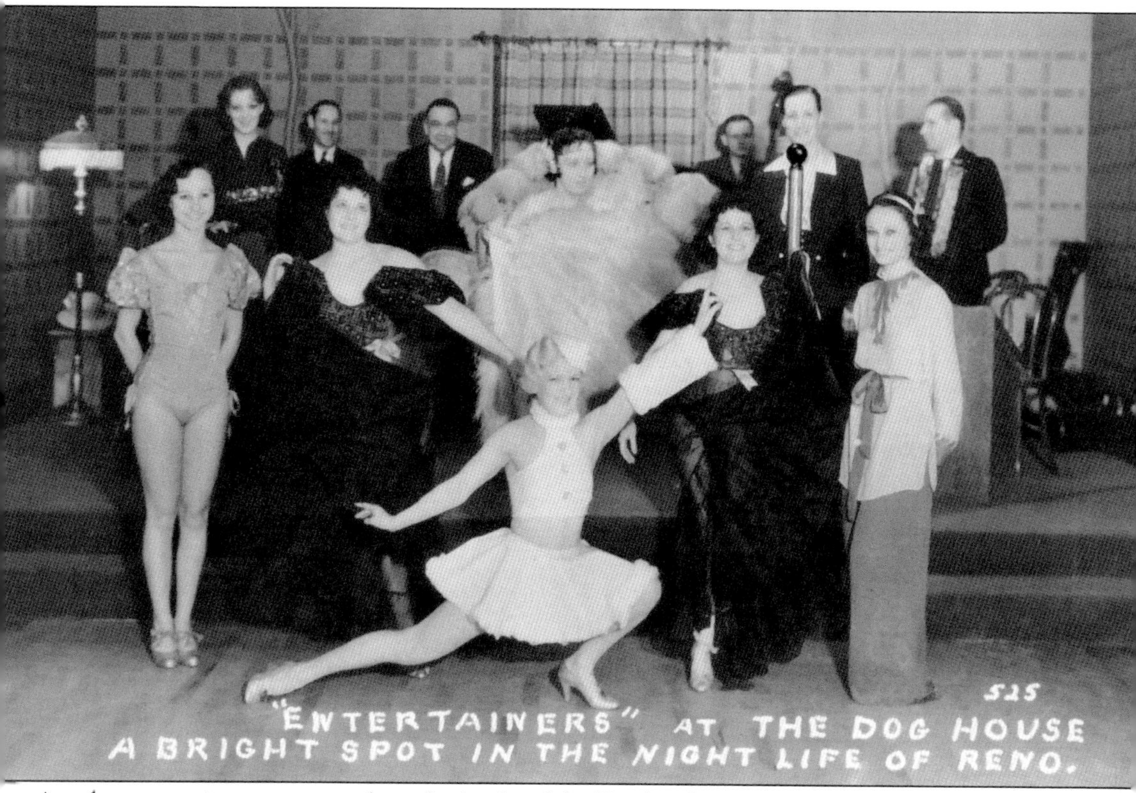

Another entertainment venue along the banks of the Truckee River was the Dog House, a very popular dance hall, theater, casino, and restaurant named in honor of a wire-haired terrier called Poochy. The club, which gained popularity during the Nevada divorce craze of the late 1930s and 1940s, often used the slogan "the Divorcee's Haven." The venue claimed to be the largest cabaret in Nevada and featured an eclectic mix of performers, often including fire dancers, hula dancers, tap dancers, magicians, oriental fan dancers, and vocalists. Many divorcees would frequent the venue as they waited for the finalization of their marriages. In 1994, the Cal Neva razed the building to create a parking garage. This image showcases a variety of entertainers at the Dog House in 1940. (WA-03435.)

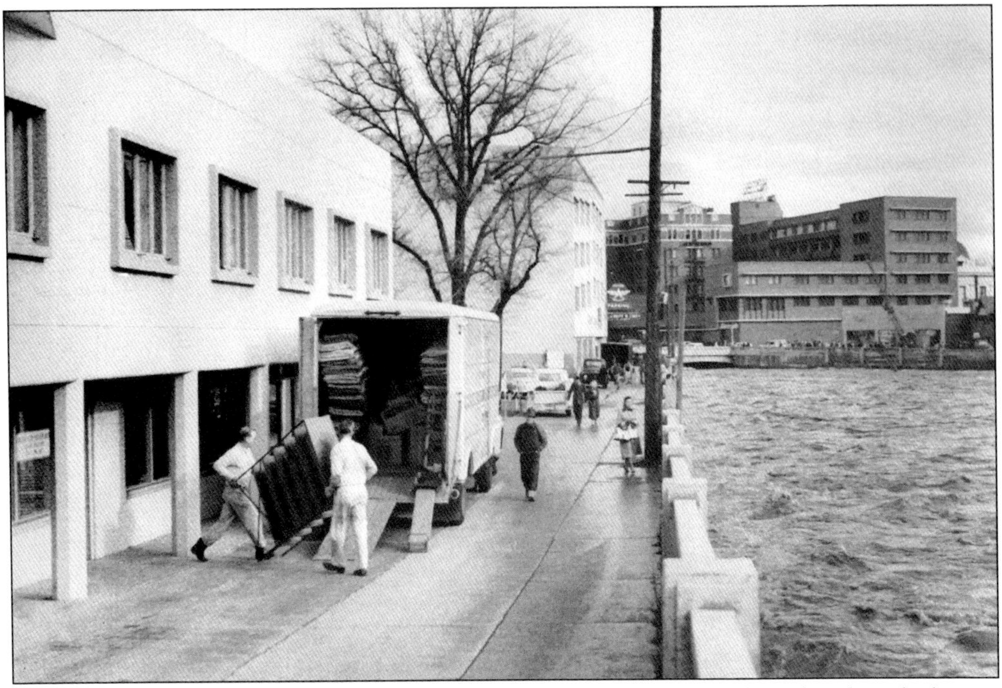

The space at 232 West First Street, across from the First United Methodist Church and adjacent to the Rialto Theater, was once home to the Hughes Porter Building and Furniture Store. This building now houses multiple retail and dining establishments, with additional apartments on the upper floors overlooking the Truckee River. This image shows movers transporting furniture from the building. (WA-10056.)

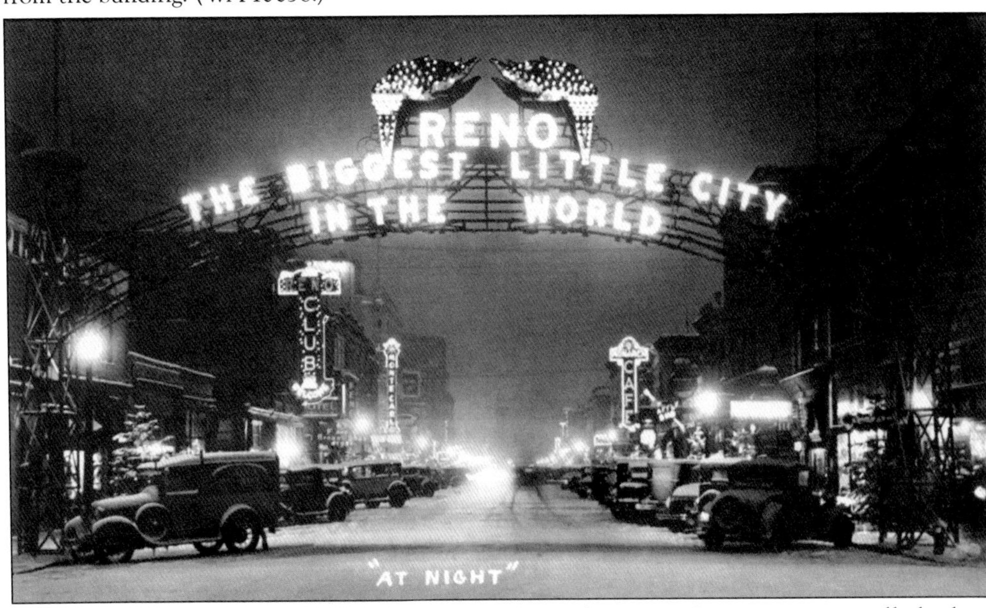

The iconic Reno Arch, located on Virginia Street in downtown Reno, was originally built in 1926 to celebrate the completion of the Lincoln and Victory Highways. From 1935 until 1963, the second version of the Reno Arch featured the city's newly adopted motto, "Reno: the biggest little city in the world." (WA-08004.)

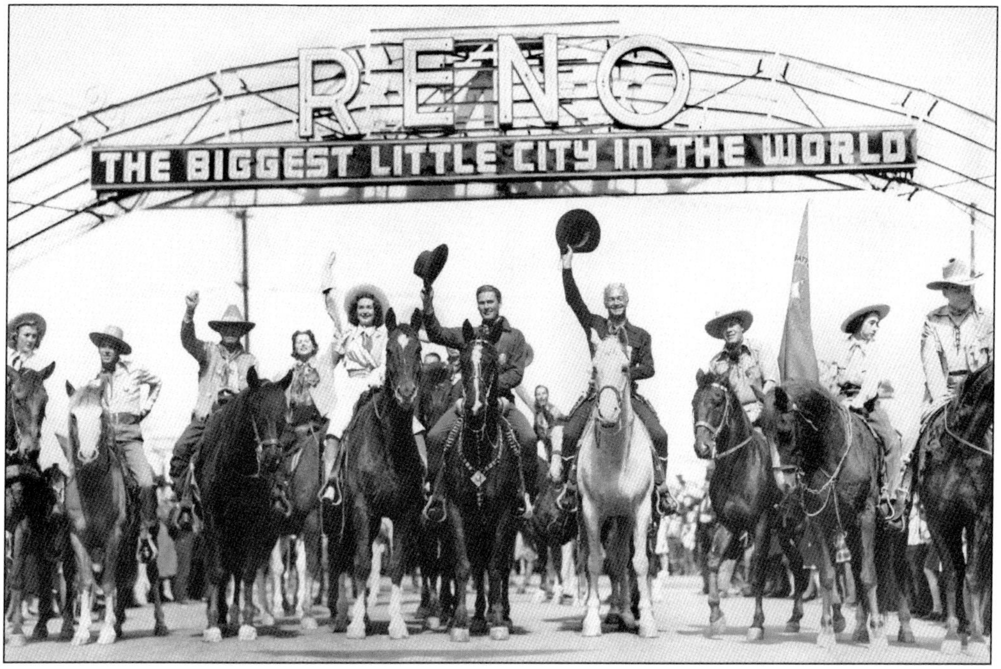

The original Reno Arch was moved to the Idlewild Park, then to Paradise Park, and then was used as a prop over east Fourth Street in the 1994 film *Cobb*. In 1995, the arch was moved to its permanent location on Lake Street, just south of the Truckee River between the National Automobile Museum and the Siena Hotel Casino. (WA-07420.)

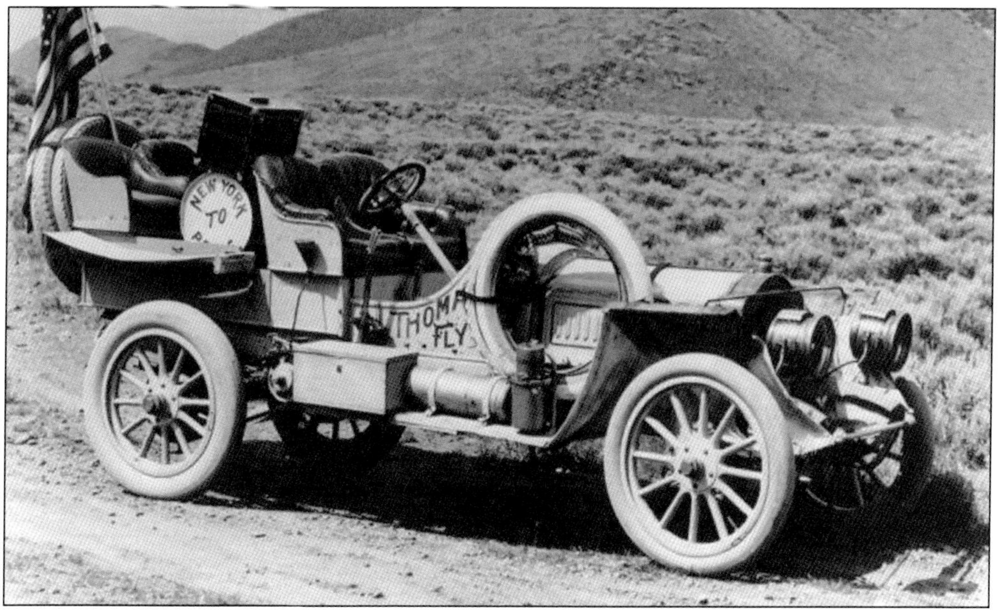

The National Automobile Museum, located on Lake Street next to Reno's iconic arch, was built in 1989 in honor of casino owner Bill Harrah. It was funded by several private grants and donations and was constructed to house over 200 historic automobiles, including the notorious Thomas Flyer (pictured), which won the around-the-world adventure, the Great Race. (Courtesy of the National Automobile Museum.)

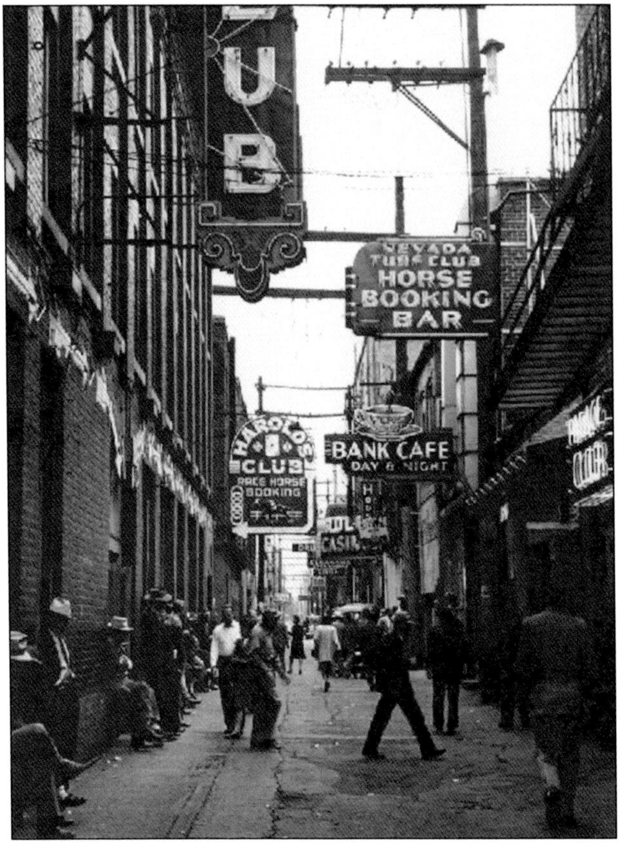

William "Bill" Harrah opened his first bingo hall (pictured at left) behind Harold's Club in Douglas Alley in 1937 and, by 1946, opened the Harrah's Club on north Virginia Street in downtown Reno. Harrah was known for breaking social barriers; he hired female dealers for the casino floor and was the first to invite African American performers to entertain in his establishment. The main theater in Harrah's casino was named Sammy's Showroom in honor of legendary entertainer Sammy Davis Jr., whose Duesenberg can be viewed inside the National Automobile Museum. The photograph below shows the soon-to-be site of the museum. (Courtesy of the National Automobile Museum.)

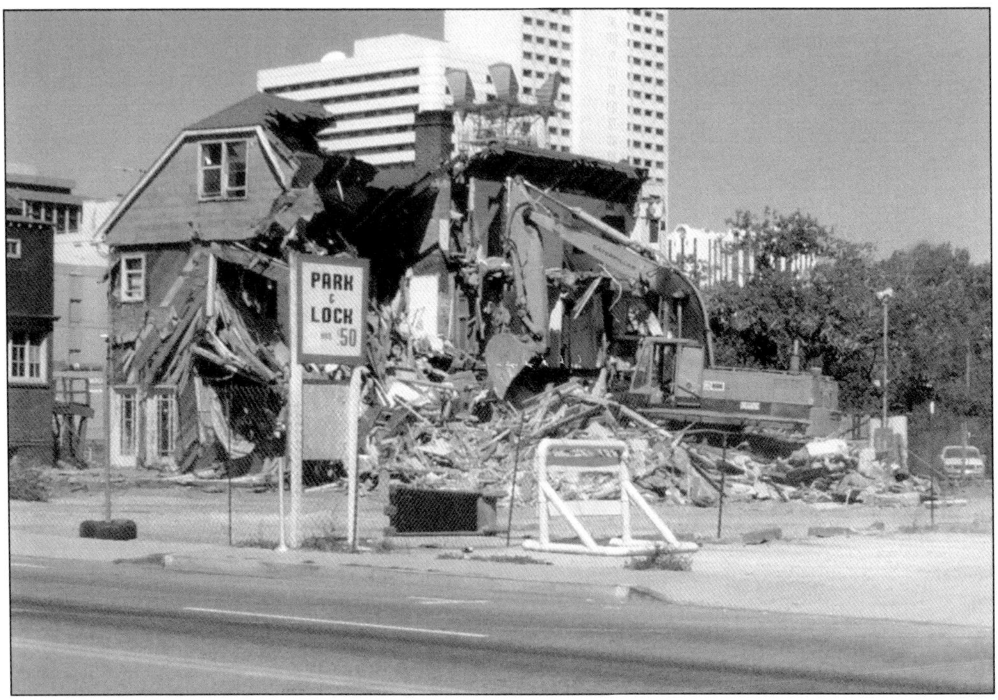

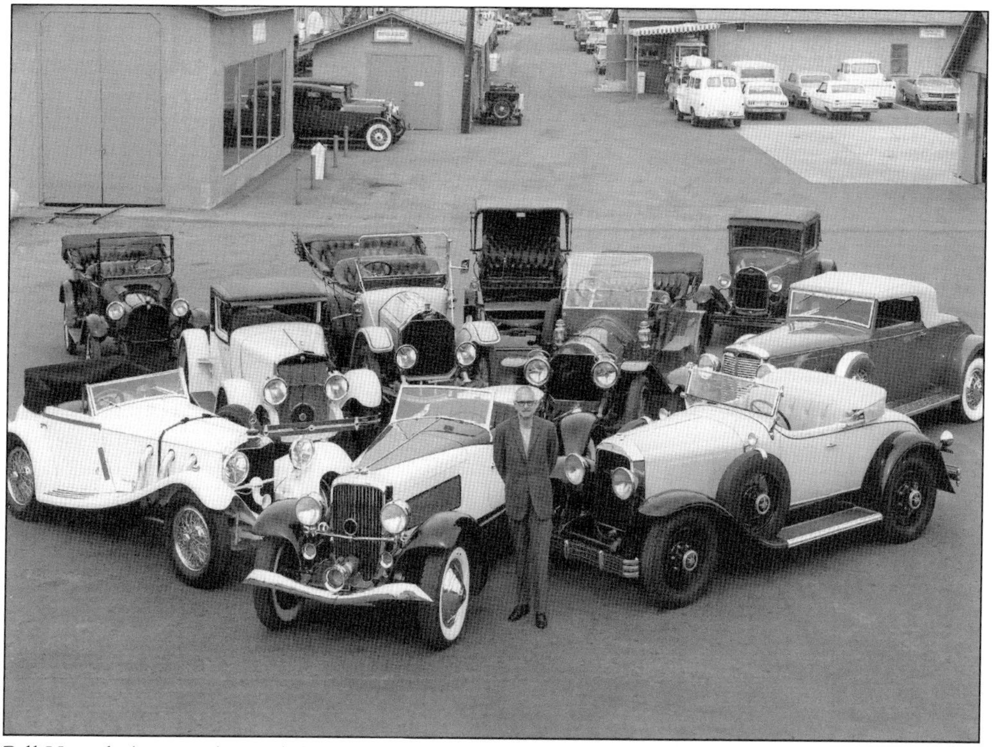

Bill Harrah (pictured at right) was known for the enormous selection of classic cars he collected during his lifetime, and it is said that, when his family car was stolen, he promised his sister that one day he would own a duplicate version of every automobile that their father had ever owned. Harrah was an incredibly prominent individual in the community and in the Nevada gaming industry; his influence led to the 1955 creation of the Nevada Gaming Control Board. The gaming commission was created with the intention to eliminate corruption and crime in the Nevada gaming scene. (Courtesy of the National Automobile Museum.)

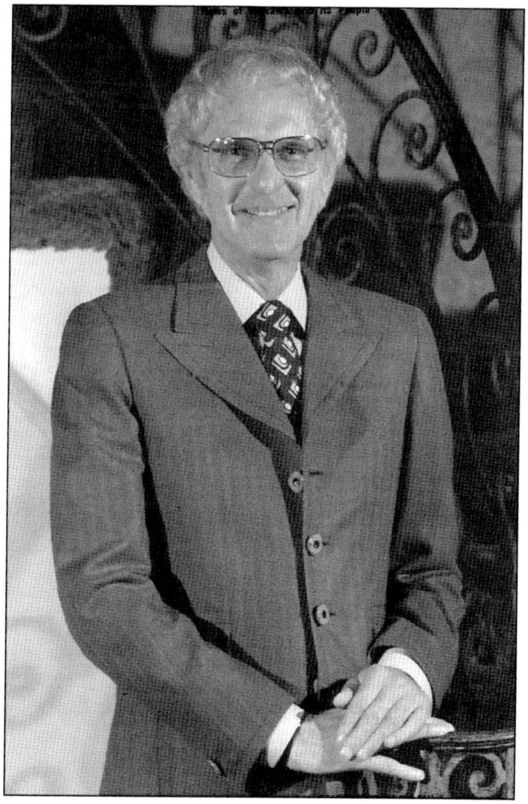

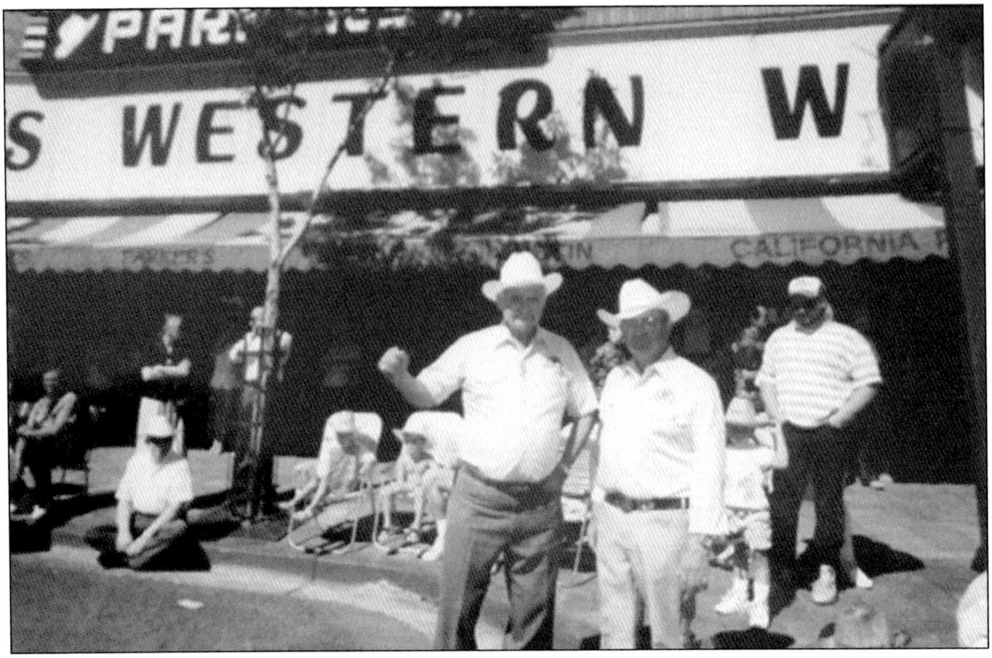

This structure in downtown Reno, built in 1929 by the Barengo family, is one of the few remaining historical buildings in downtown Reno. It sits along Sierra Street and now houses Antiques & Treasures. The original plans for the site involved the construction of a multi-level hotel, but it instead became the home of the National Dollar Store, which operated until the 1970s. In the late 1970s, the building was leased to Harry Parker, who opened the world-renowned Parker's Western Wear Store. It was renamed the Antiques Emporium in 1999. (Above, courtesy of Antiques and Treasures; below, courtesy of the Riverwalk Merchants Association.)

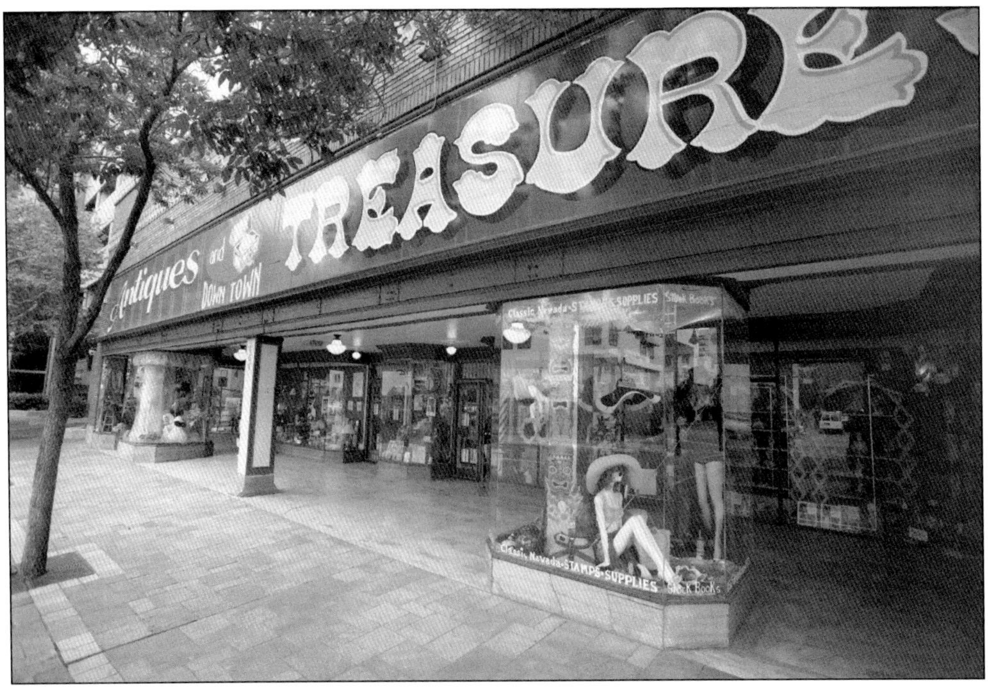

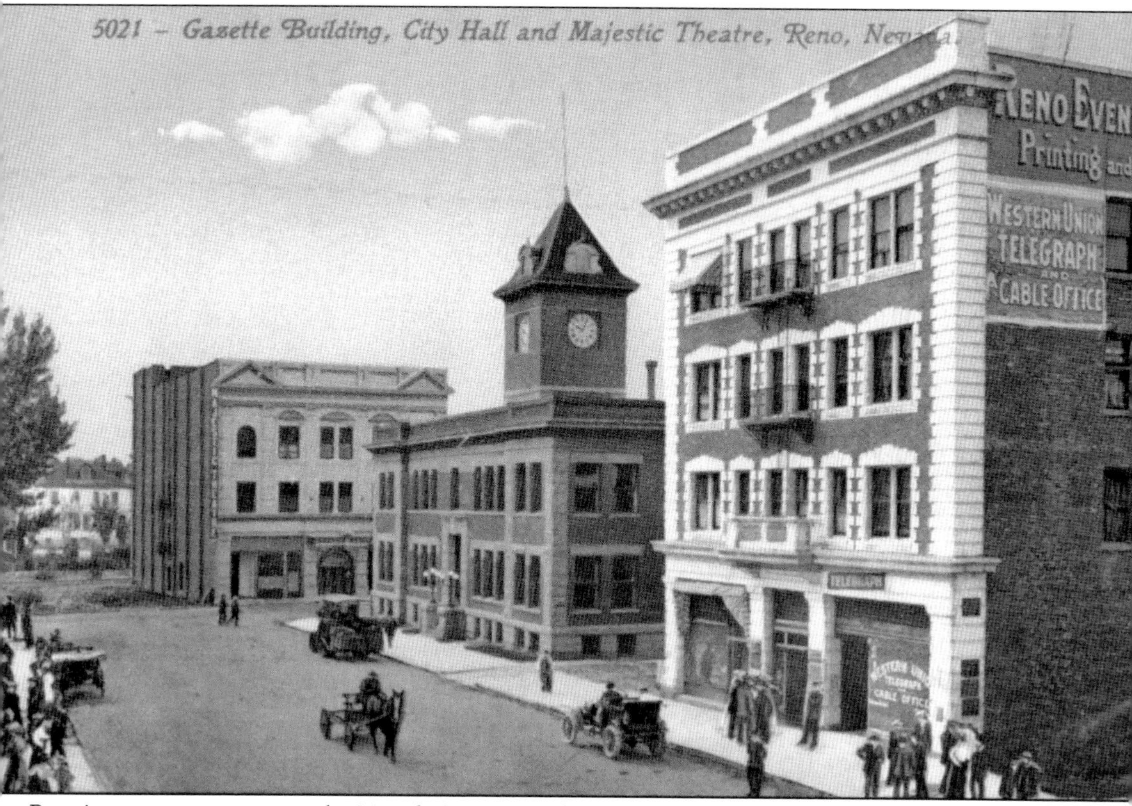

Reno's morning newspaper, the *Nevada State Journal*, was located for a brief time on East Second Street in downtown Reno. After a fire devastated the building, the paper was forced to move to a remodeled garage that later became a dance hall, an automobile showroom, and then the popular Dog House night club. After being taken over by a variety of different owners through the years, the *Journal* established itself inside a former bowling alley at 124 North Center Street. Later, it moved into the former Western Union office where the *Nevada State Journal* and the *Reno Evening Gazette* news staffs shared office space on the second floor. The *Nevada State Journal* and the *Gazette* operated as separate publications, and competition was fierce. Each paper had its own news and advertising staff, and they each had their own editorial policy. In 1977, the Pulitzer Prize was awarded to the *Reno Evening Gazette* and *Nevada State Journal*. On September 30, 1983, the last *Reno Evening Gazette* was printed and replaced by the *Reno Gazette-Journal*, a seven-day morning newspaper. (UNRS-P1992-03-205.)

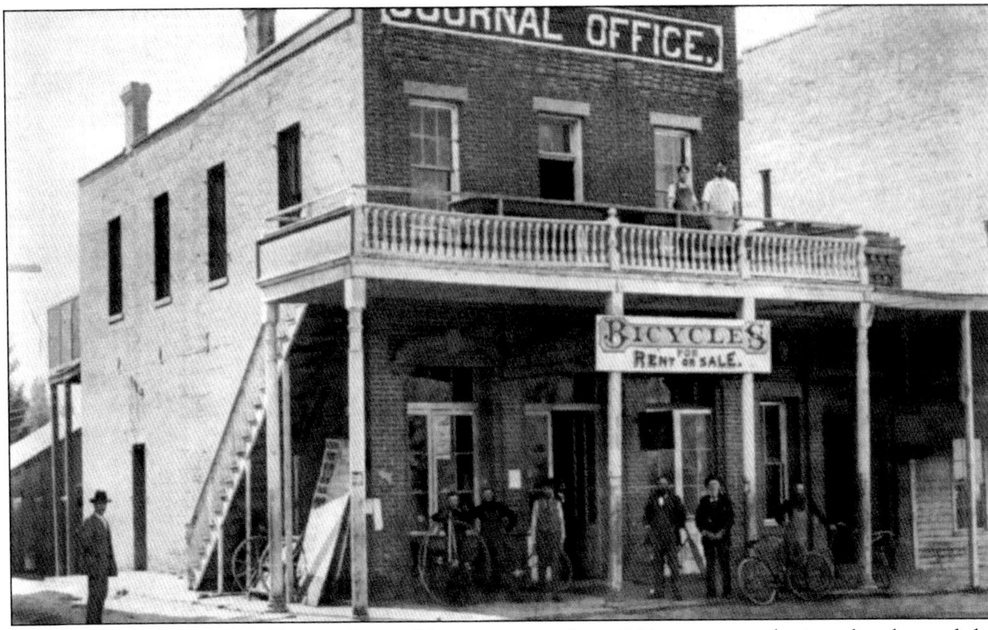

The history of the *Reno Gazette-Journal* began more than 125 years ago during the days of the bustling Comstock, when journalists such as Mark Twain, Dan De Quille, Joe Goodman, and Alf Doten roamed the dusty streets. During this time Reno's first newspaper was operating in a small area on East Second Street. The *Journal* office produced a small newspaper upstairs while a bicycle shop sold and rented bicycles below. Bicycles were an important means of transportation for those who could afford them.

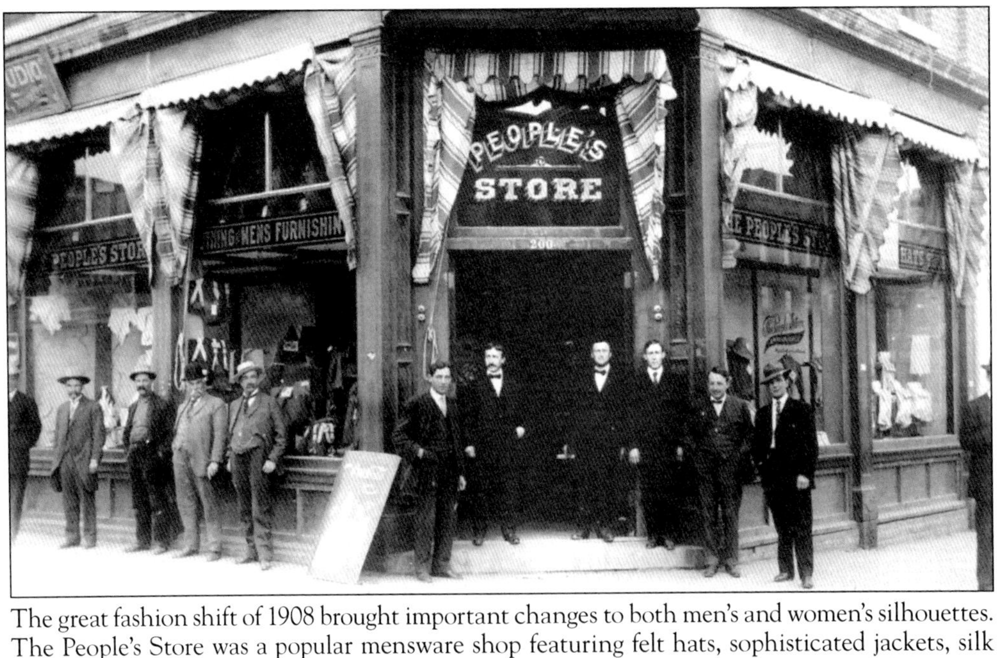

The great fashion shift of 1908 brought important changes to both men's and women's silhouettes. The People's Store was a popular mensware shop featuring felt hats, sophisticated jackets, silk ties, shoes, and accessories that added a rare spark to the rather dull men's clothing of the time. The People's Store was a brief stroll from the Virginia Street Bridge on the corner of Second and Virginia Streets.

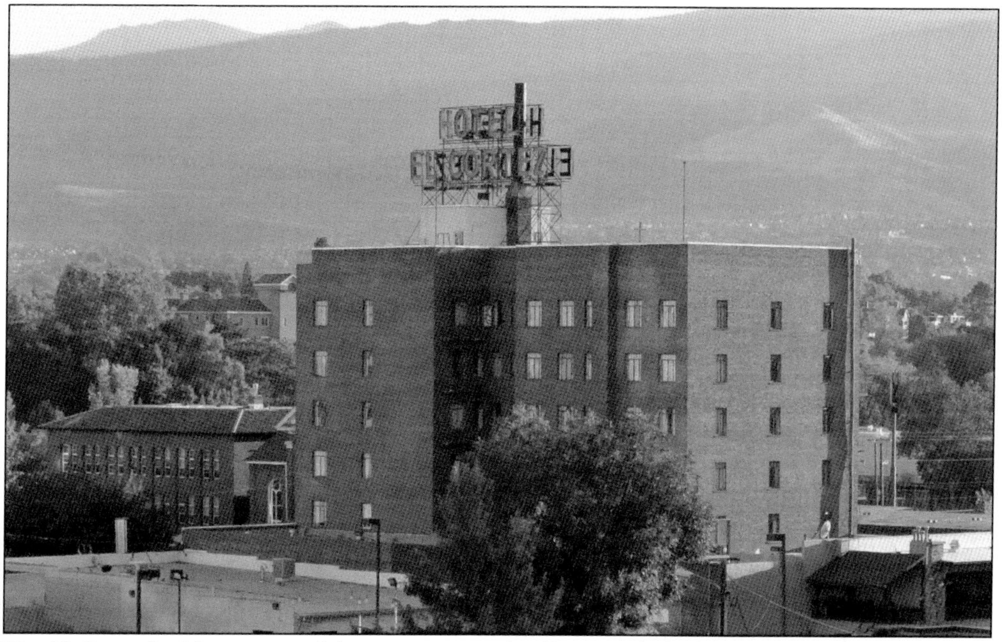

The El Cortez building is one of three remaining Art Deco–style buildings in Reno. The building, built on West Second Street in the Riverwalk District in 1931, offered high-class accommodations for a rate of $6 per night. This rate was much higher than that of competitors, who were charging only $2.50 per night.

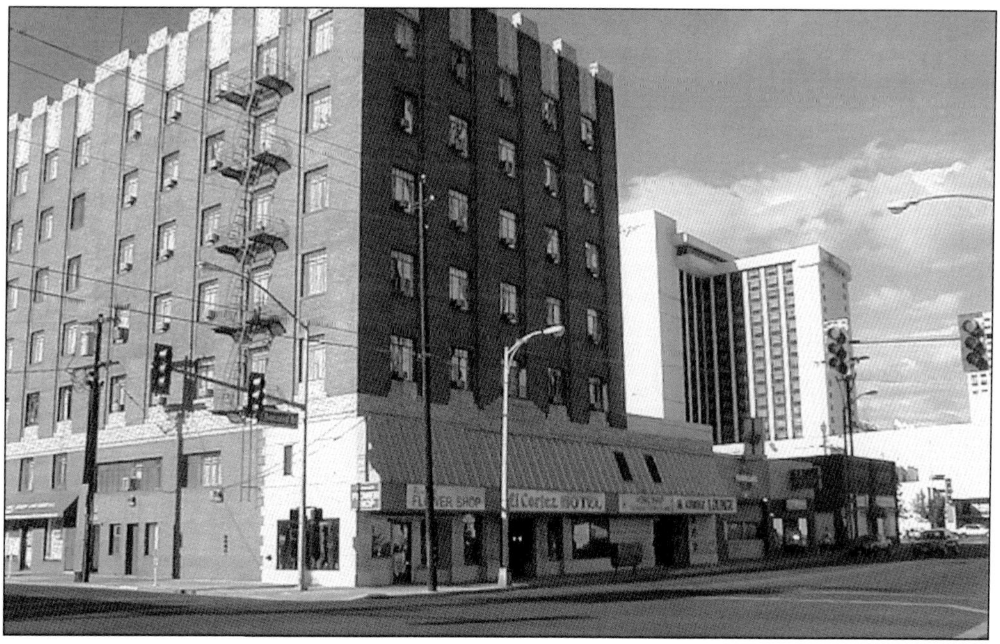

The El Cortez Hotel included a fashionable bar, the Orchid Room, and a very popular restaurant, the Trocadero Room, all elegantly constructed with Art Deco ornamentation. George Ferris and his son, Lehman A. "Monk" Ferris, were hired to design the hotel-casino for investor Abe Zetooney. Lehman was the first architect in Nevada to specialize in steel-frame construction and studied for a brief time with Frederic DeLongchamps.

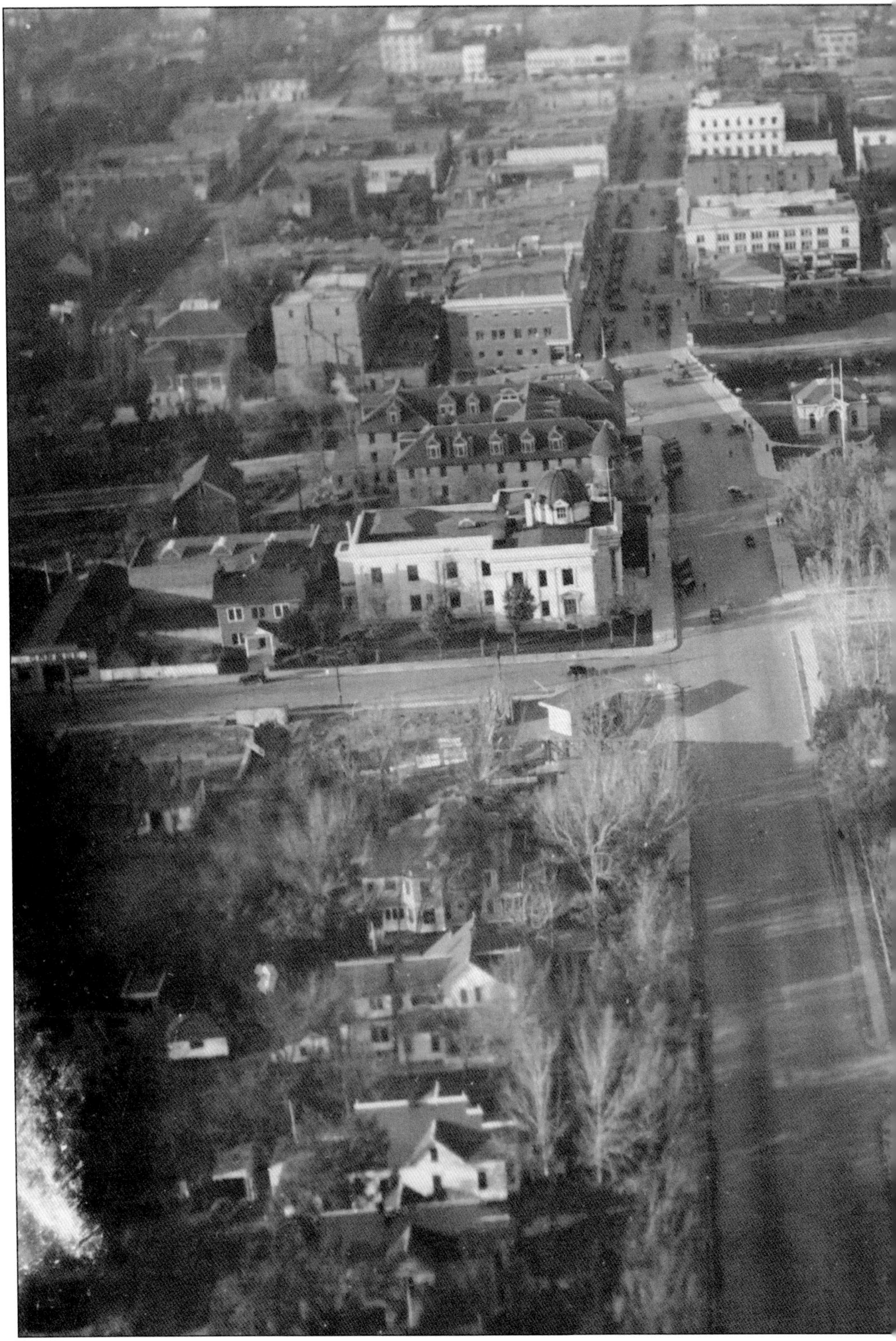

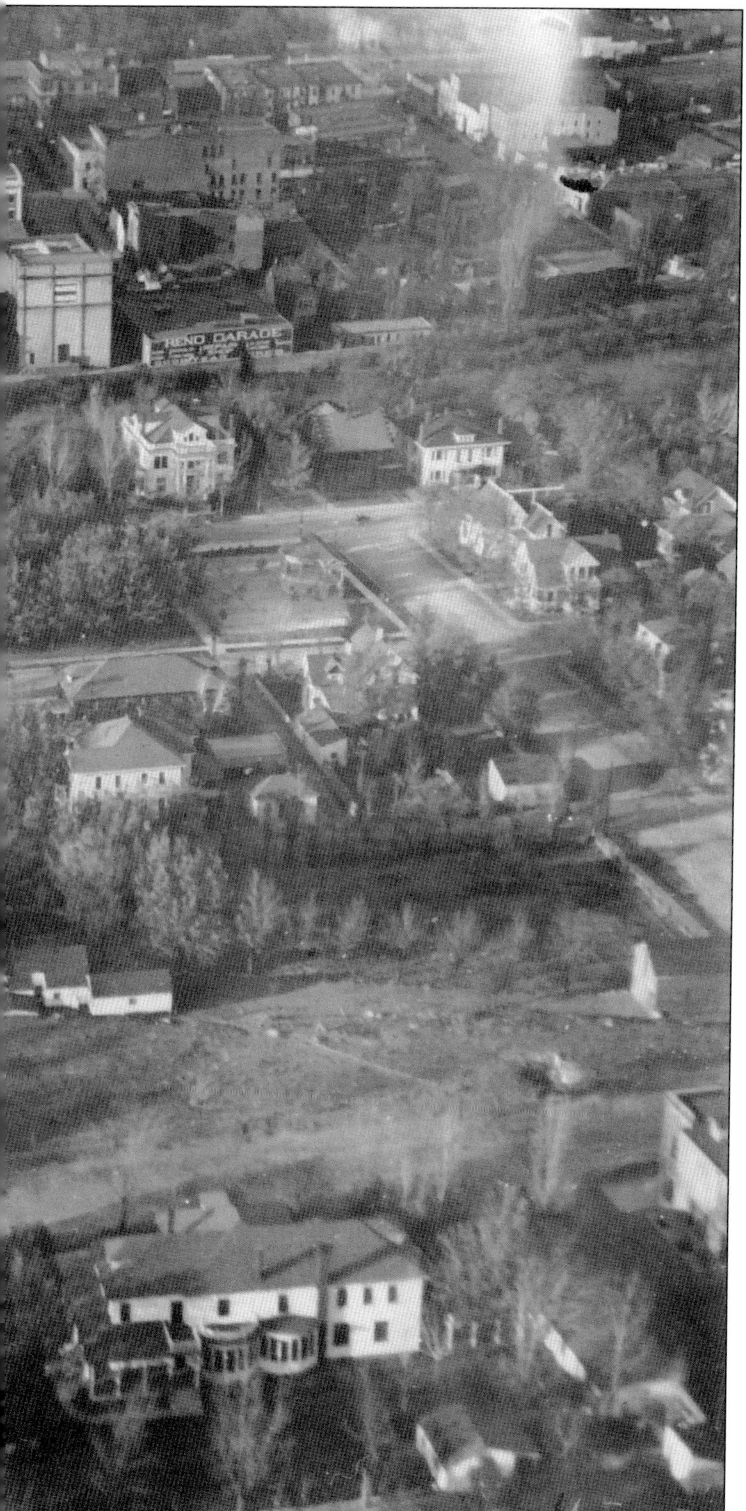

This 1922 aerial photograph shows Reno looking north on Virginia Street. The Washoe County Courthouse is the large, domed structure to the left, and just above the dome is the Riverside Hotel. The Masonic building sits on the opposite side of the Truckee River, which can be seen running through the center of the photograph. Opposite of the Masonic building sits the Carnegie Library, and next to that is the Majestic Theater. (UNRS-P1010-5.)

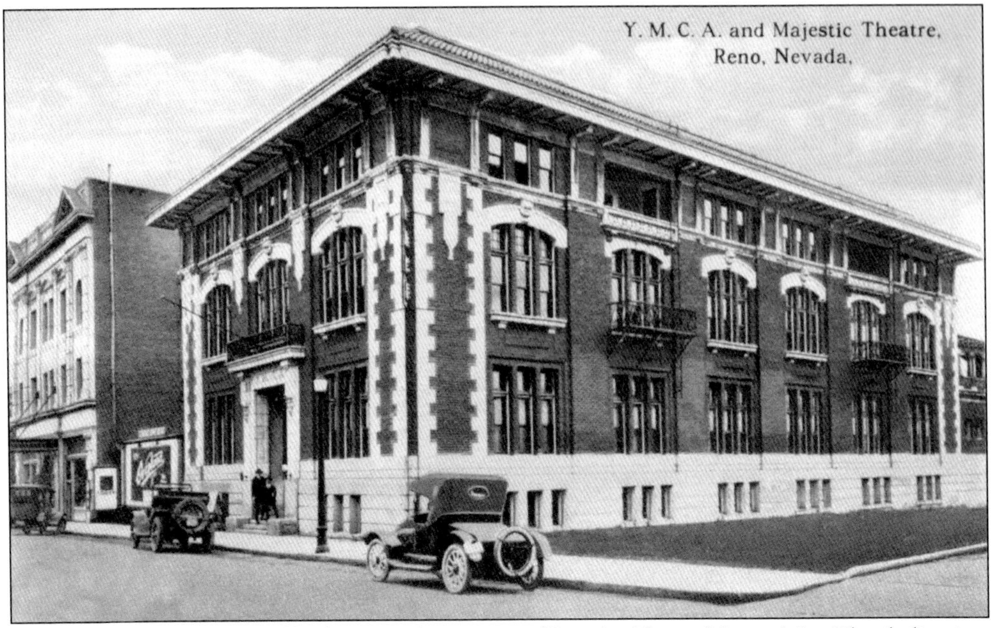

Located along the Riverwalk, the YMCA was one of Reno's oldest athletic clubs. The dedication of the new facility on November 12, 1911, included the placement of a time capsule (whose contents were never documented) behind the stones in the building. The YMCA resided in Reno for over 100 years and later moved to Foster Drive in 1956, where it remained until closing in 2012. (WA-01755.)

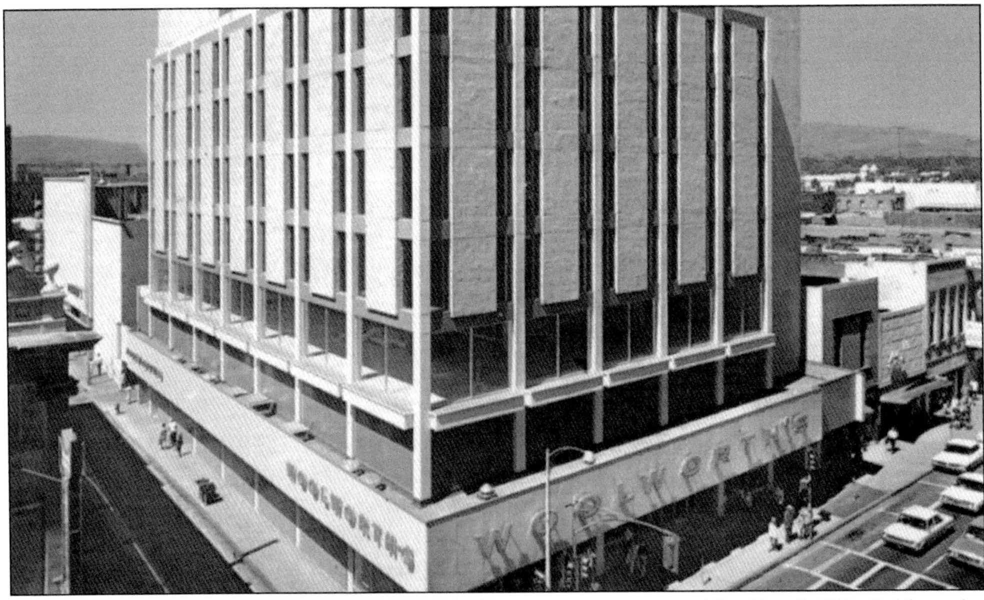

In February 1878, the first F.W. Woolworth Company was opened by Frank Winfield as the "Woolworth's Great Five Cent Store" in Utica, New York. Woolworth's was one of the original (and most successful) five-and-dime stores in the United States. Reno's Riverwalk was one of many locations where Woolworth's would open for business. The 60,000-square-foot Woolworth's building was located at 101 North Virginia Street across from the Mapes Hotel-Casino. This building can still be seen today. (UNRS-P1992-03-40.)

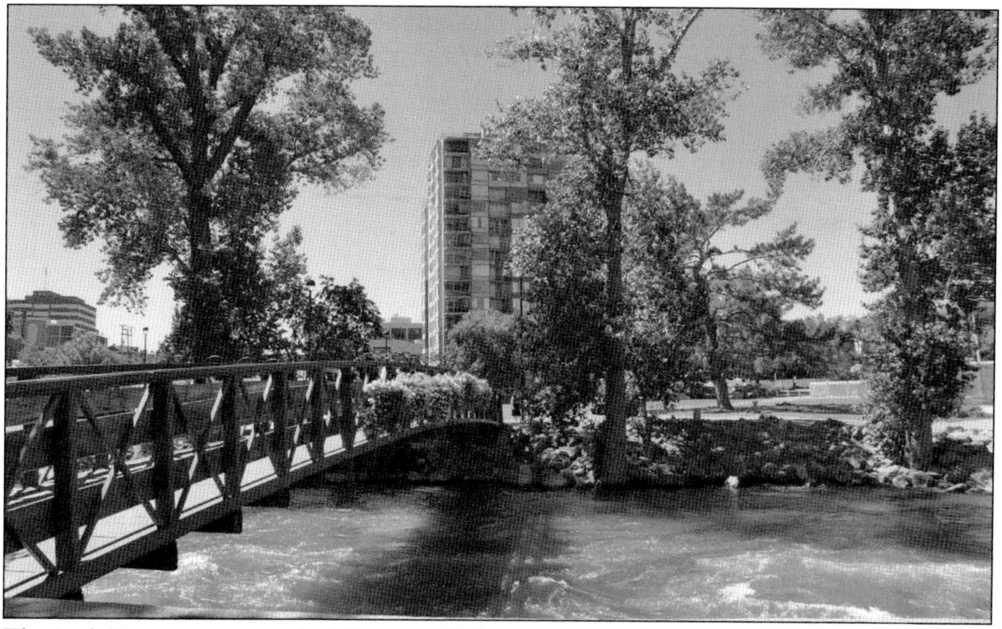

The Park Tower apartment building is a 17-floor structure that sits on the south bank of the Truckee River at Island Street and Arlington Avenue along the edge of Wingfield Park. The complex opened in 1962 as a residential apartment building; since 2000, it has been converted to condominiums. This photograph shows the Park Tower in the background. (Courtesy of the Riverwalk Merchants Association.)

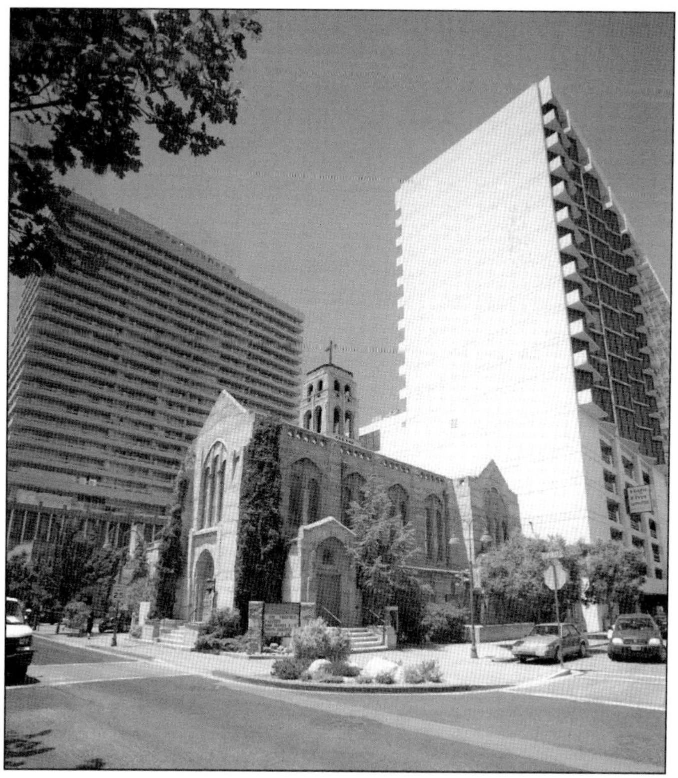

Across the river, at Arlington Avenue and First Street, sits the 22-story Arlington Towers. The building was constructed in 1968 and converted to residential condominiums in 1984. The lower level of the property features a variety of retail establishments. Pictured are the Arlington Towers (left), First United Methodist Church (center), and the Residences at Riverwalk (right). (Courtesy of the Riverwalk Merchants Association.)

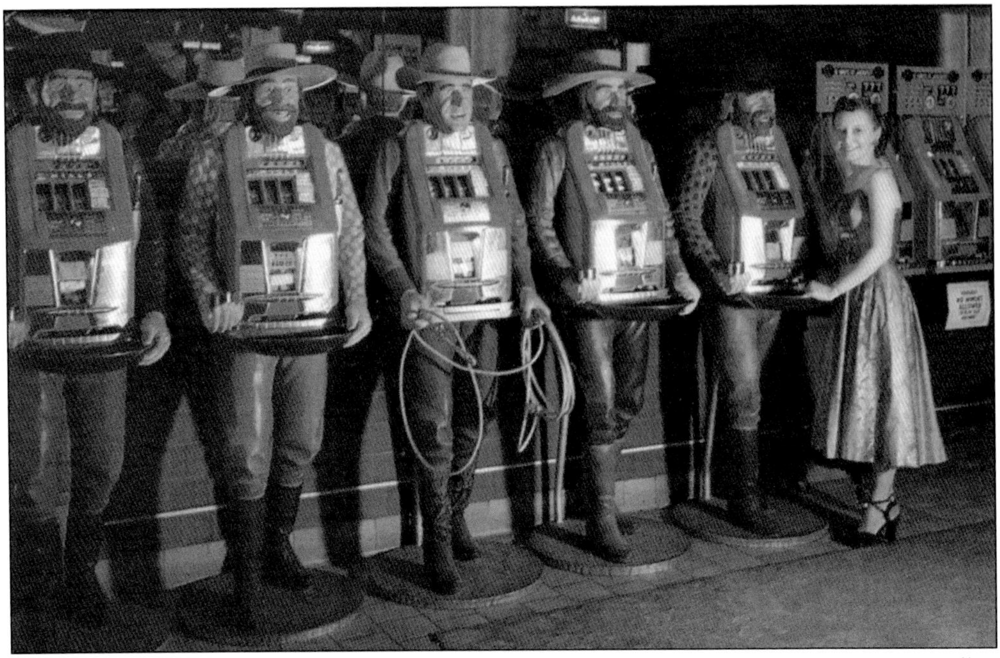

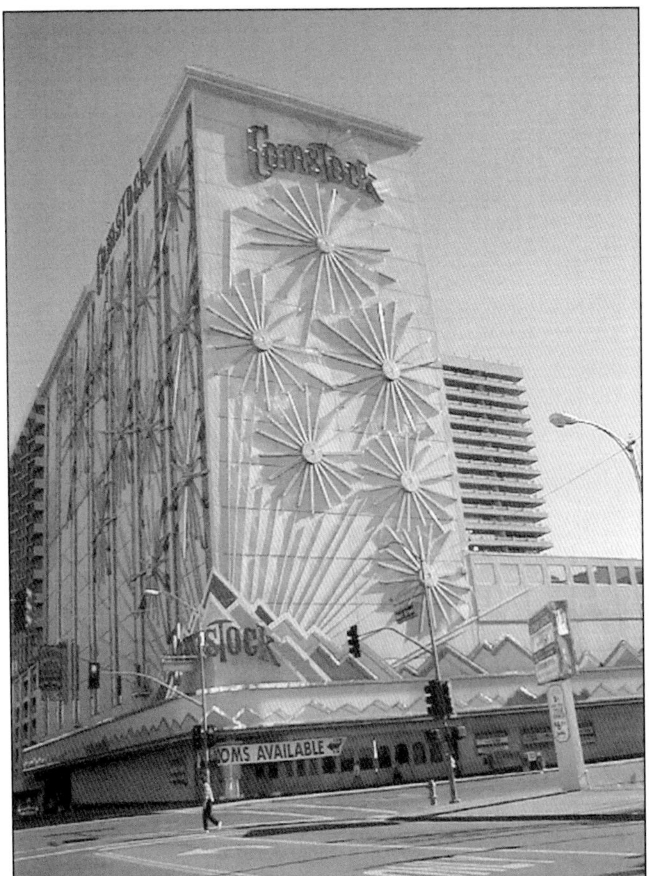

The Residences at Riverwalk Towers, on the corner of West and Second Streets, was renovated in 2004 to house 125 condominiums featuring oversized whirlpool tubs, slab granite countertops, nine-foot ceilings, and some of the most beautiful views in the city. Prior to catering to local residents, the property was known as the Comstock Hotel-Casino, which opened its doors in May 1978 with 160 rooms on nine floors, with an additional expansion in 1984 bringing the room count to 320. The casino featured a western motif with a spectacular light show, restaurants, an outdoor swimming pool with a jacuzzi, a sauna, and exercise room. The lower level featured a bustling casino with 710 slot machines, 22 gaming tables, keno, and a sports book. The property was sold in May 1999. (UNRS-P1992-03-0138, Nevada Historical Society.)

Five

20TH-CENTURY DIVORCE CAPITAL

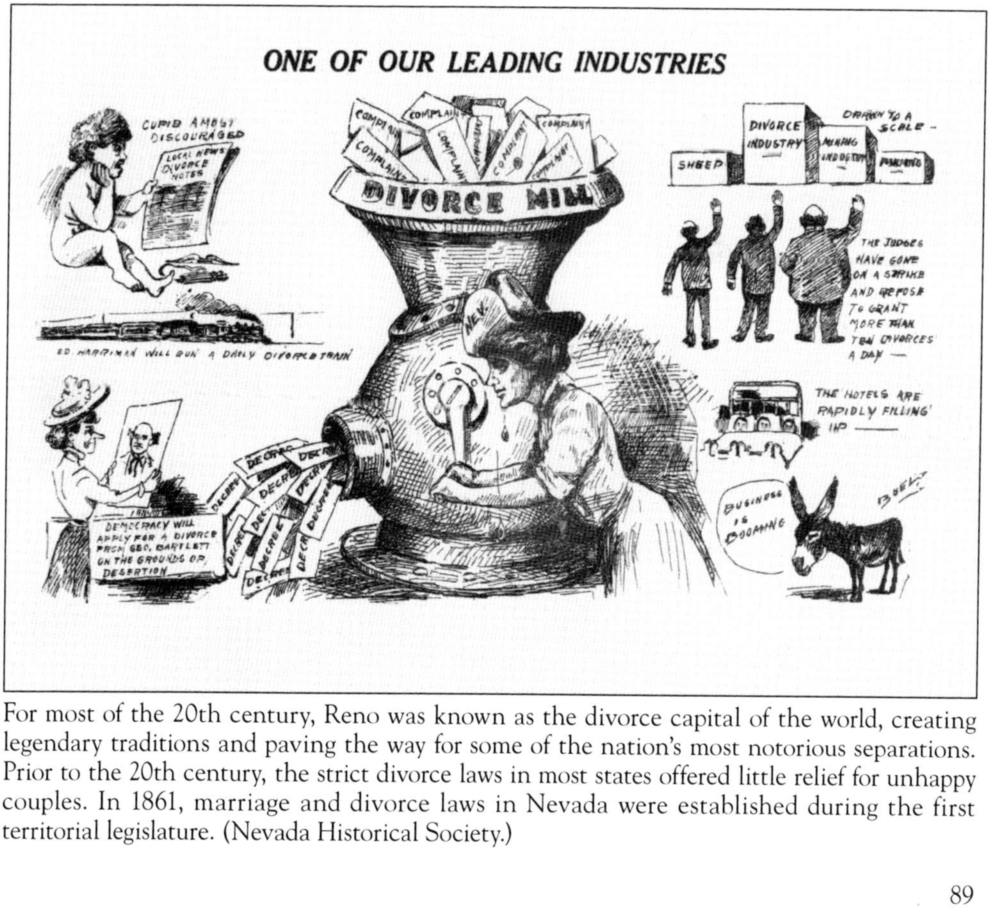

For most of the 20th century, Reno was known as the divorce capital of the world, creating legendary traditions and paving the way for some of the nation's most notorious separations. Prior to the 20th century, the strict divorce laws in most states offered little relief for unhappy couples. In 1861, marriage and divorce laws in Nevada were established during the first territorial legislature. (Nevada Historical Society.)

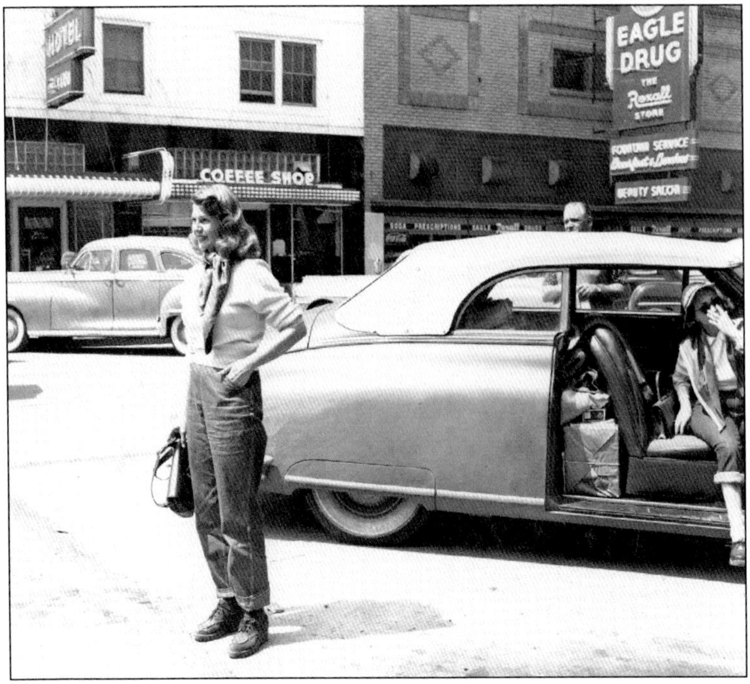

This image features well-known actress Rita Hayworth getting out of a car in Reno on May 10, 1951. Hayworth established a temporary residence in Nevada while awaiting her divorce from her third husband, Prince Aly Khan (Pakistan's representative to the United Nations, and a socialite). (UNRS-P1989-51-225.)

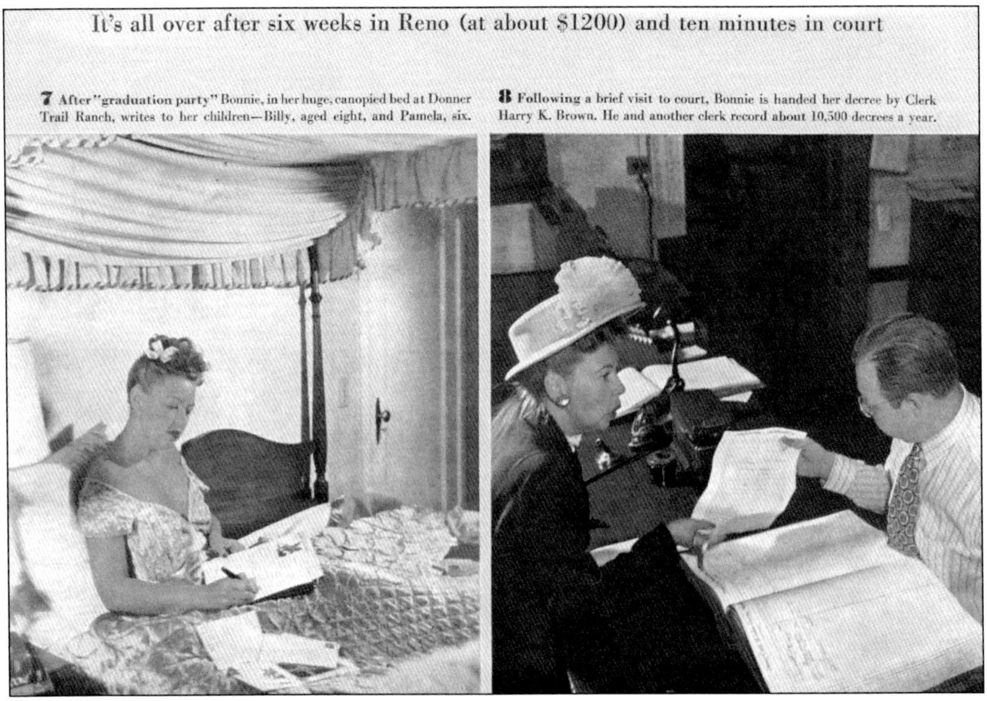

It's all over after six weeks in Reno (at about $1200) and ten minutes in court

7 After "graduation party" Bonnie, in her huge, canopied bed at Donner Trail Ranch, writes to her children—Billy, aged eight, and Pamela, six.

8 Following a brief visit to court, Bonnie is handed her decree by Clerk Harry K. Brown. He and another clerk record about 10,500 decrees a year.

One of the requirements for receiving a divorce decree was the establishment of residency in the state of Nevada. Divorce seekers could choose to stay at nearby boardinghouses, divorce ranches, private homes, or any one of Reno's five hotels, such as the ever-popular Riverside Hotel and Casino, El Cortez, and Colonial Apartments. This postcard touts the ease of getting a divorce. (UNRS-P1992-01-2004.)

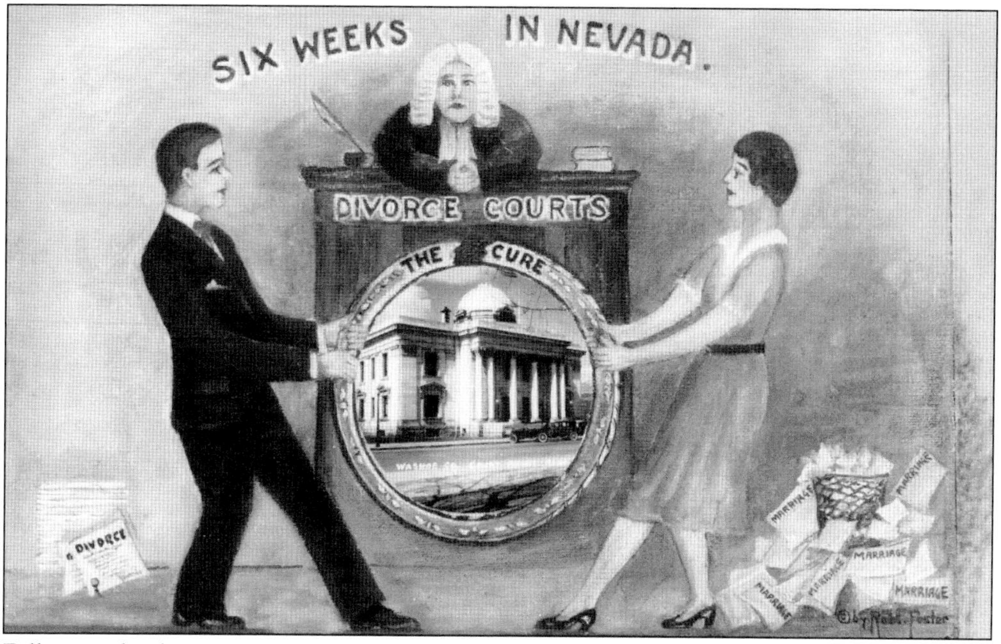

Following the devastating crash of the stock exchange on October 24, 1929, the state of Nevada passed a law reducing the divorce residency requirement from three months to six weeks. This new change not only increased awareness of Nevada's lenient laws but also supported Nevada's economy through the Depression. During the next 10 years, the Washoe County Courthouse would grant more than 30,000 divorces. Reno quickly became known as Nevada's sin city. Reno gained notoriety for a number of famous divorces, including those of silent film star Mary Pickford, Cornelius Vanderbilt Jr., boxer Jack Dempsey (pictured below), Estelle Taylor, Earl Russel, and Laura B. Corey.

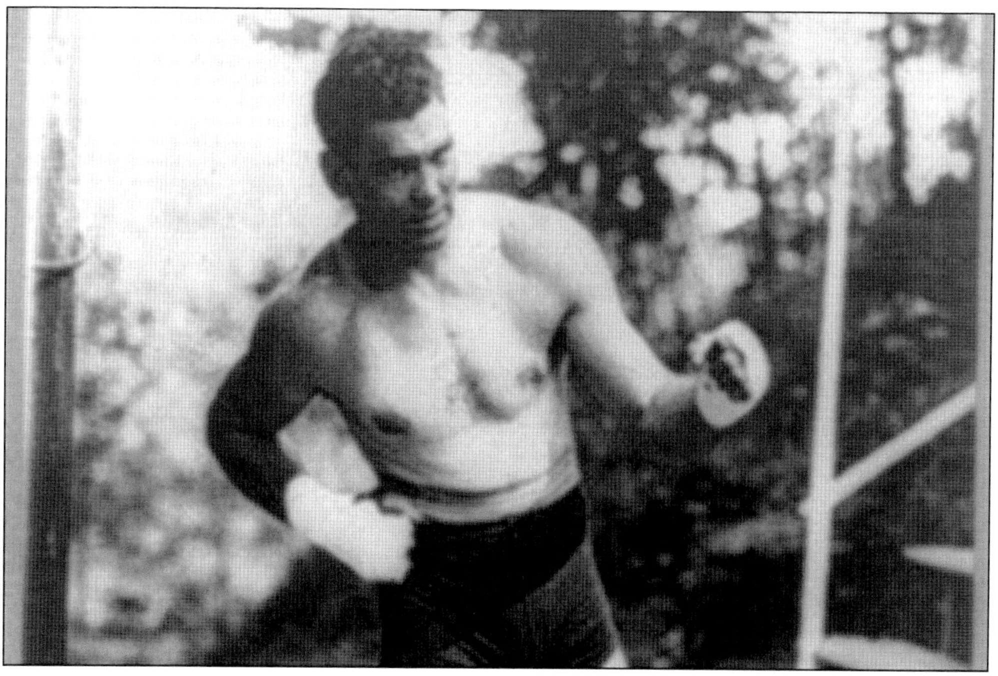

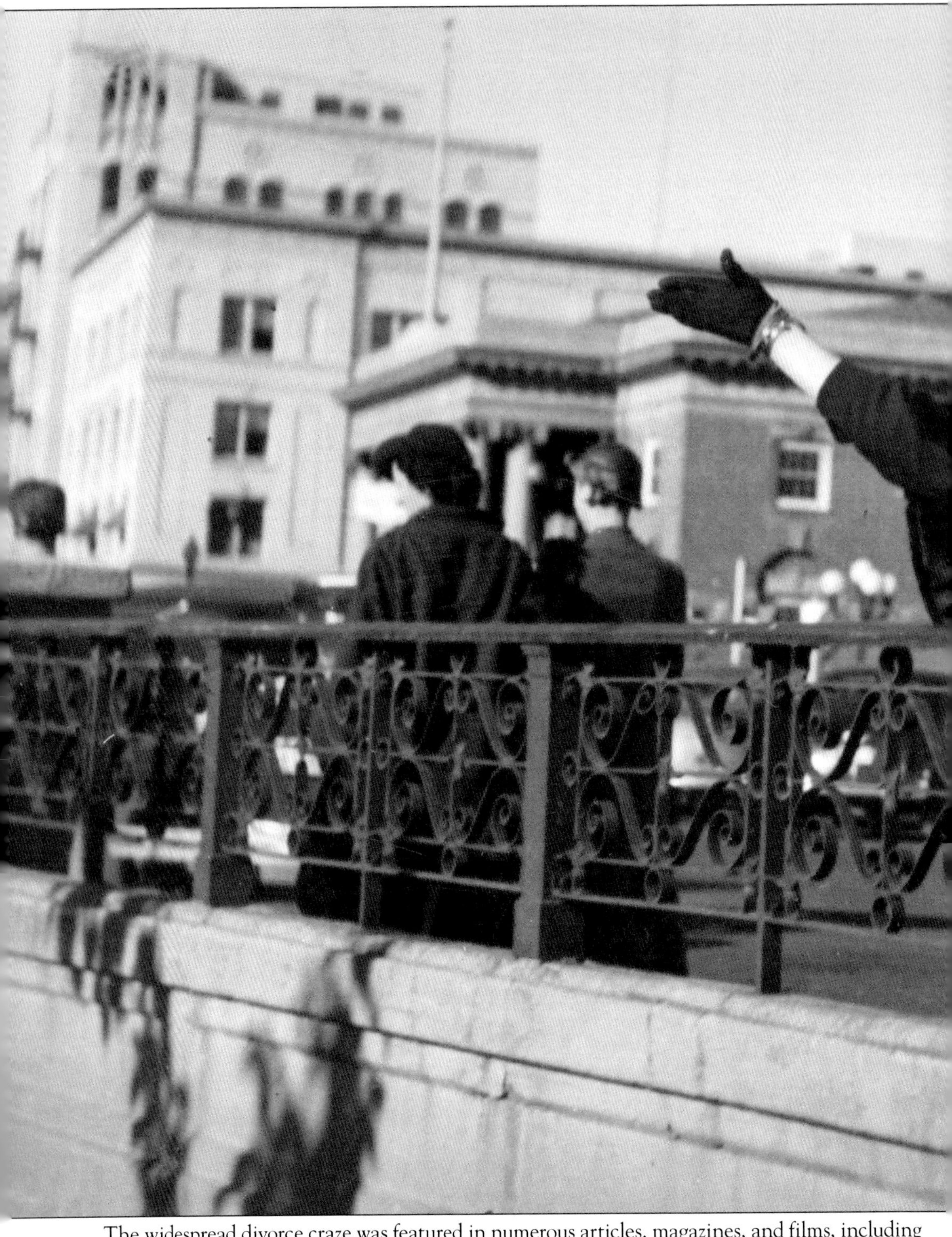

The widespread divorce craze was featured in numerous articles, magazines, and films, including Arthur Miller's 1961 film *The Misfits*, starring Clark Gable and Marilyn Monroe. During the film, Monroe tosses her ring into the river from the Virginia Street "Bridge of Sighs." According

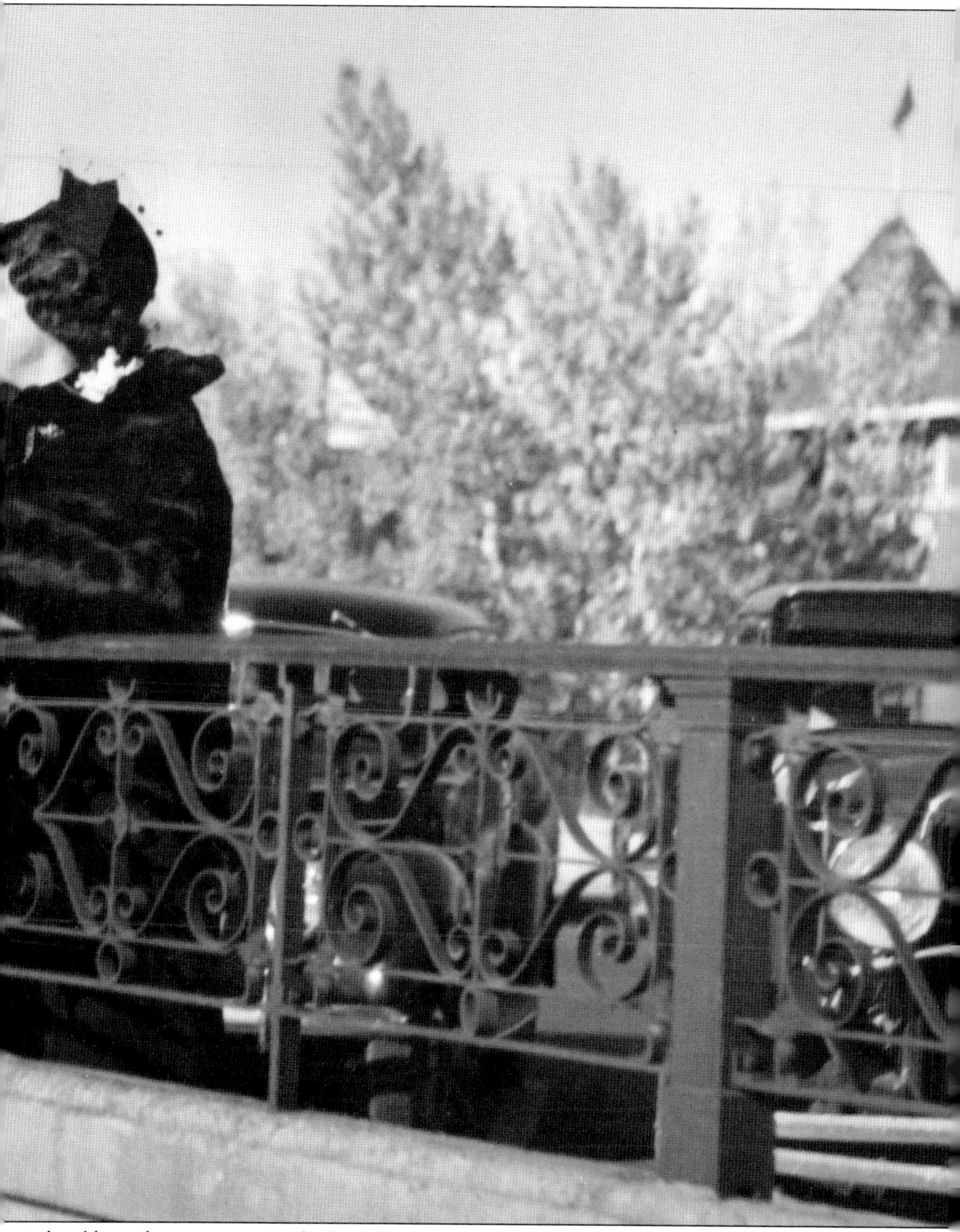

to local legend, upon receiving the final divorce decree, divorcees should kiss the columns at the courthouse steps and toss their wedding rings into the Truckee River. This image shows a recent divorcee enthusiastically taking part in this custom. (Dave Stafford Collection.)

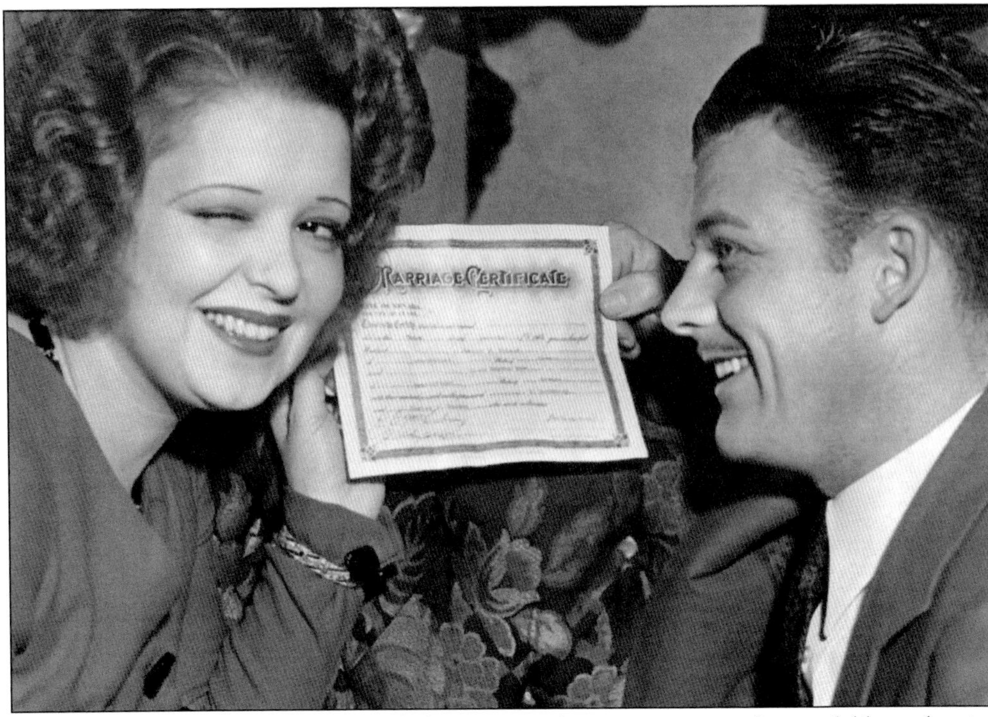

Reno was not only known for its quick divorces; quick marriages were also available at the city courthouse. Such elopements were celebrated by well-known celebrities, including silent film stars Clara Bow and Rex Bell (pictured here), and Yvonne DeCarlo (Lilly Munster in the television series *The Munsters*) who married Bob Morgan on November 21, 1955. (BIO-B-561.)

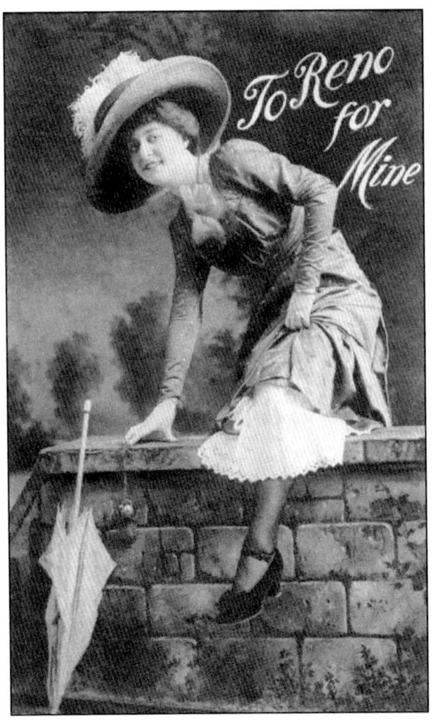

The popularity of divorce in Nevada brought what seemed to be a never-ending stream of income into the downtown Reno community. It was estimated that guests, by staying in hotels, playing the casinos, and paying attorneys' fees, brought an estimated $5 million annually to the Silver State. This 1907 postcard depicts a woman eager to receive a divorce decree in Reno. (WA-10686.)

Six

Casinos and Gaming Along the Riverwalk

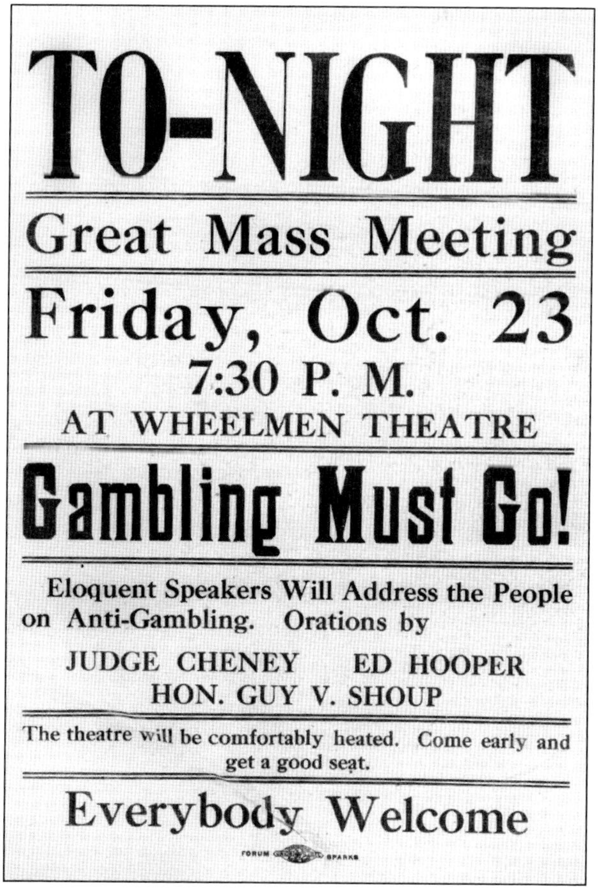

Reno's Riverwalk has always catered to locals and visitors alike by providing entertainment and opportunity. After the great Comstock Lode, Reno began to offer gaming as a viable source of revenue for the city's economy. Reno had often been known for activities that other states would not traditionally allow, such as the famous Jeffries-Jackson boxing match in 1910, prostitution, divorce, and gaming. This antigambling poster was generated from the Reno Wheelmen's club to promote a ban on gambling in the city. (WA-04368.)

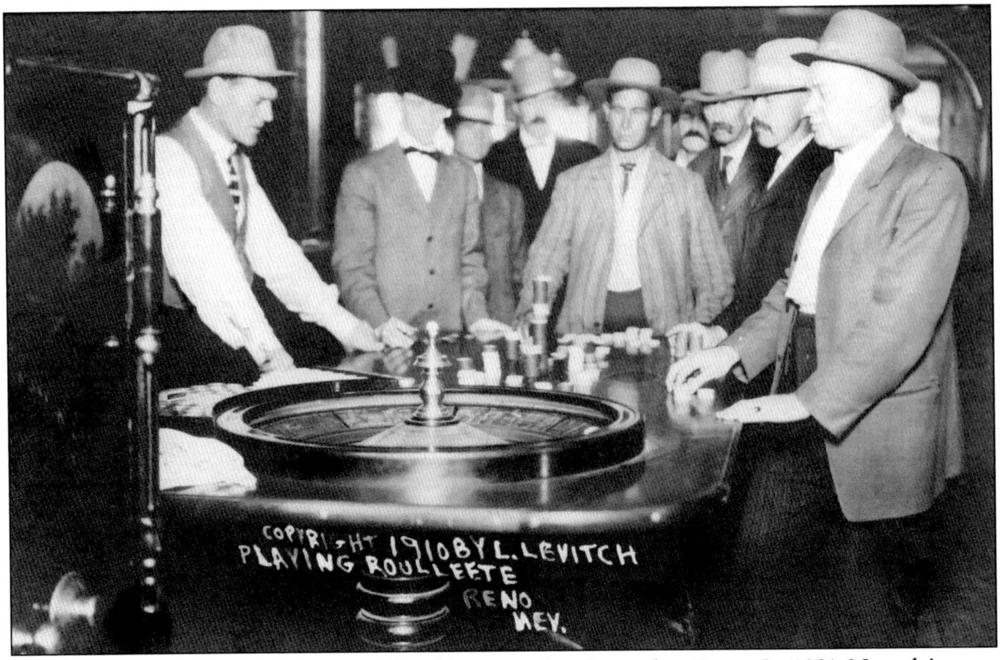

From 1910 to 1931, gaming became illegal but openly tolerated in Reno. In 1931, Nevada's state legislature passed a wide-open casino bill, making Reno the primary city in the United States to offer legal gaming. Reno maintained its gaming reputation through the 1950s with the assistance of the Mapes and Riverside Hotels on lower Virginia Street, which offered luxury accommodations and a casino. The Riverwalk was home to some of the more prominent casinos during the 1950s and 1960s, including the Holiday and the Dog House. (UNRS-P1992-03-360, LC-3B12224R.)

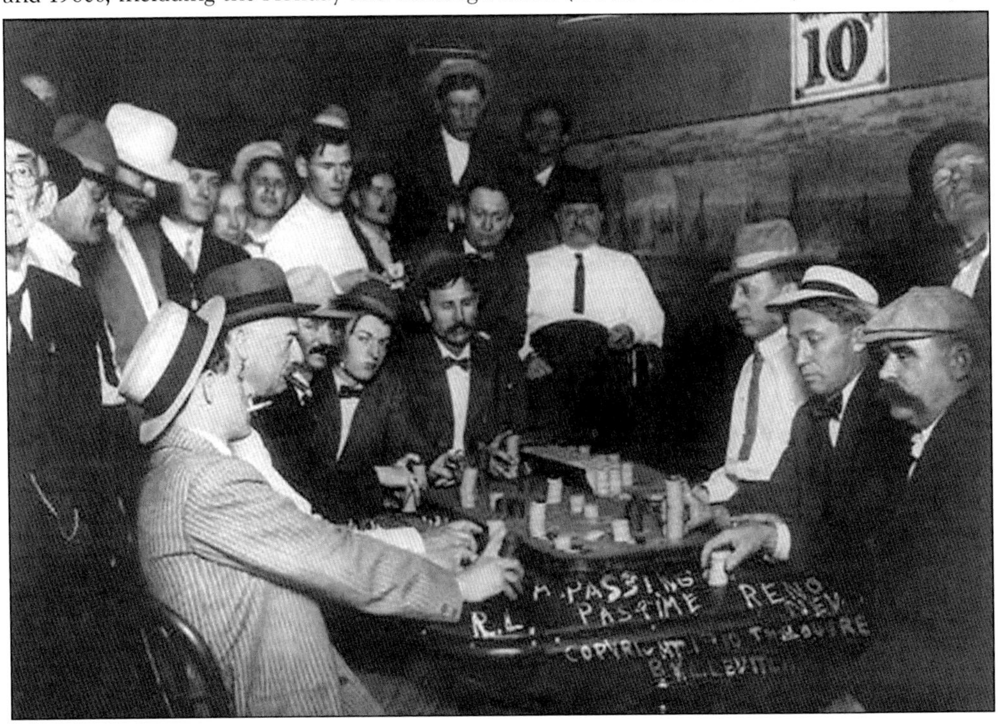

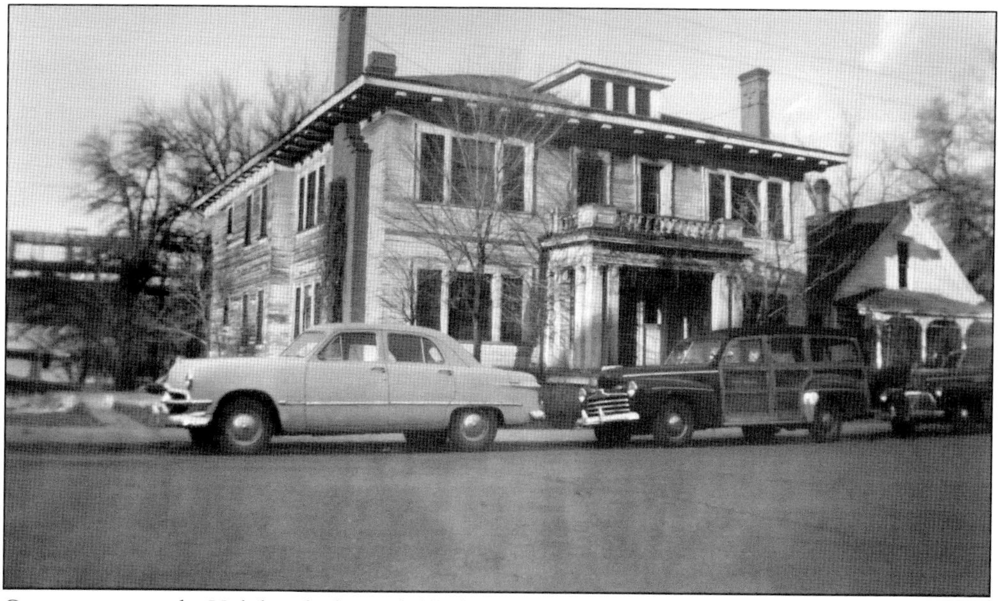

Construction on the Holiday, the brainchild of Norman Biltz and Stanley Dollar, began in December 1956. The property, on the corner of Mill and Lake Streets, was originally the site of a small home. Dollar pulled out of the endeavor at the last minute before investing any money. (WA-04521.)

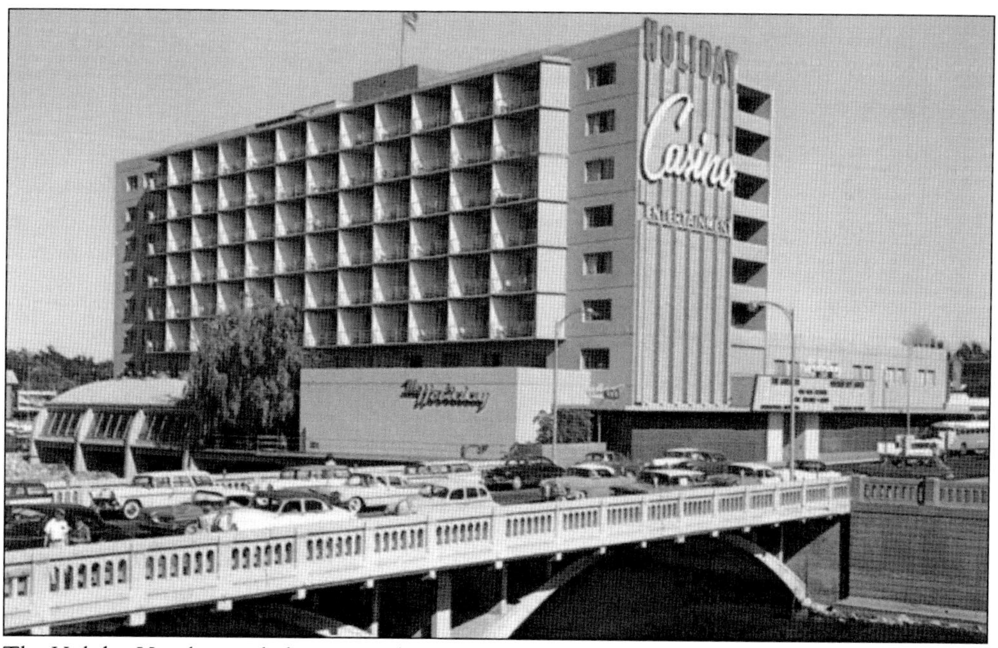

The Holiday Hotel provided guests with comfortable accommodations in one of their 200 rooms, many of which had views of the Truckee River. The first floor held 50 slot machines; however, since none of the original owners were licensed for gaming, the property could not hold any table games. The property was sold to new owners after one year. (UNRS-P1992-03-517.)

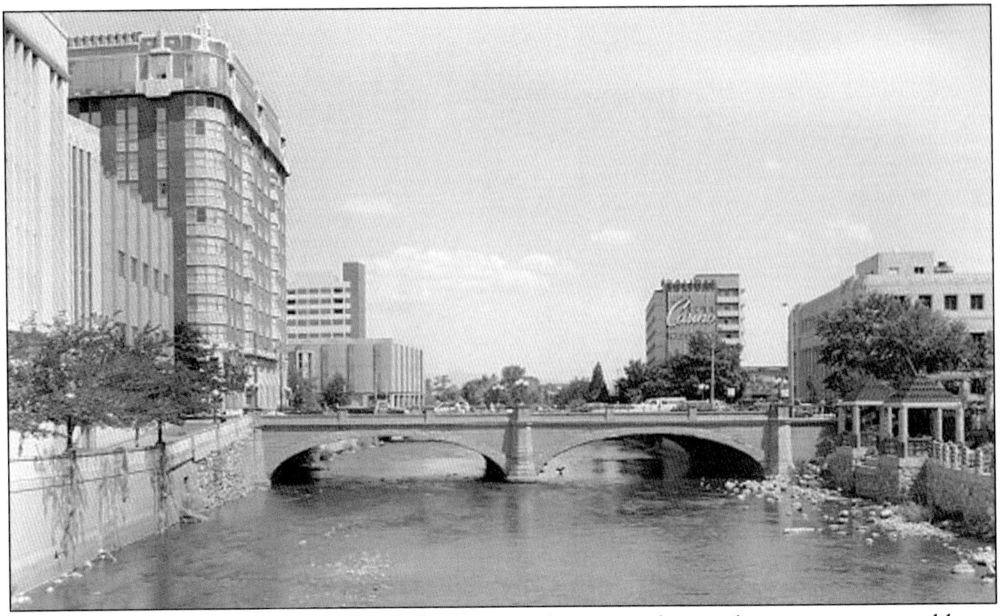

The new owners of the Holiday decided to license their own slot machines, two craps tables, a roulette wheel, and four 21 tables for the casino floor. The property struggled through the years and was sold during a public auction in 1999 for $2.5 million. In 2001, new owners Barney Ng and architect Peter Wilday rebuilt the property as the Siena. The Holiday can be seen in the distance in this photograph. (UNRS-P1992-01-9023.)

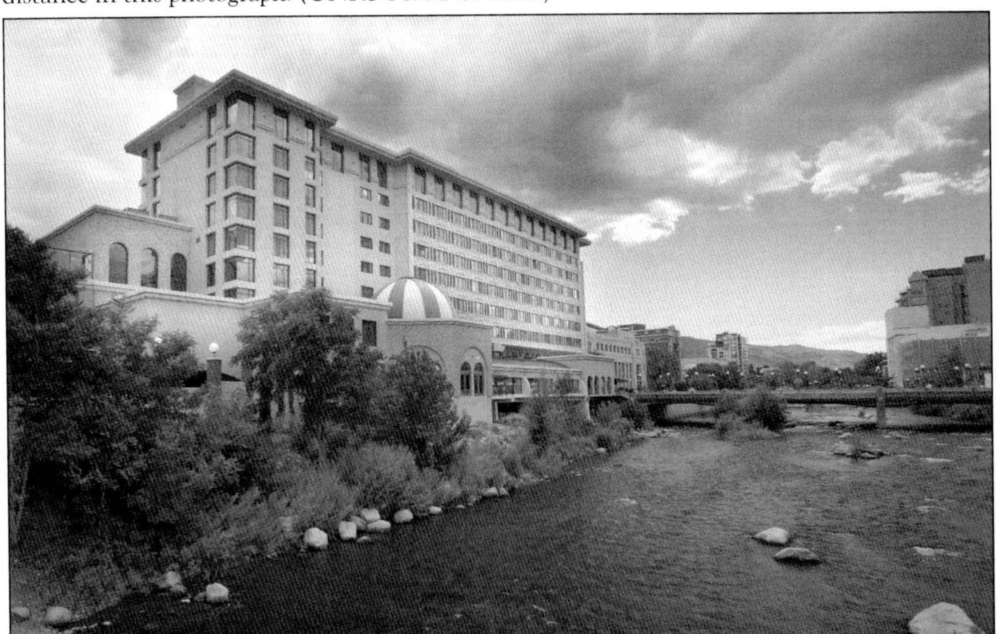

The new Siena projected a Tuscan-style theme and strove to brand itself as the "locals' casino." The Siena offered two restaurants, a wine bar, and a larger lounge area overlooking the Truckee River. The project struggled to gain momentum, and, 10 years later, the property was sold for $3.9 million during public auction. It reopened in 2011 as the Grand Siena. (Courtesy of the Riverwalk Merchants Association.)

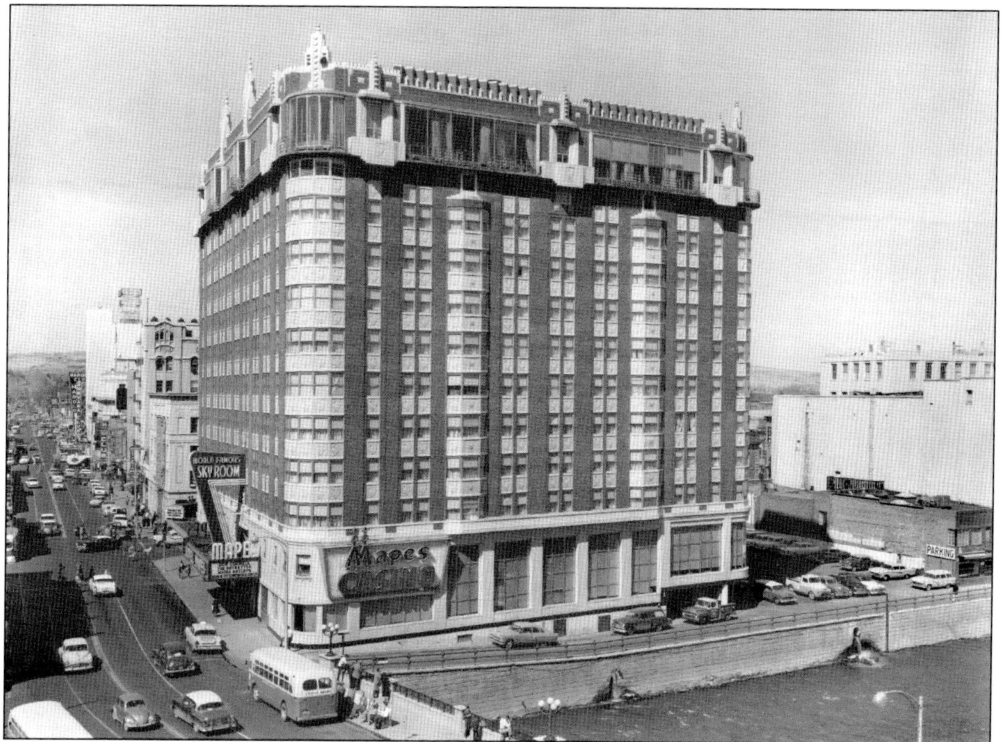

The Mapes was considered to be the most popular resort-casino hotel in the nation, offering amenities unlike any of its competitors. The building is believed to be the first high-rise in the world to be completed after World War II, and was Nevada's tallest building until the 1956 opening of the 15-story Fremont Hotel and Casino in Las Vegas. Charlie Mapes Jr. often referred to the Mapes as the "jeweled corner of Reno." The basement of the Mapes featured a nightclub, and the entrance was exquisitely decorated for its time. The property offered a wonderful array of gaming, dining, and world-renowned entertainment. (WA-04356, WA-10689.)

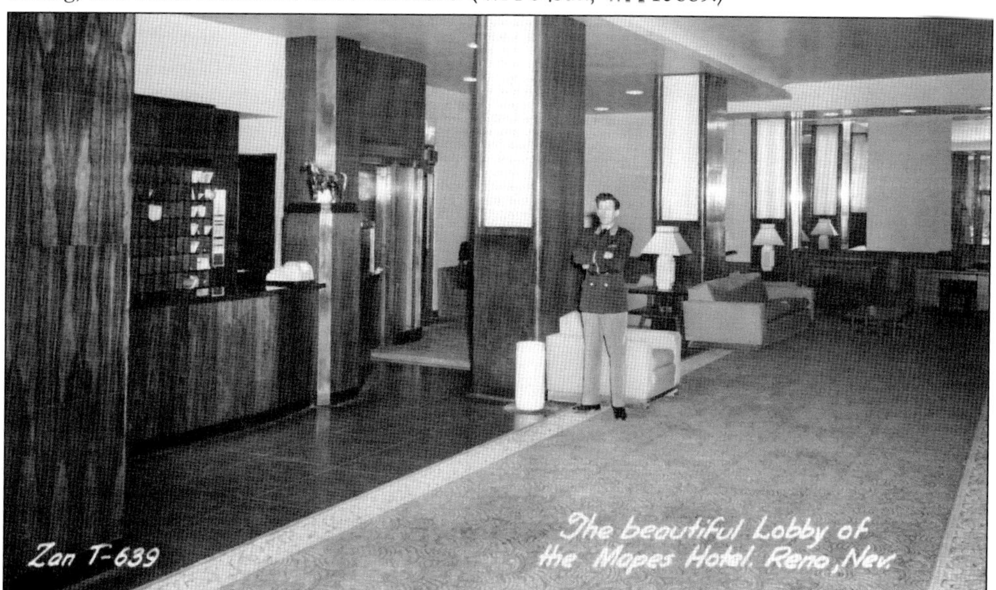

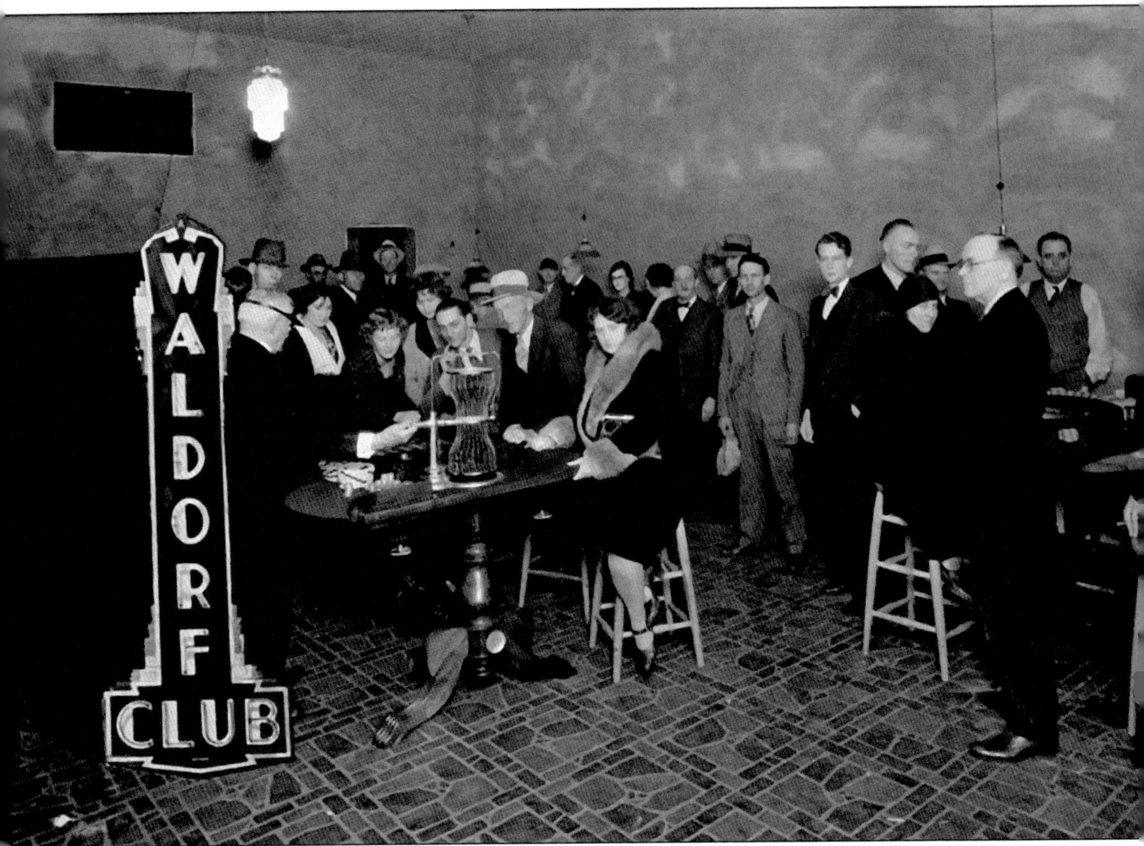

The Riverwalk was home to an assortment of casinos. One, the Town House Casino, at 39 West First Street, remained successful until a fire destroyed the building in 1955. Another, the unique Merry-Go-Round Bar (opened in 1946 at 26 West Second Street), was licensed for slots, craps, 21, and roulette. Its most iconic feature, however, was that the bar stools were on a carousel base and would revolve around the center part of the bar while patrons enjoyed their cocktails. The establishment operated under several owners for 10 years before having its license revoked in August 1965. Between First and Second Streets was the Waldorf Club, which had originally opened in 1910 and, in 1929, moved to 142 North Virginia Street. The Waldorf opened and closed several times until it permanently closed on July 28, 1979. (UNRS-P1992-01-1989.)

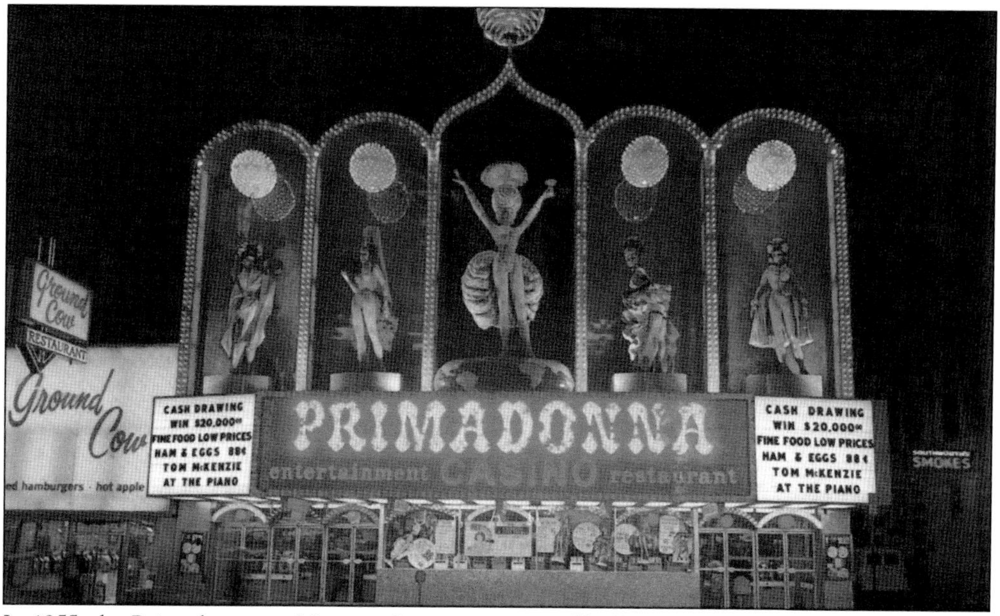

In 1955, the Primadonna on Virginia Street was opened by Ernie Primm, with 50 slot machines, 3 craps games, 3 roulette tables, and 9 twenty-one games. Primm placed an iconic showgirl at the casino entrance, and the second floor showroom featured an all-adult revue called *Paree, Ooh Laa Laa* that gave three performances nightly. Primm purchased property on the west side of Sierra Street and created a covered walkway between the two sites. The properties were sold in 1974 to the Del Webb Corporation, and the Primadonna was renamed Del Webb's Sahara Reno in 1978. (UNRS-P1992-03-111.)

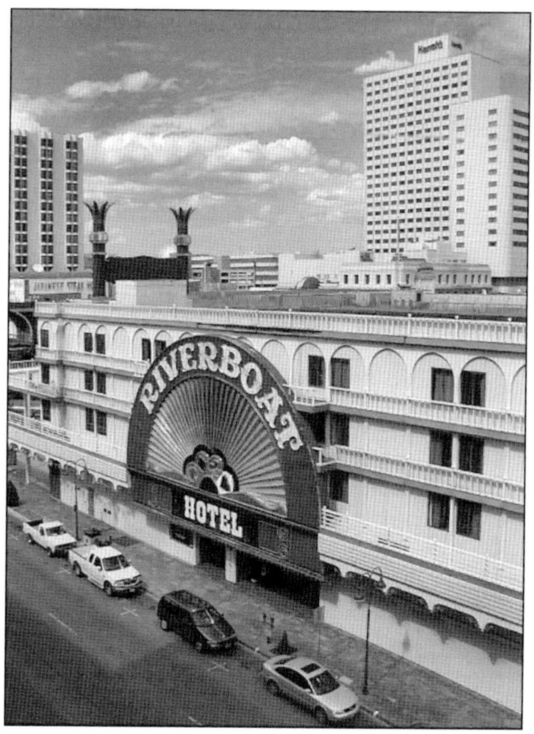

The Riverboat Hotel and Casino located at 34 West Second Street opened its doors in 1988 with 120 hotel rooms and a full casino. The owners constructed a walkway in the early 1990s to what became known as the Onslow Tower, which provided an additional 182 rooms. The building closed in 1998 and was renovated into the Riverboat Apartments.

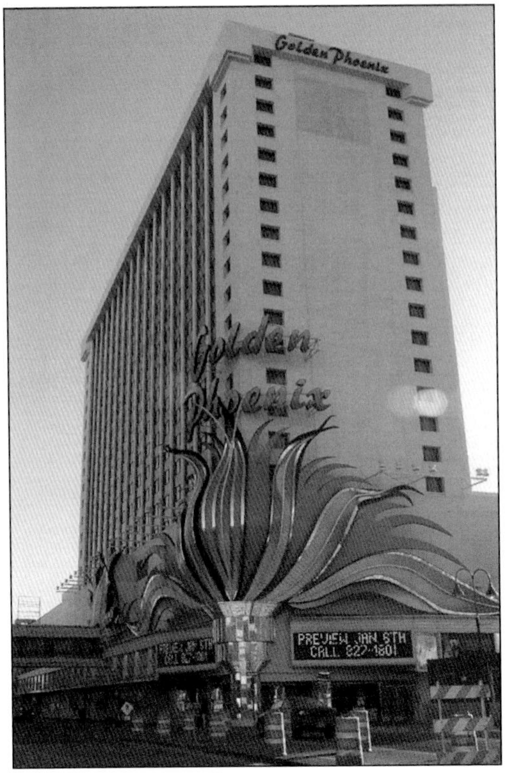

In 1988, the Virginia Street Casino, once owned by Ernie Primm, was renamed Pacos; in 1989, the 602-room hotel and casino was reopened as the Flamingo Hilton. The Flamingo Hilton was a deluxe hotel with full casino, sports book, and showroom. It also featured Reno's only rooftop restaurant at the time, as well as six restaurants, a lounge, and 24-hour room service. The Flamingo remained open until October 2001, when it was sold and reopened as the Golden Phoenix.

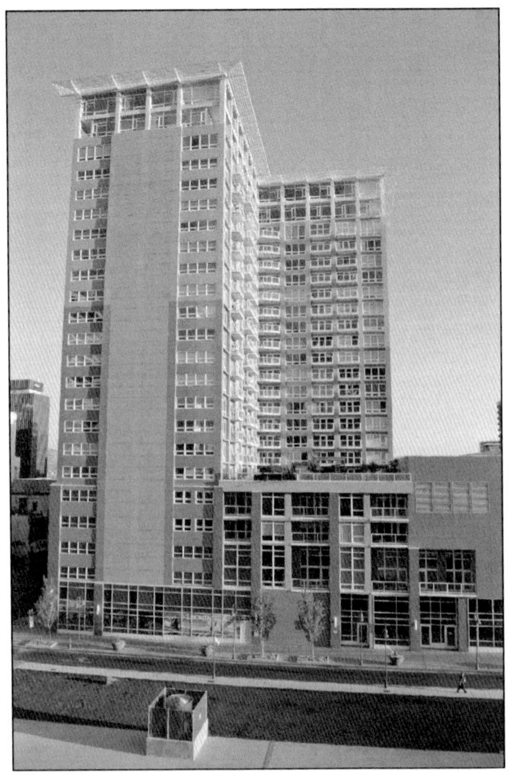

The Golden Phoenix made its place in history in November 2003 when it reportedly hosted the longest craps roll in Nevada history. It was estimated that the casino lost approximately $70,000 that evening. In 2005, the Golden Phoenix closed and was converted into the Montage luxury condominiums, seen here. (Photograph by Courtney Meredith.)

Seven

Fires and Floods

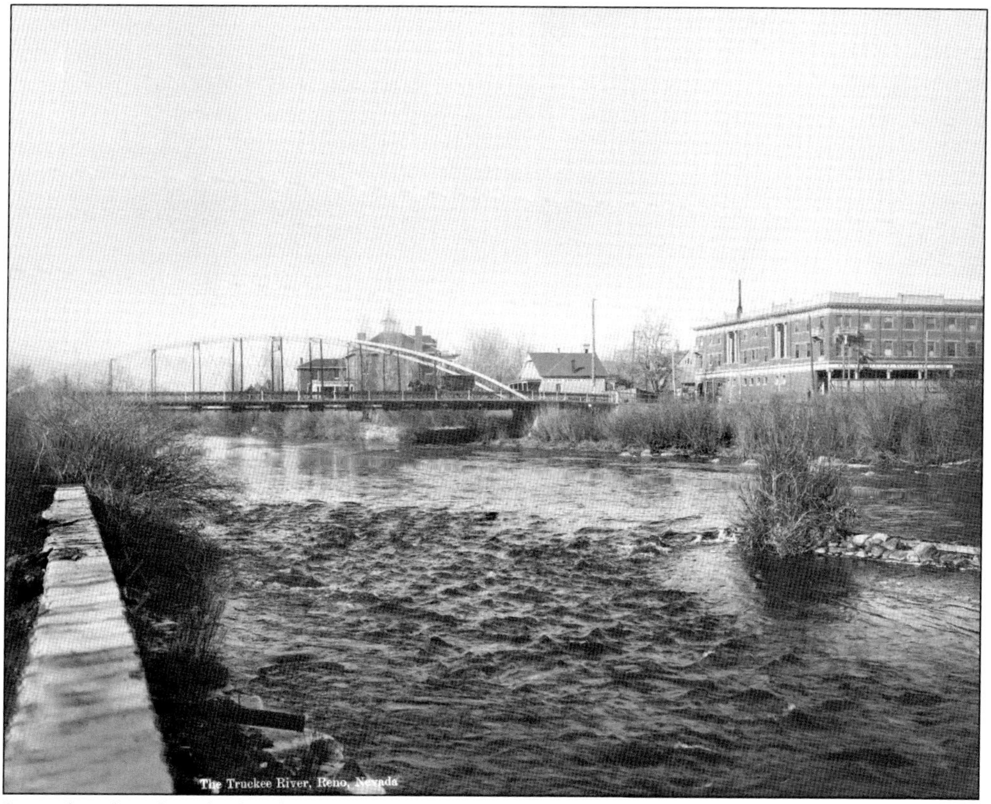

Reno has lived with the devastation of fires and floods from its earliest days. Many of the businesses along the Riverwalk have been rebuilt and rehabilitated over the years. Few buildings and bridges have survived these bouts of disaster, but Reno continues to thrive as a vibrant community. (WA-4034.)

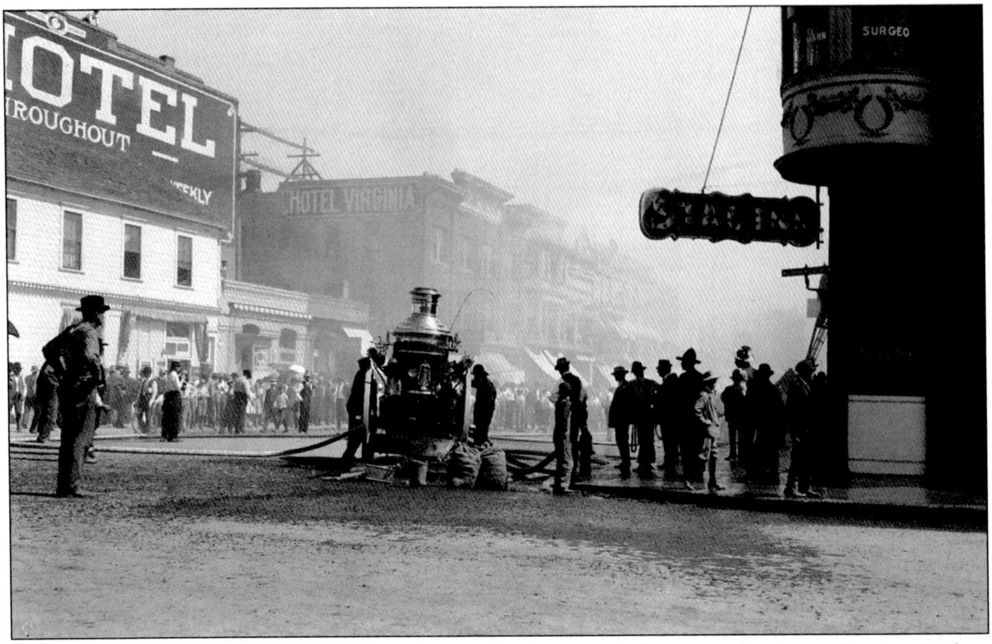

At 10:30 p.m. on October 29, 1873, a fire nearly destroyed the entire business district. Before volunteers could acquire buckets and cisterns, the fire had burned an entire block of Commercial Row. The blaze destroyed over 100 buildings and did an estimated $100,000 in damage; only two buildings were left standing. Additional support from the Central Pacific Railroad fire engines out of Wadsworth and Truckee and the S.T. Swift steam engine helped to eliminate the blaze. Shortly after the fire had been exhausted, a small truck carrying ladders, buckets, and hooks was delivered to the city, paid for by money collected from citizens and property owners. (UNRS-P1989-55-3155, UNRS-P2006-05-4.)

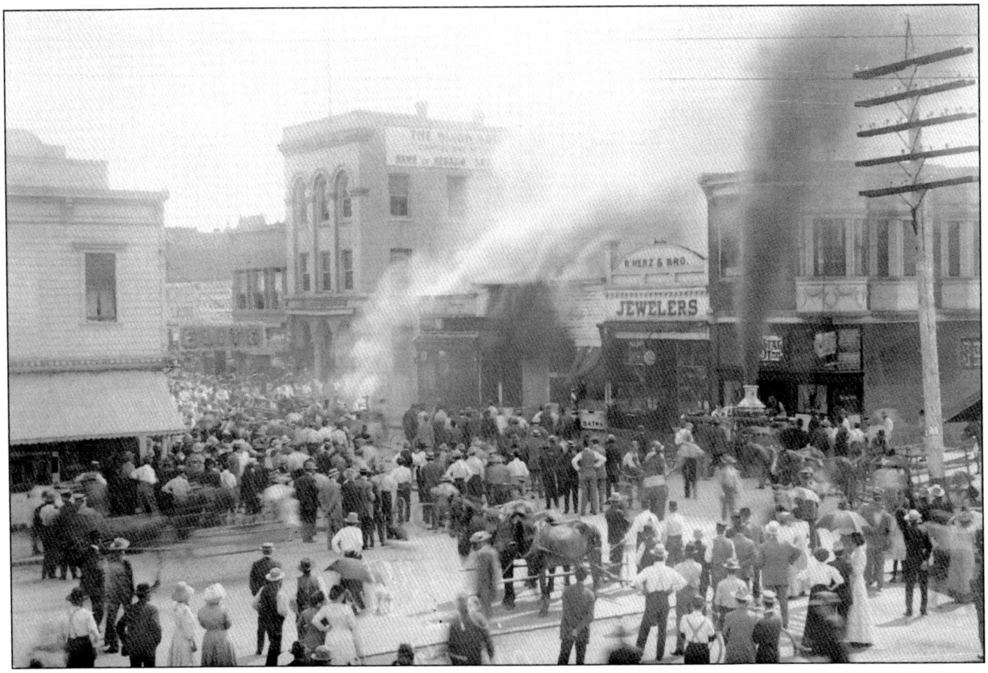

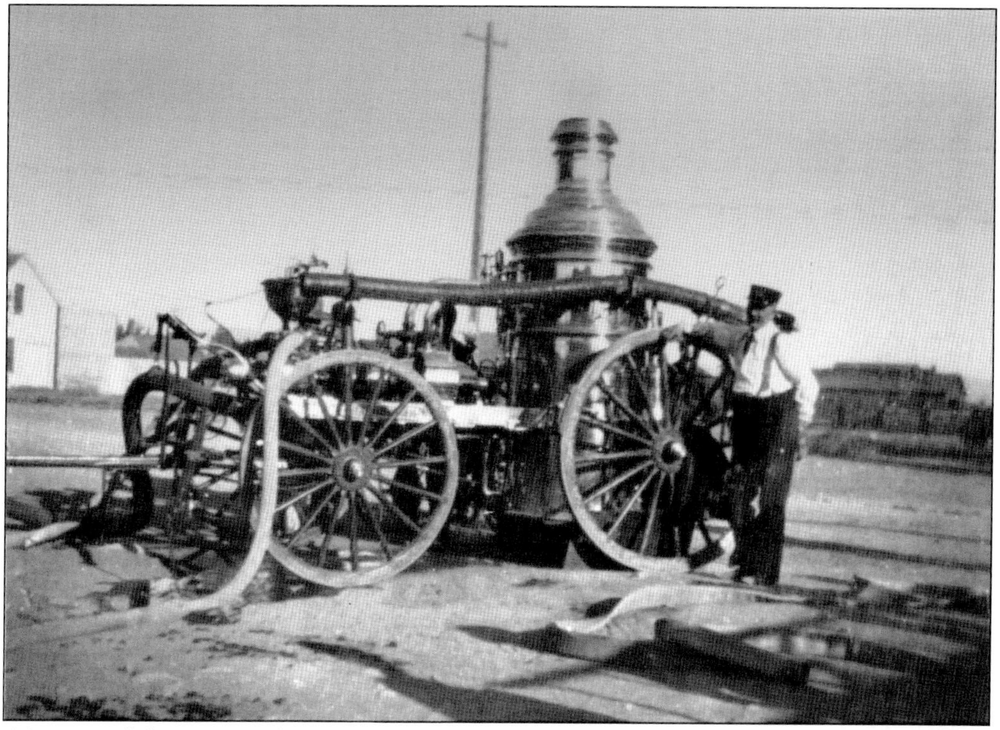

After a small fire in a nearby stable (caused by an intoxicated teamster who discarded his lit cigar), several cisterns were installed in the business district along the Truckee River, and buckets were strategically located for the use of volunteers. The community came to a general consensus that, in the event of a fire, all able-bodied citizens should render help. The Reno Hook and Ladder Company No. 1 was established in 1878 and, for over 120 years, organized the service of local fire fighters who have risked their lives to protect the citizens, visitors, and property of downtown Reno. The photograph to the right is of James Malone, an early fireman from Eagle Company No. 3. (WA-05977, UNRS-P0227-1.)

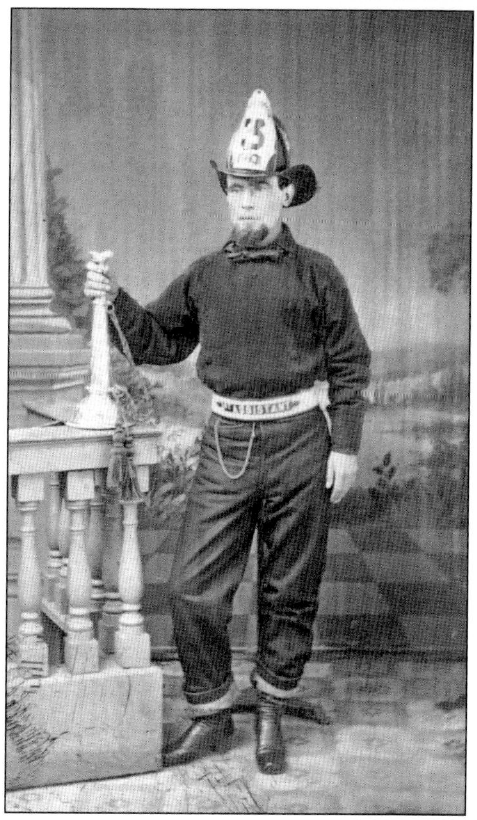

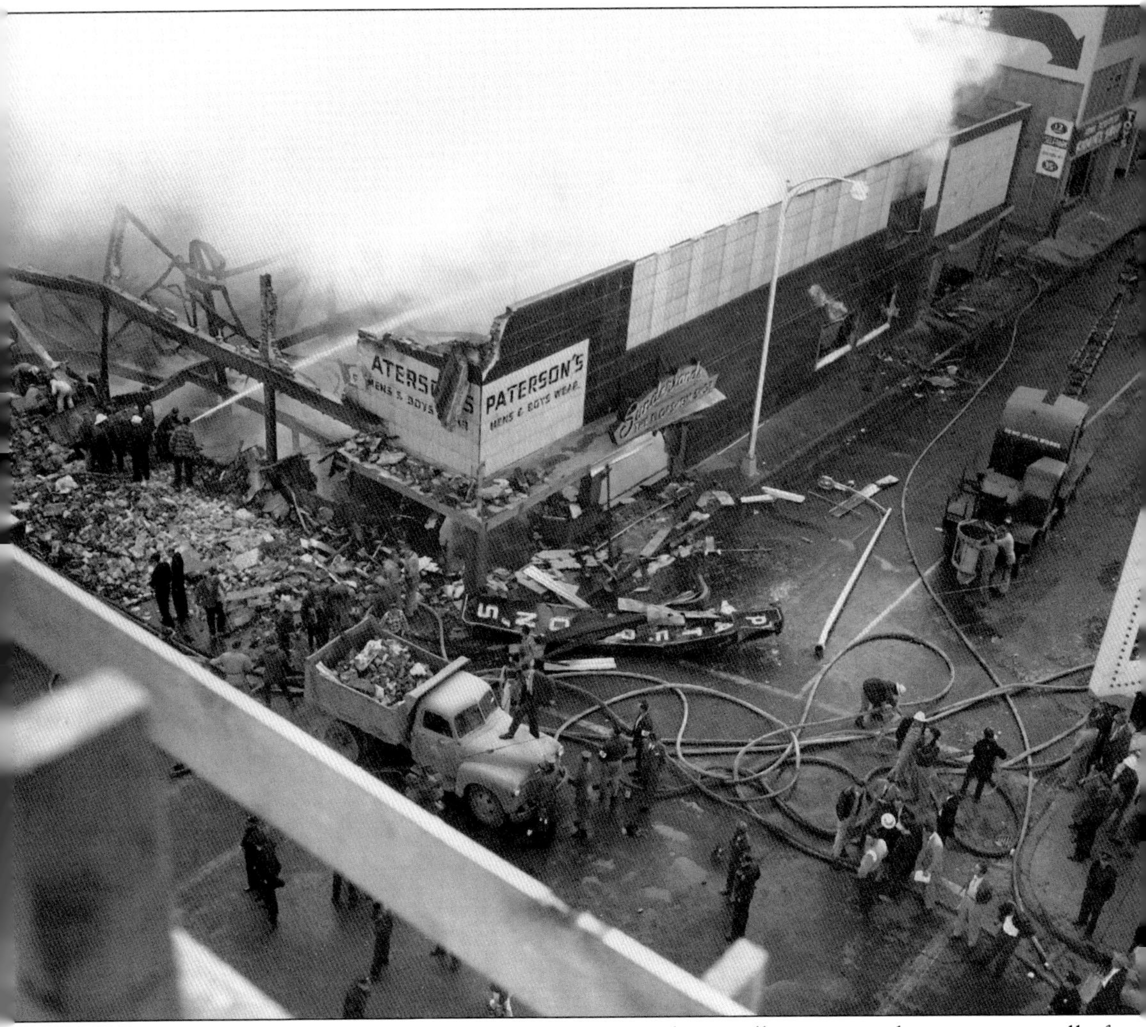

In February 1957, the Reno Fire Department received two calls reporting that a strong smell of gas was coming from Spina's Nevada Shoe Factory and the Paterson's Men's Store, both located on the west side of Sierra Street between the Truckee River and First Street. The manager of the Elk's Club, J.C. Kumle, began evacuating the lunch crowd from the building because of the odor. Soon after the first engines arrived on the scene, a violent explosion blew the windows from some of the surrounding buildings; two smaller explosions followed. Five buildings (Paterson's, the Bankers Trust, the Blitz/Sanford building, the Gray-Reid's department store and the Elk's Home) were damaged and destroyed in the explosion, which caused over $5 million in damages. (UNRS-P2012-07-55.)

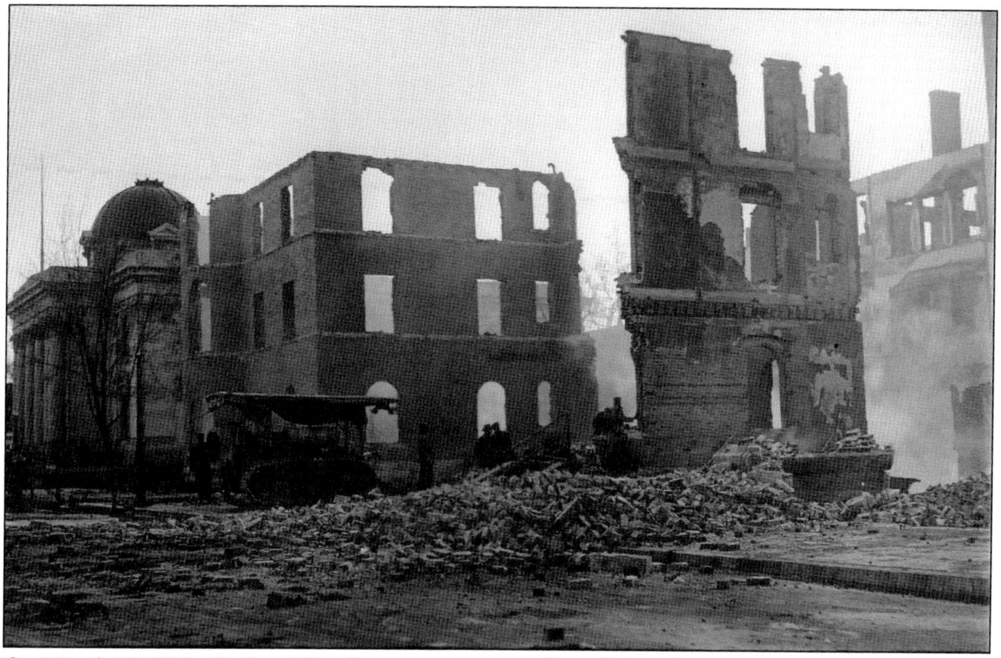

On March 15, 1922, the local fire department received a call that the popular Riverside Hotel had been completely destroyed by a fire that was reportedly started in the basement of the building at approximately 2:00 a.m. Many of the hotel guests were rescued by ladders, and by 4:00 a.m. the fire department discontinued attempts to extinguish the fire, instead turning their attention to saving the neighboring structures. During the fire, two steam engines were on the scene, and 21 firemen were working. L.A. Sheppard, the engine driver, was said to have been injured by a loose nozzle/hose. The estimated damage was $250,000. (UNRS-P1986-19-6, UNRS-P2006-05-024.)

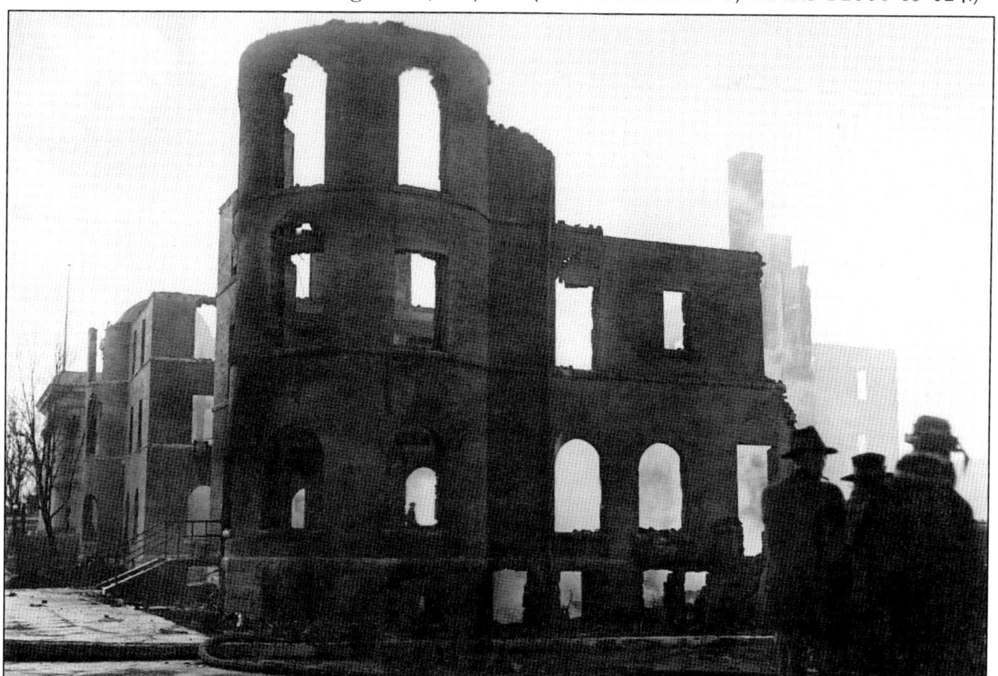

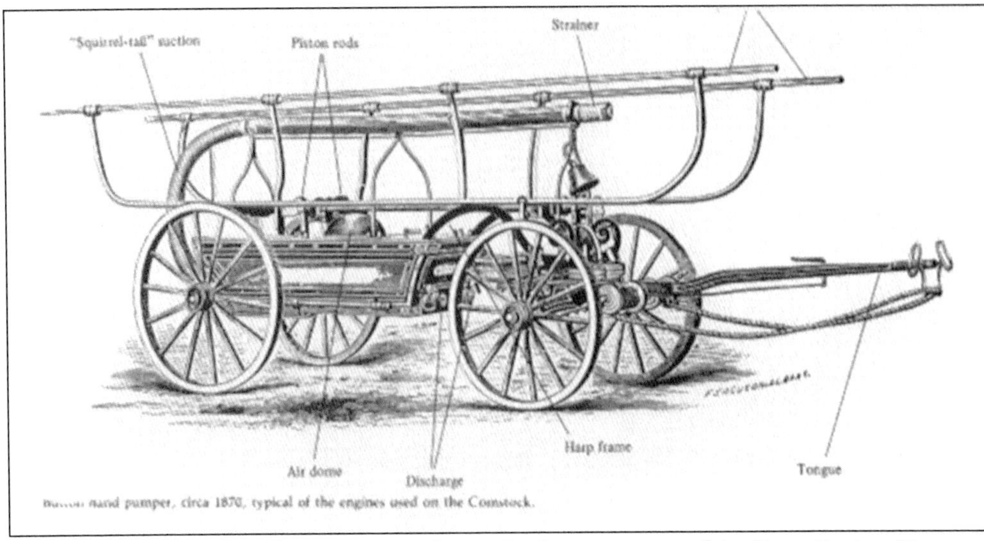

This drawing illustrates a fire engine similar to the first apparatus of the Reno Engine Company No 1—an 1863 Button and Blake Hand Pumper. The Hand Pumper was purchased on November 10, 1875, from Virginia Cities Washoe Engine Company No. 4 for $800. It had 9.5-inch cylinders and a 7.5-foot stroke. The drawing is from *Red Shirts and Leather Helmets* by Steve Frady. (Courtesy of Reno Fire Department and IAFF Local 731.)

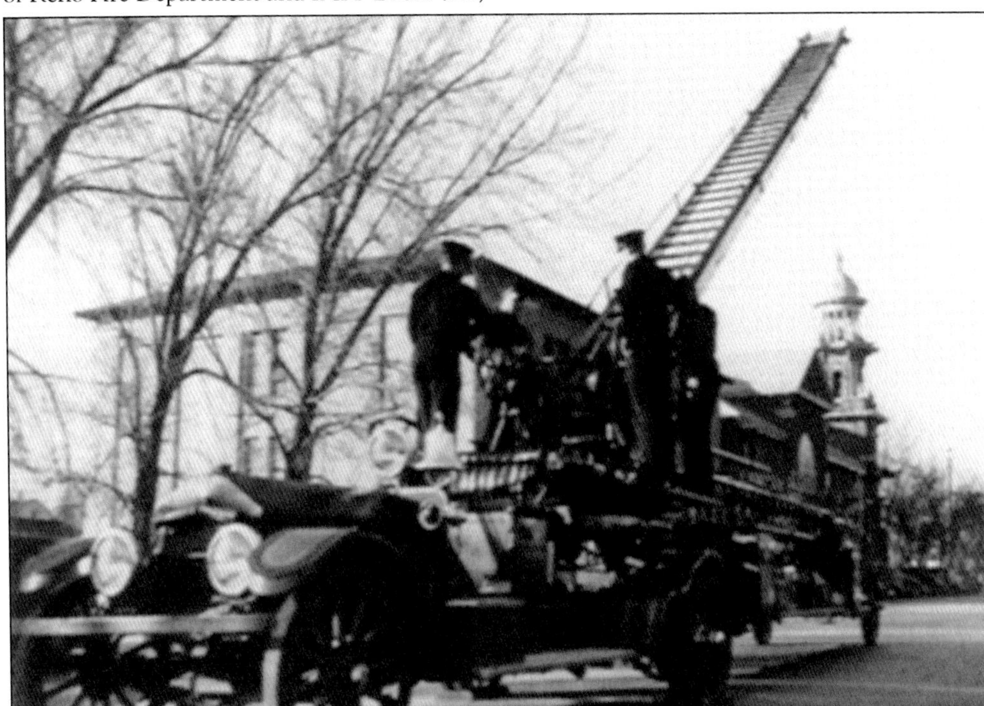

Over the years apparatuses have dramatically evolved from horse-drawn carriages to advanced motorized vehicles. This image shows the 1917 ALF Aerial with the ladder being raised, on Arlington Avenue near the Truckee River looking north. The bell tower of St. Thomas Aquinas Catholic Church on Second Street is visible in the background. (Courtesy of Reno Fire Department and IAFF Local 731.)

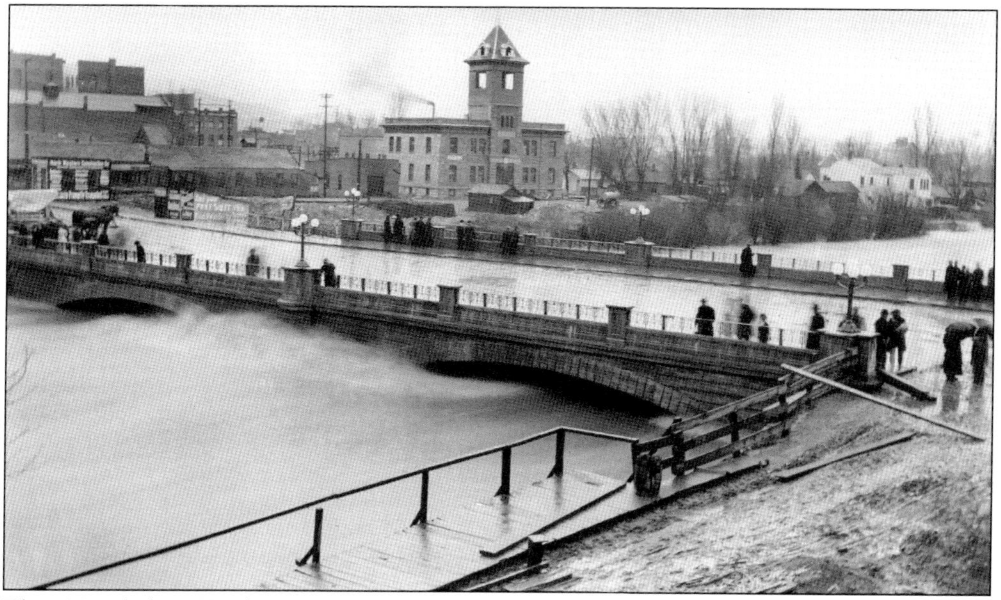

The 120-mile-long Truckee River has been the cause of devastating floods throughout its history. The floods are brought about by winter rainstorms, which melt the snowpack in the Sierras. There have been major floods recorded in the Truckee Meadows in 1862, 1875, 1890, 1904, 1907, 1928, 1937, 1943, 1950, 1955, 1963, 1986, 1997, and 2005. This photograph is of the March 19, 1907, flood. (WA-05952.)

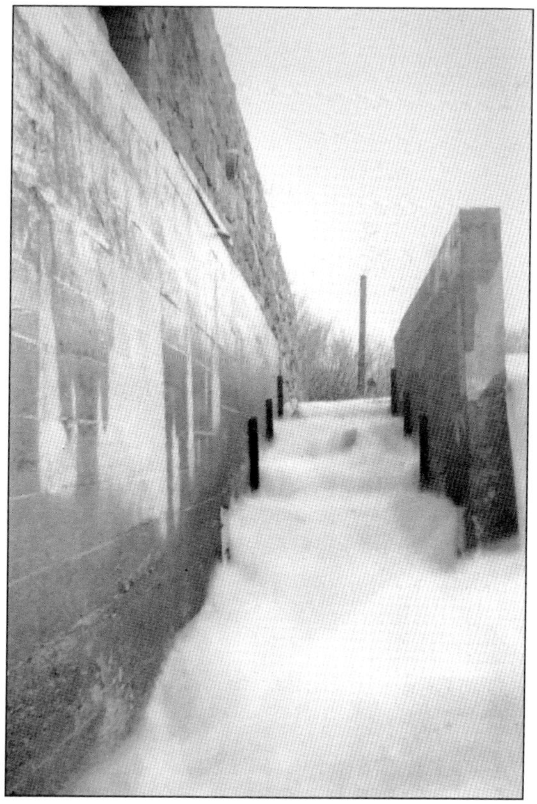

In March 1928, Reno was affected by another flood for five days. At the time, the flood was considered the third worst in recorded history. The storm began on March 23 and was deemed the "drought-breaker" because, up until then, Reno had been fairly dry. Residents in the lower Truckee Meadows and along the river were evacuated by March 25. (WA-04008.)

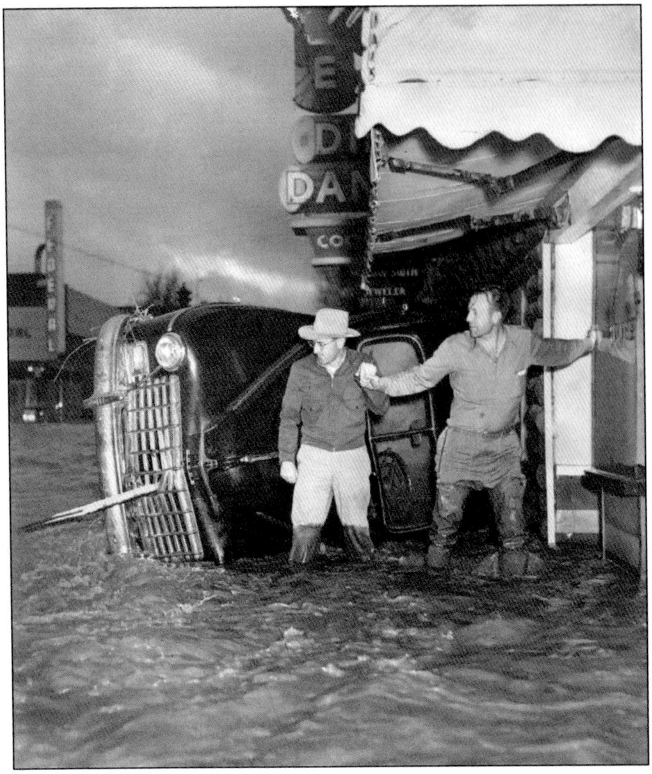

In November 1950, Reno was hit by a severe storm that caused up to $3 million in damages. The water ran four feet deep in the downtown area, and many of the homes on Riverside Drive were ruined. A portion of the bridge on Second Street was washed out by floodwaters, and remnants of the structure ended up on the Rock Street Bridge. Some areas in the Sierras were noted as receiving 17.67 inches of rain over an eight-day period. Pictured here are two men hanging on to a building beside a car that was overturned by flood waters in front of the Reno Garage. The Gray Reid Wright building is in the distance. (WA-04107.)

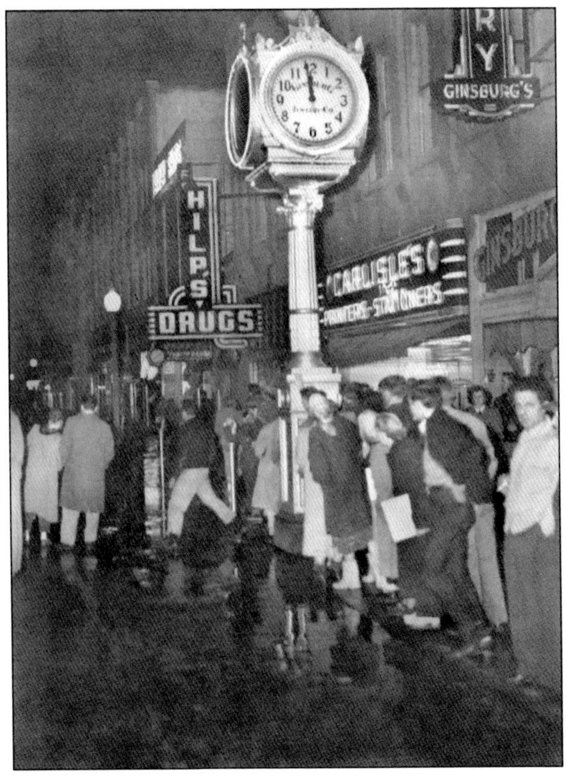

This image shows individuals on the corner of Second and Virginia Streets watching the waters rise during the 1950 flood. Hilps Drug Store can be seen towards the back. The historic street clock seen here first appeared on Virginia Street in front of Ginsburg Jewelry Company in early 1920. Years later, Reno's clock was moved to a shopping mall and now is preserved downtown. The street clock served as the town's indicator of accurate time since most people did not carry watches. (WA-4116.)

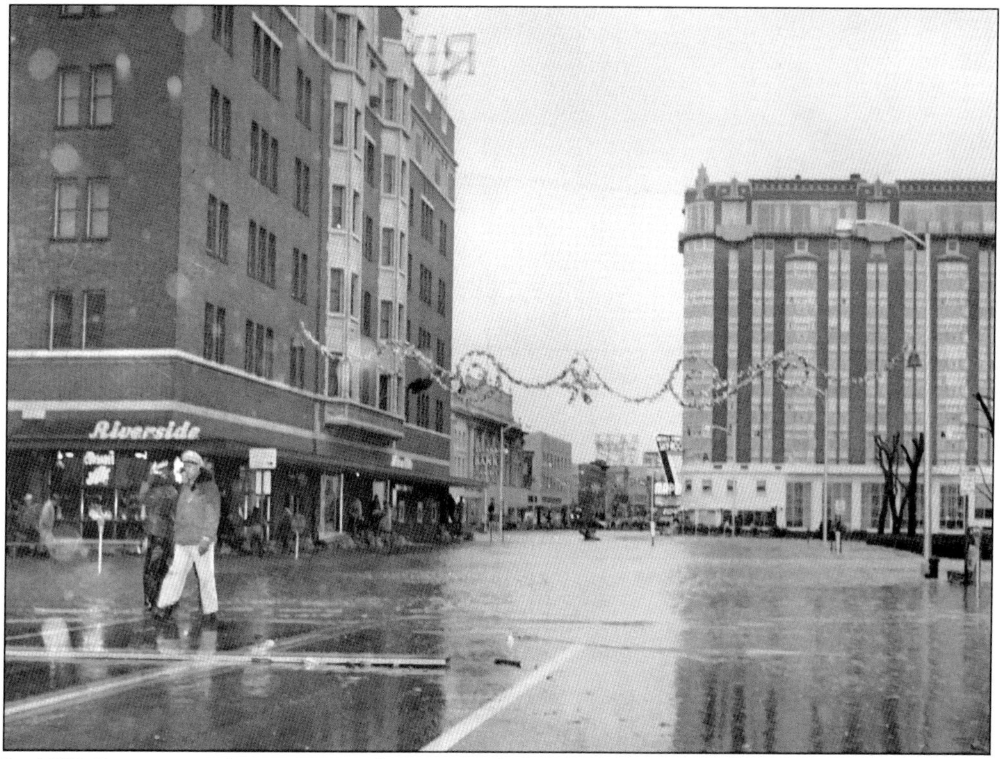

In 1955, Reno was subject to a 10-day series of storms that poured down on the Sierras. The community, remembering the heavy damage of the flood only five years earlier, began working to protect downtown Reno from what was dubbed the "Storm of the Century." (WA-04147.)

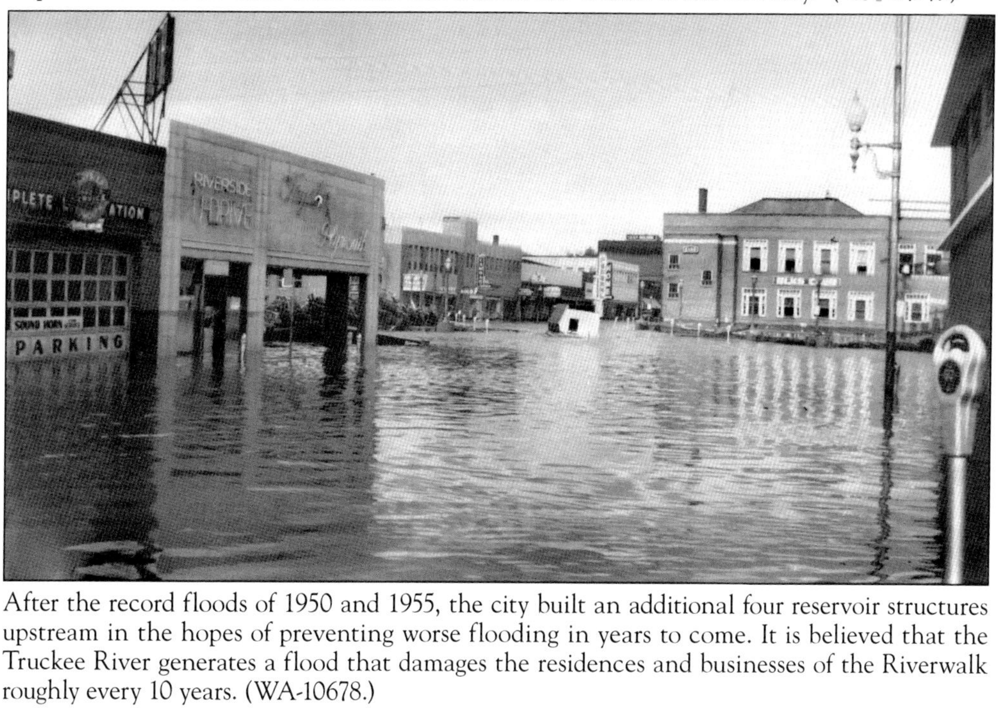

After the record floods of 1950 and 1955, the city built an additional four reservoir structures upstream in the hopes of preventing worse flooding in years to come. It is believed that the Truckee River generates a flood that damages the residences and businesses of the Riverwalk roughly every 10 years. (WA-10678.)

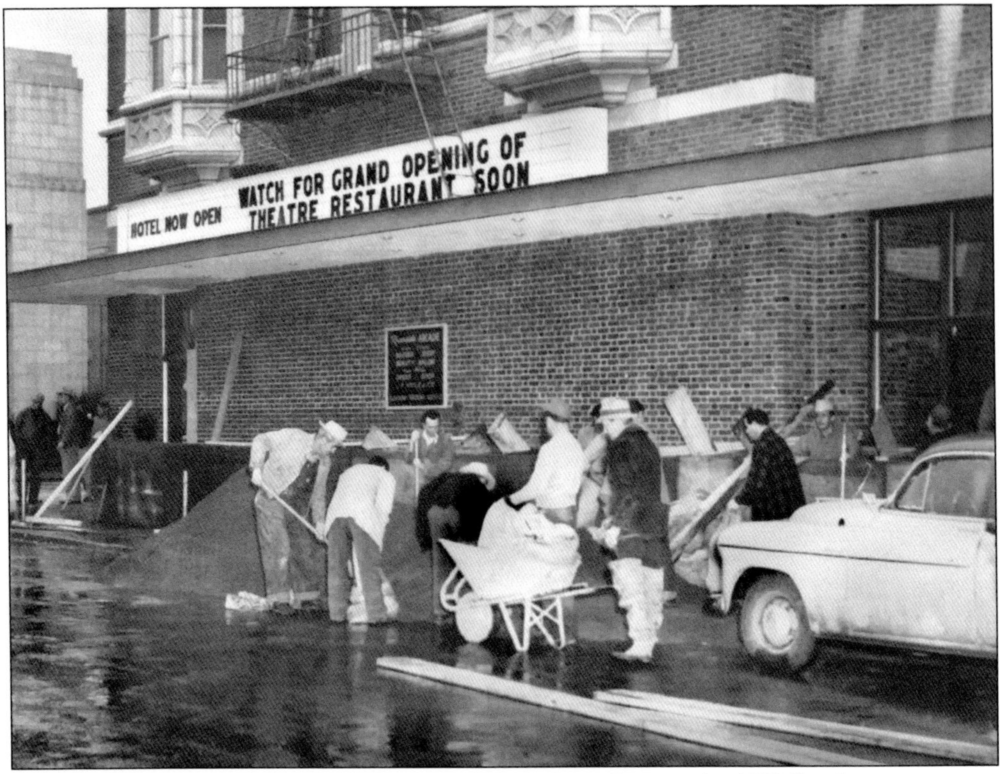

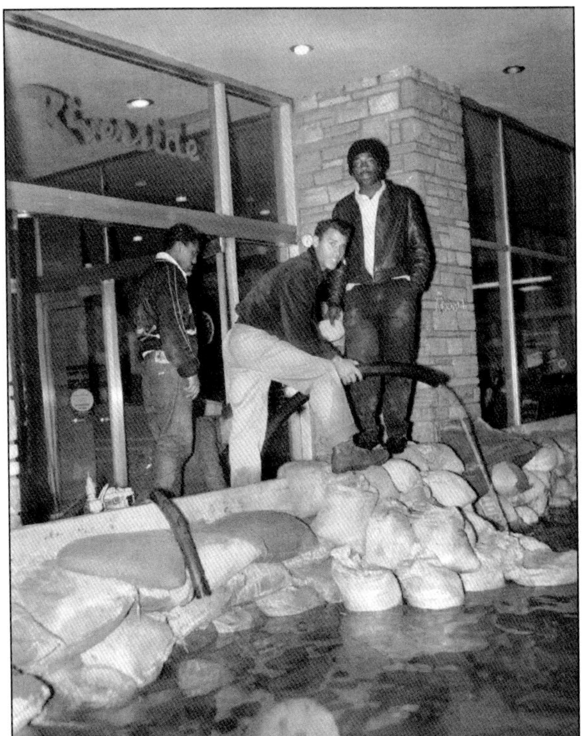

During the 1955 flood, city volunteers and the National Guard began stacking sandbags along the riverbanks, casinos, hotels, and many of the store entrances to help prevent additional damage to downtown businesses. Contractors were hired to clear out areas where wood and debris had started to block the flow of water. Only two days after Christmas, more than two inches of rain fell on Reno in less than 24 hours. The damage was so bad that communication was lost entirely between western Nevada and California due to fallen power lines. Over four feet of water engulfed downtown Reno's bustling businesses. Many of the residents fled the city, first hanging their gifts high inside their Christmas trees to save them from ruin. Prior to the flood, the weather bureau sent a notice stating that "no menacing storms appear on the weather maps and a series of storms appear unlikely." (WA-4121, WA-4152.)

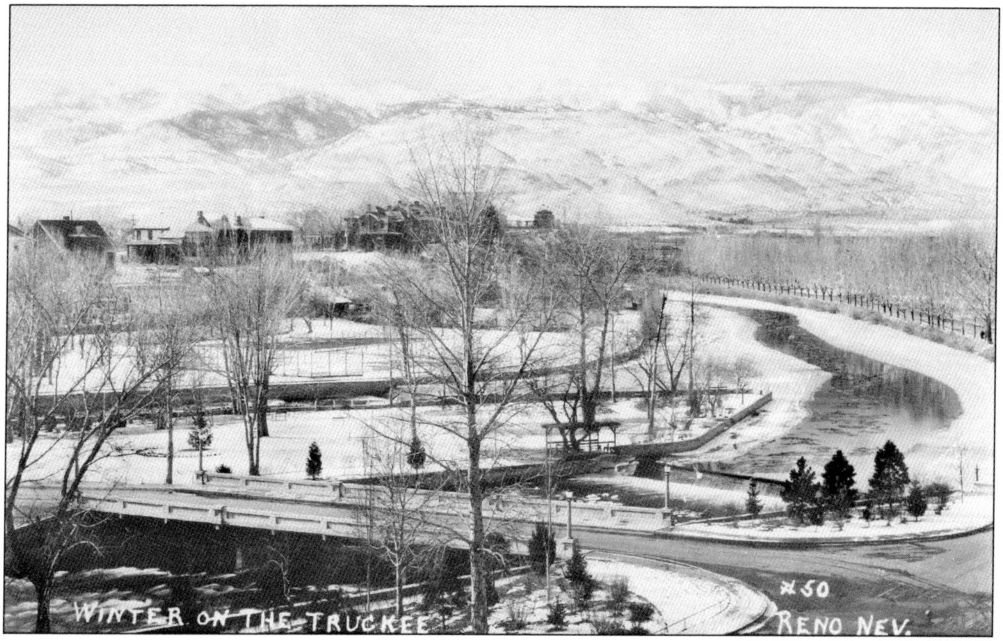

On Christmas Eve 1955, the rain finally stopped and turned into snow from a storm that came through the Gulf of Alaska. The floodwaters began to recede, and overnight Reno received a full snowstorm covering everything in the city. The residents awoke to the first white Christmas in years. (WA-09129.)

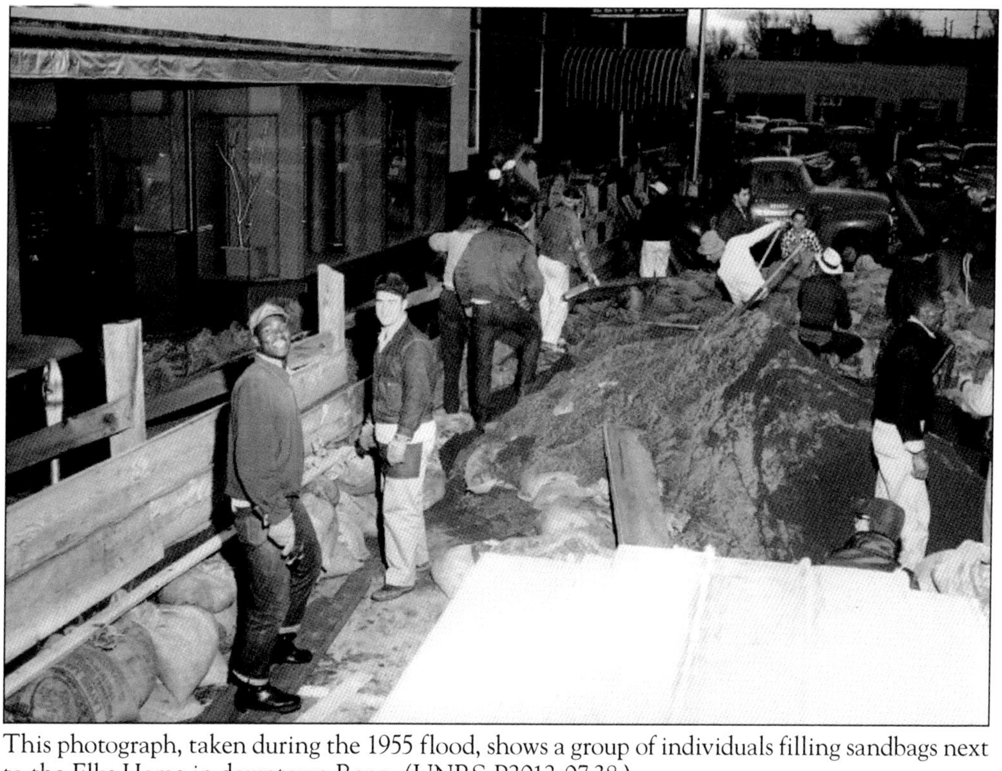

This photograph, taken during the 1955 flood, shows a group of individuals filling sandbags next to the Elks Home in downtown Reno. (UNRS-P2012-07-38.)

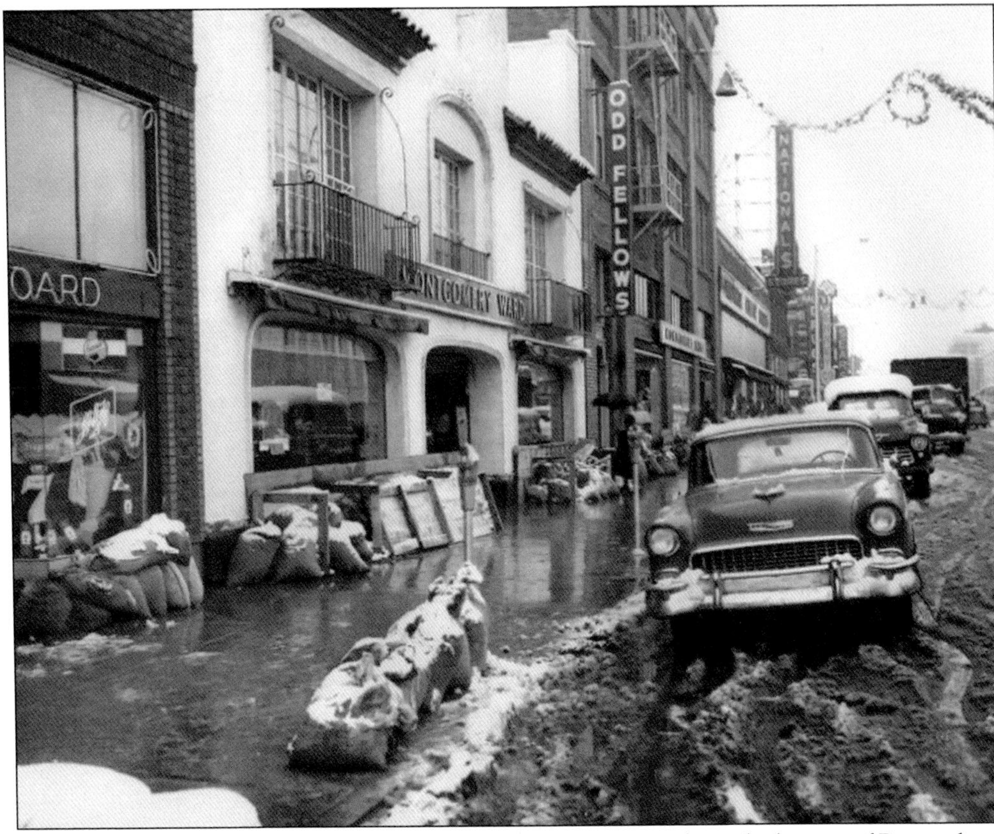

This photograph was taken after the floodwaters of 1955 swept through the city of Reno where Mongomery, Oddfellows, and the National Store once stood. (UNRS-P2012-07-46.)

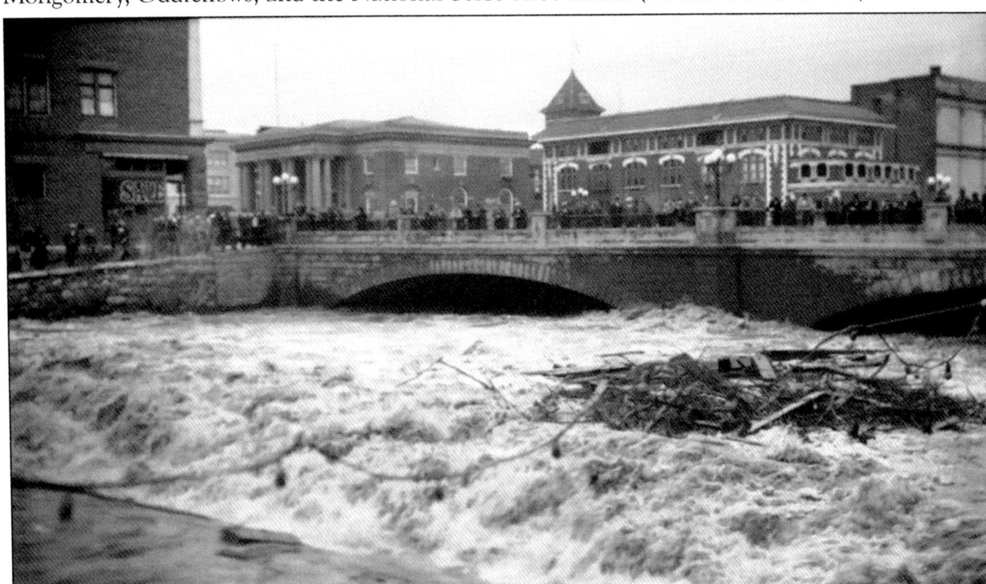
This photograph shows individuals looking over the Virginia Street Bridge during the flood of 1920 with the Riverside Hotel in the background. (UNRS-P1992-01-1942.)

Eight

Forming of the Riverwalk

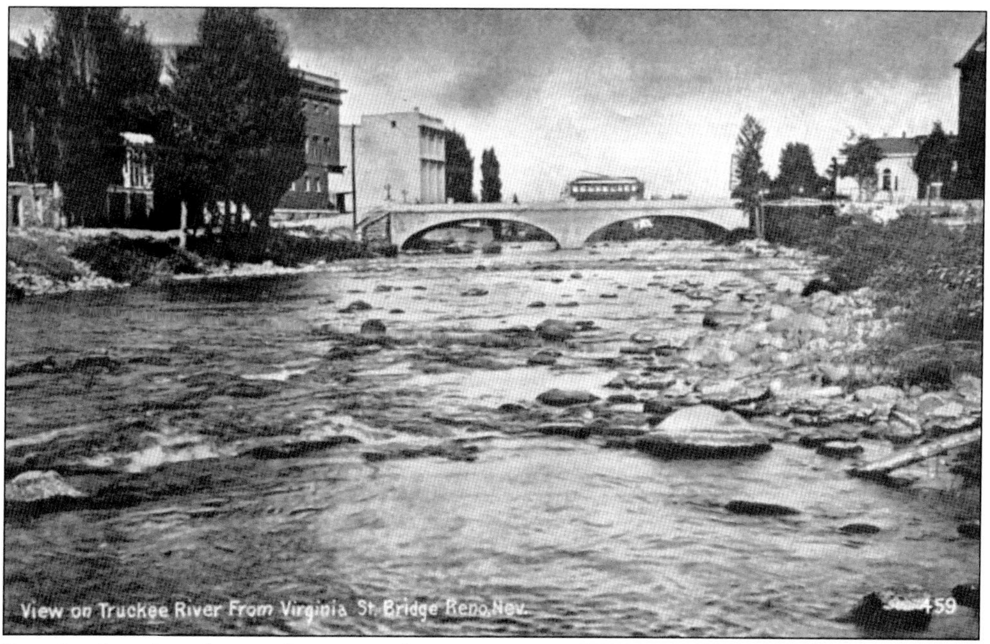

Reno has long been known for constantly reinventing itself, from the beginning of the Comstock Lode through the popular 1930s and 1940s gaming and divorce era. The area along the banks of the Truckee River has been home to some of the state's most historical treasures. Over time, the area has been reestablished and renamed the Riverwalk. The Riverwalk encompasses hotels, restaurants, entertainment venues, and a lovely park upon an island.

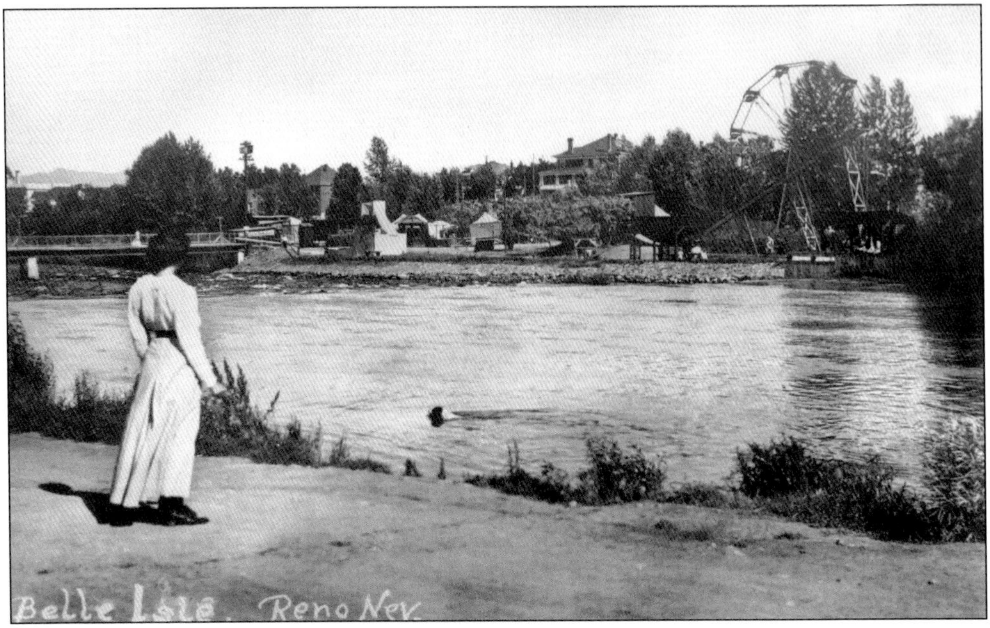

In 1910, local Reno attorney Lewis E. Hinkley planned to transform the area around a small island not far from the city's main Virginia Street Bridge. Hinkley constructed walkways from the natural foliage, such as the wild rosebushes, willows, cottonwoods, and poplars. A wooden dancing pavilion was built in the center island, which was called Belle Isle (French for "beautiful island"). The park officially opened in July 1911. Belle Isle guests were able to enjoy the latest motion pictures, accompanied by a live orchestra, inside a 700-seat open-air theater. The island would hold weekly concerts and dances and, on occasion, served as a venue for traveling carnivals. A 60-foot Ferris wheel was built on the island, and in the winter months there was an area for ice skating. (WA-02934.)

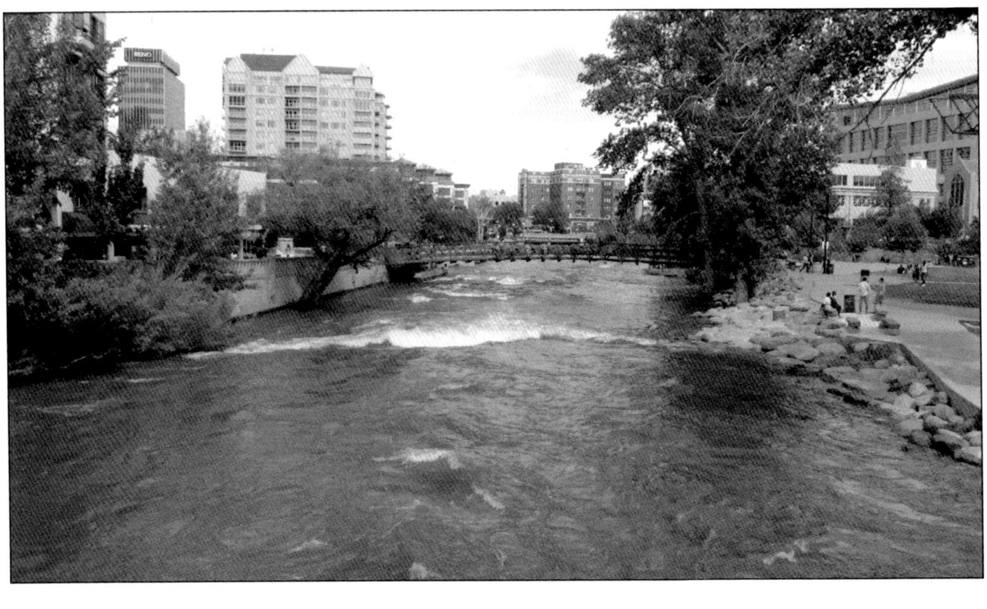

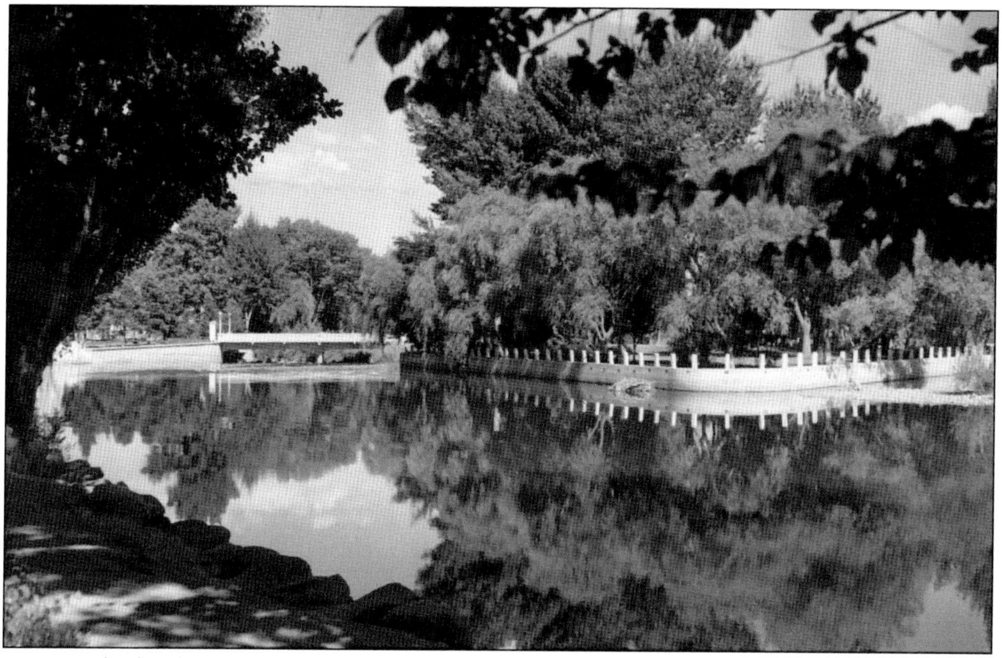

In 1920, the land was purchased by hotel owner, banker, and businessman George Wingfield, a tremendous political power in Reno during the first half of the 20th century. Wingfield generously donated the park (subsequently renamed in his honor) back to the city for public use. (Dave Stafford Collection.)

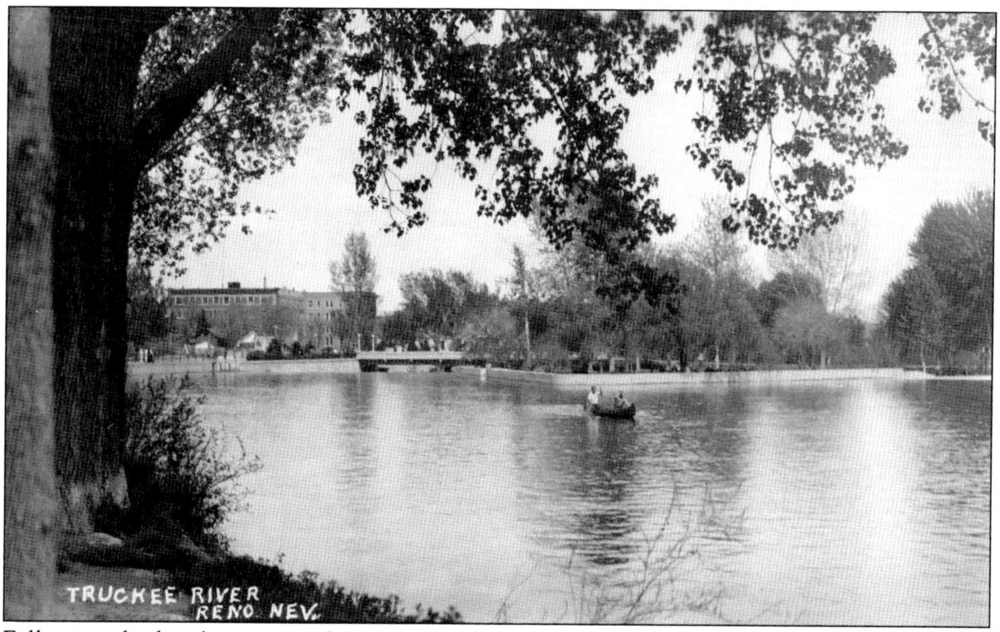

Following the bustling years of the Comstock Lode and the early divorce craze, Reno's image along the banks of the Truckee River began to deteriorate, and the once-lovely areas around it began to suffer. In the mid-1990s, Reno proposed a plan to redevelop the area along the river into the official Riverwalk. Since this time, downtown Reno has undergone a steady revitalization. (Dave Stafford Collection.)

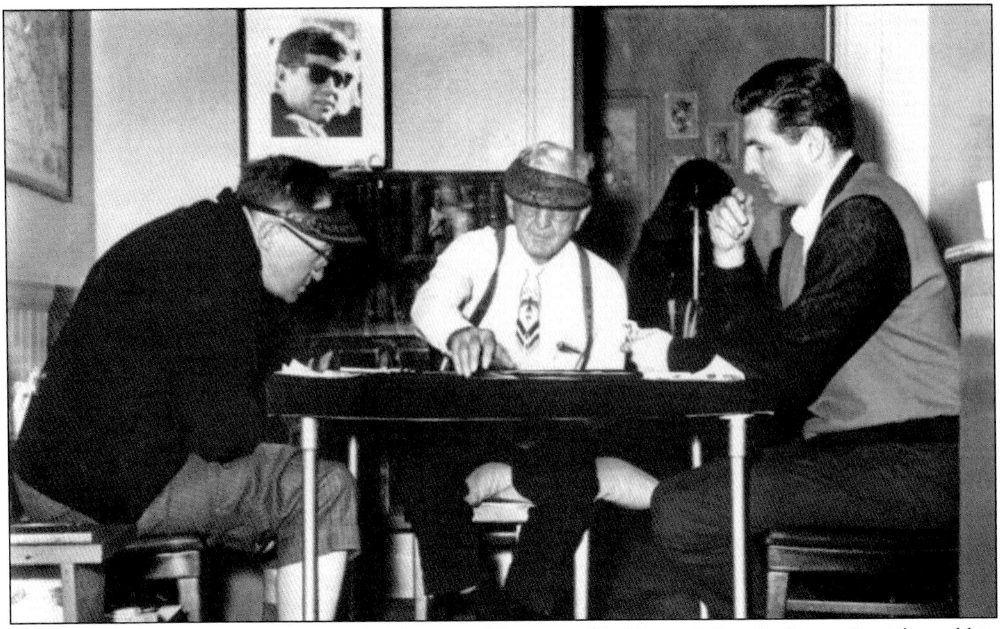

The Truckee Riverwalk was named in honor of Raymond I. "Pappy" Smith. Pappy Smith and his brother Harold ran carnival games along the boardwalks and beaches in San Francisco before coming to Reno in 1935 to establish the Harolds Club, which was the largest casino operation in the world prior to the 1960s. The Smiths were generous supporters of their community and donated money back into the churches, clubs, and facilities that needed their help. They also funded a yearly $90,000 scholarship for local high school seniors. The photograph above shows Harold S. Smith Sr., Pappy Smith, and Harold Smith Jr. gambling. The image below shows Pappy Smith in front of the world-famous Harolds Club. (UNRS-P1212-1, UNRS-P1992-03-488.)

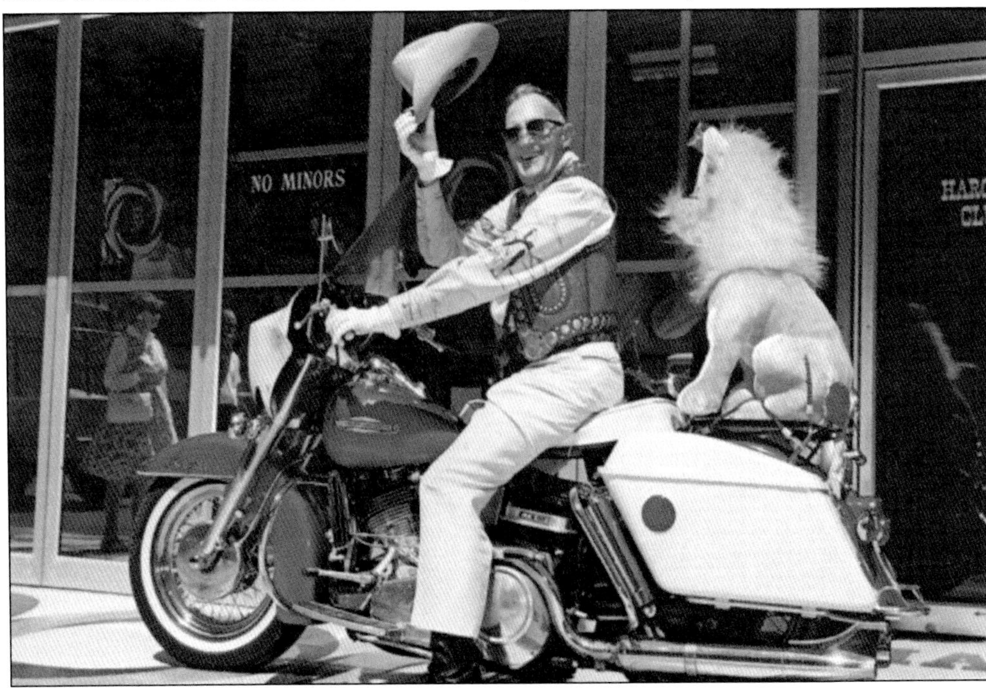

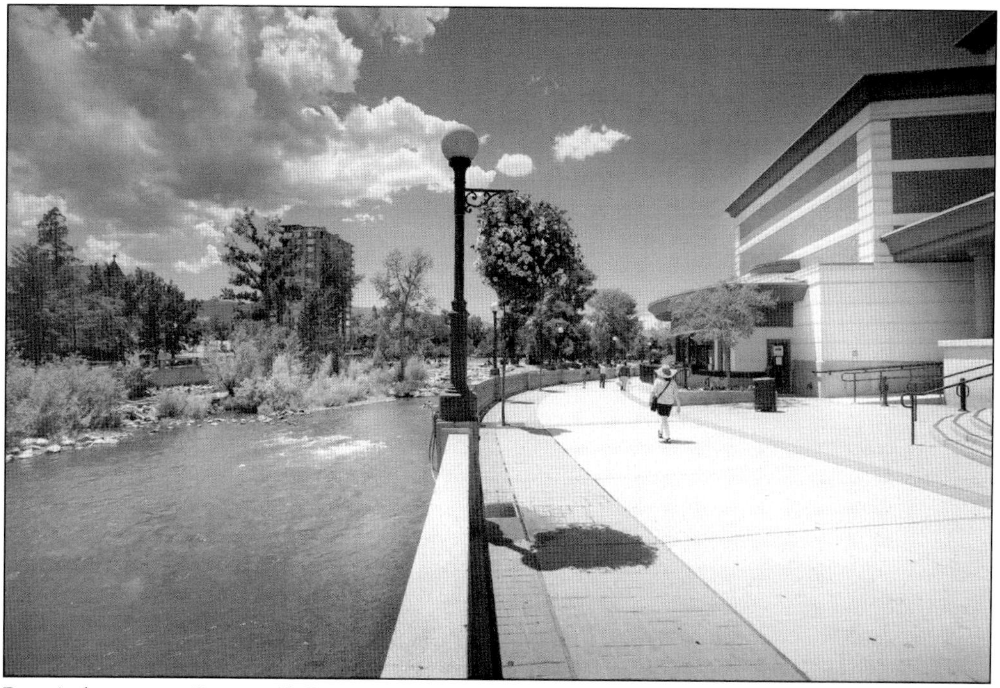

Reno's downtown Riverwalk District is typically defined as the area spanning the Truckee River between Arlington Avenue and Lake Street. The modern-day Riverwalk features over three-dozen restaurants, pubs, nationally recognized museums and galleries, retail shops, boutiques, salons, restaurants, lounges, and unique locally owned retailers. The northern end of the Riverwalk District along First Street, between Lake Street (east) and Arlington Street (west), overlooks Reno's beautiful Truckee River where a few historical buildings, such as the Hughes Porter Building, the Colonial Apartments, and the Twentieth Century Club still stand. Reno's very popular Truckee River Whitewater Park runs directly through this area, offering visitors a variety of fun outdoor activities. (Courtesy of the Riverwalk Merchants Association.)

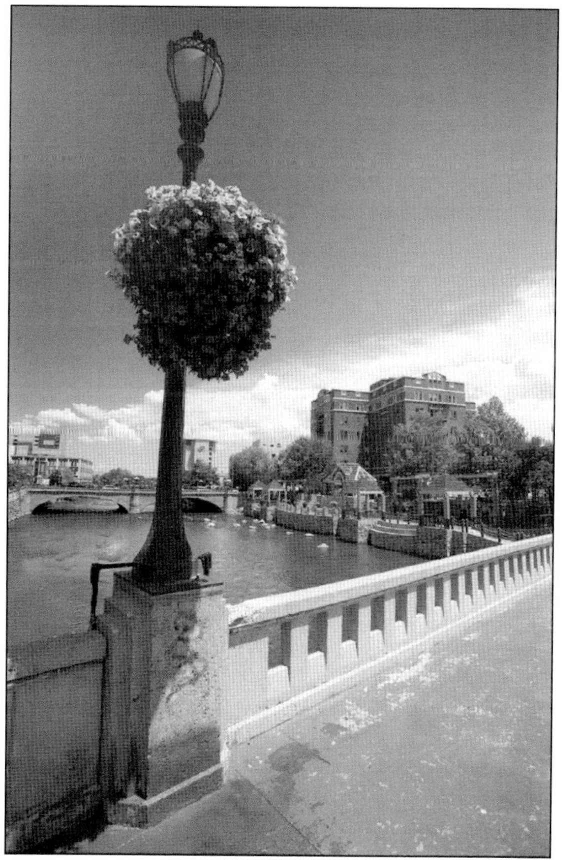

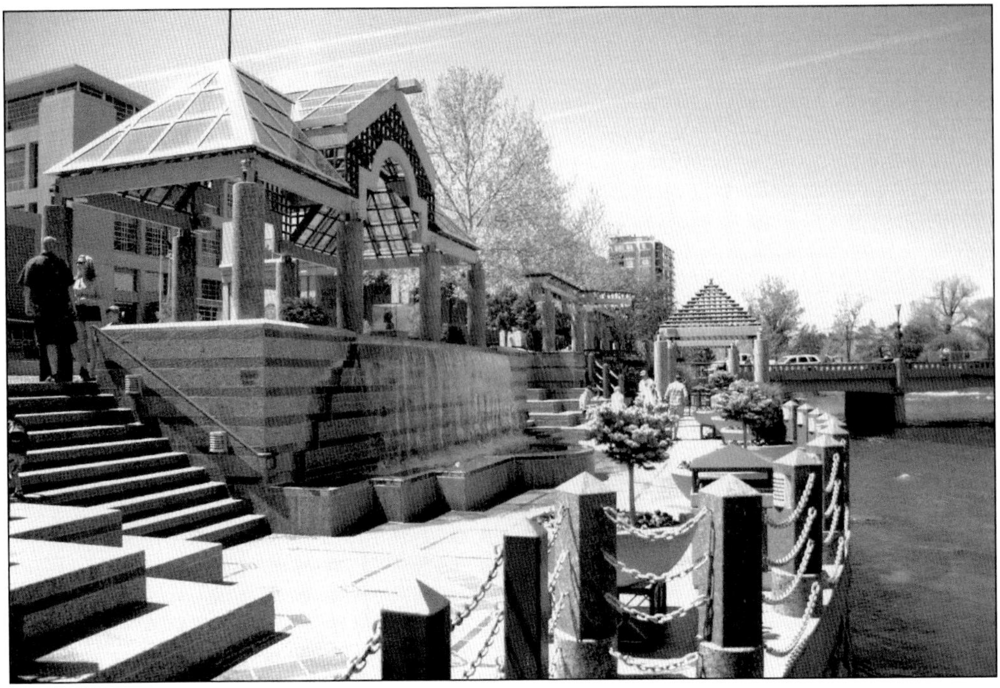

The newly redeveloped Riverwalk area showcases a series of seven different water features and original sculptures featuring native Nevada wildlife, including the *Creatures of Nevada* by artist John Battenberg. Passersby can walk from street level down to a variety of seating areas overlooking the Truckee River. The Riverwalk can be accessed from the Virginia Street Bridge or Wingfield Park. (Courtesy of the Meredith family.)

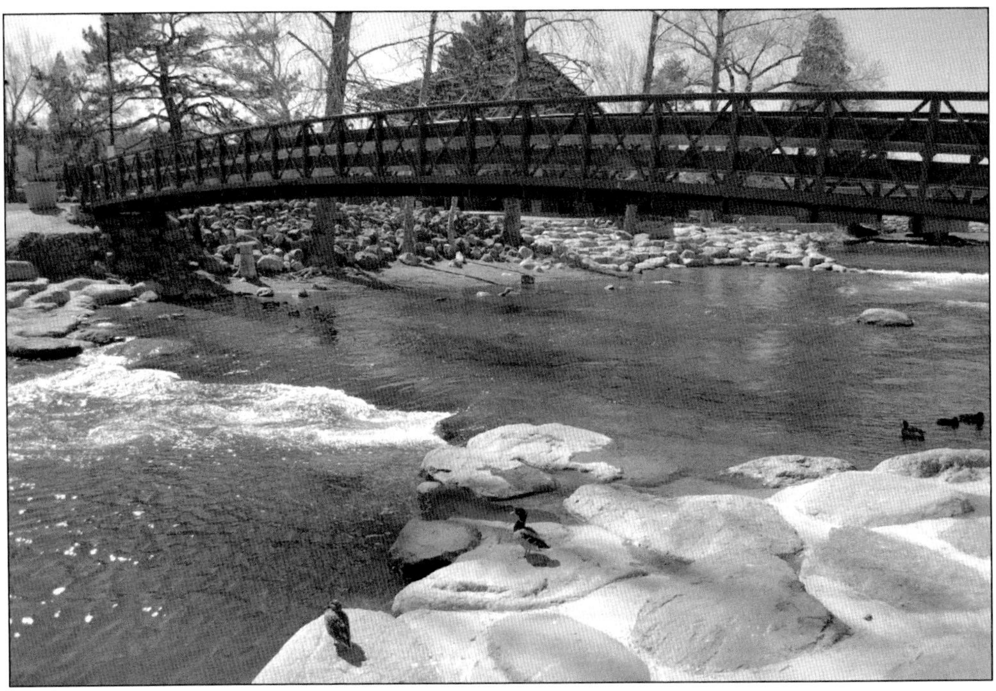

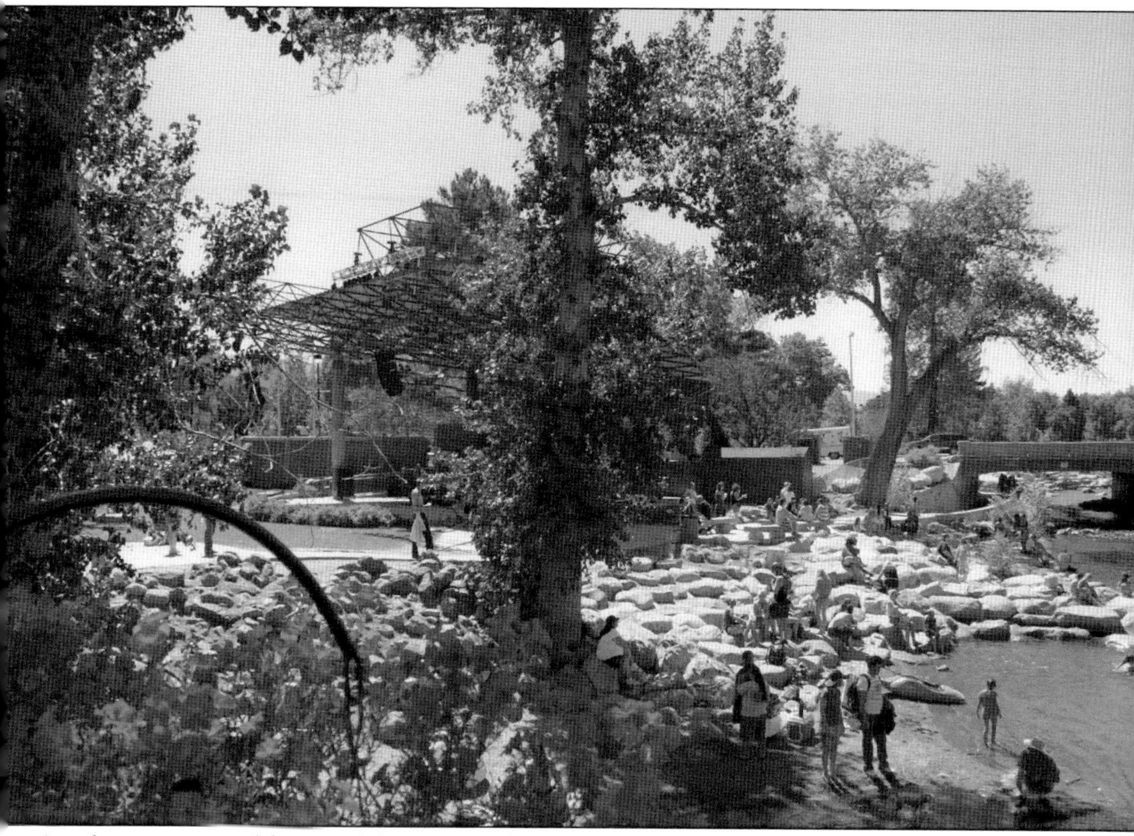

Another monumental feature of the area was the installation of a whitewater park, which allowed for the opening up of the riverbanks for public use. During construction, the river was temporarily drained, and 7,000 tons of smooth, flat-top rocks and boulders were installed along the riverbanks and in-stream. The dynamic park features 11 drop-pools and is 2,600 feet in length.

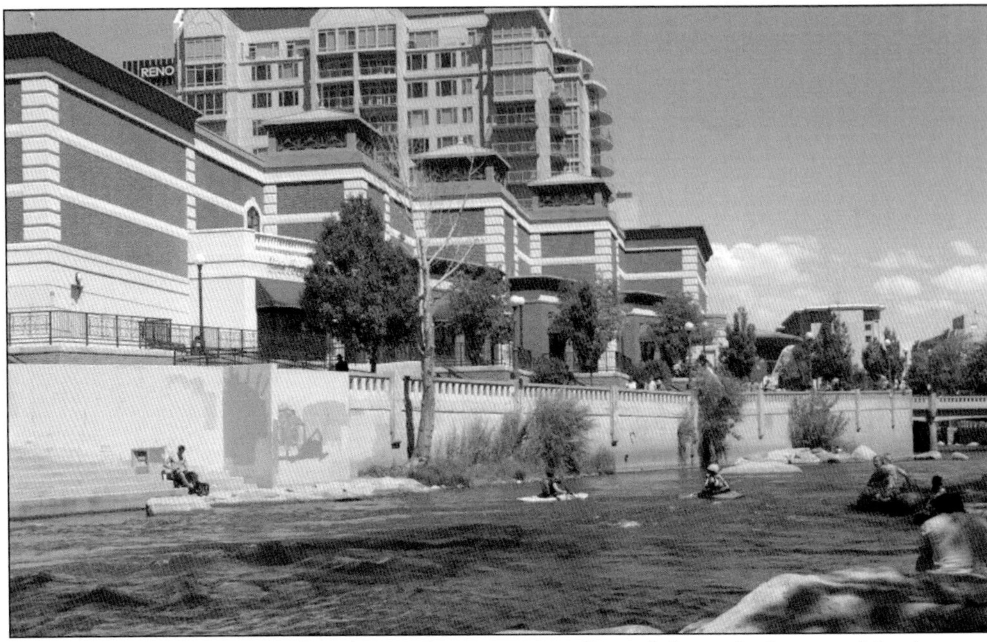

The park is open year-round and provides a constant flow of clean, fresh water. Nearly every summer, crowds of people can be found enjoying the river; many come from around the globe to take pleasure in swimming, kayaking, and various performances that take place on a stage on the island in Wingfield Park.

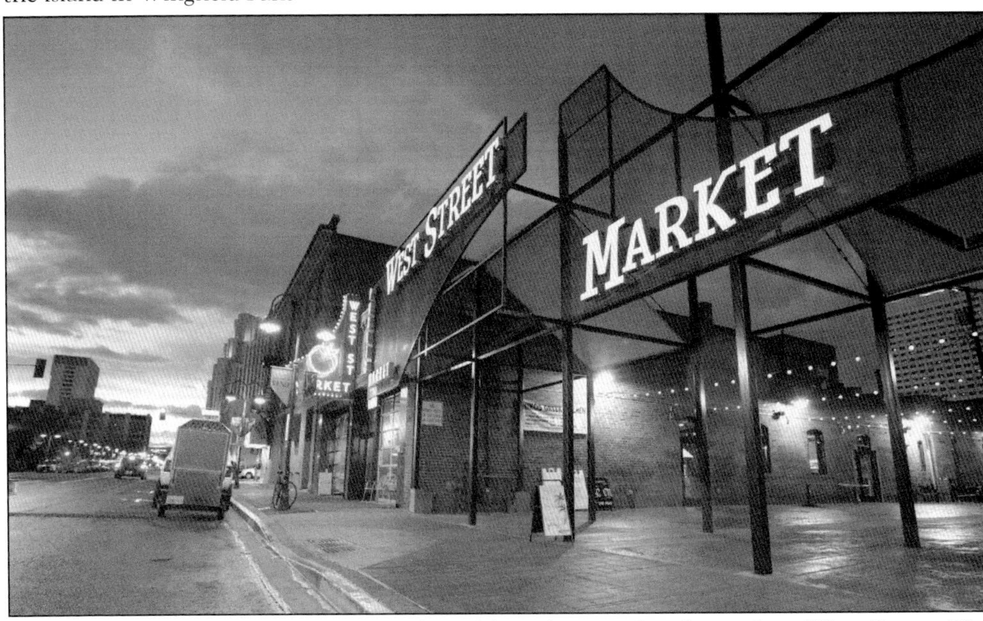

In 2010, Reno initiated the creation of a public urban market, located on West Street. The project was funded by community development block grants, the Reno Redevelopment Agency, and investments by individual tenants. The West Street Market features a variety of shops, bars, and dining options. Prior to its opening, it housed smaller establishments, at one time operating as the Ferrier Horse and Cart stables that serviced the Ross Manor. (Courtesy of the Riverwalk Merchants Association.)

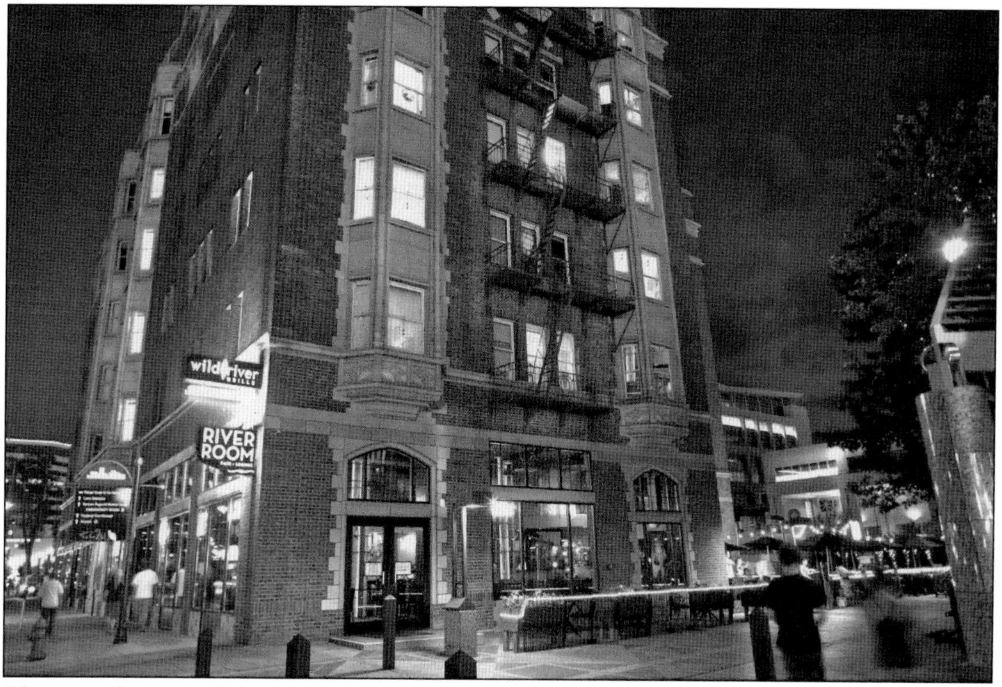

The revitalization of downtown Reno included the rehabilitation of the old Riverside Hotel, which had remained vacant for some time. The building, located on Virginia Street south of the Riverwalk, served as a popular casino and hotel before its closure. It was ultimately converted into 35 lofts for local artists, aptly renamed the Riverside Artists Lofts. It is also home to retail establishments, restaurants, and art galleries. (Courtesy of Wild River Grille.)

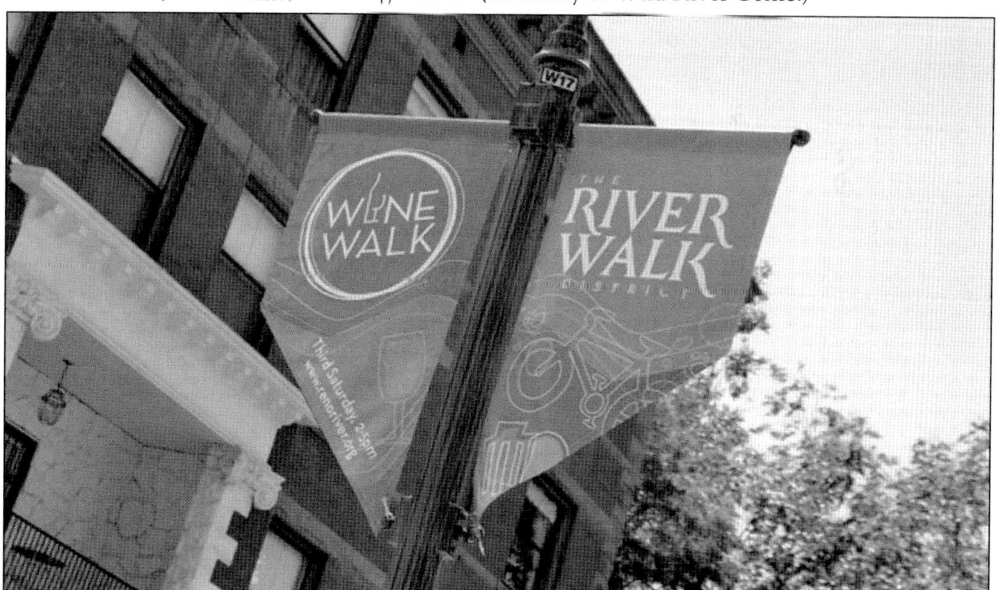

In the early 1990s, a new business association was formed by the residents and business owners of the newly renovated Riverwalk District. The Riverwalk Merchants Association holds popular monthly and annual events that help to generate additional funds to continue the revitalization of downtown Reno. (Courtesy of the Riverwalk Merchants Association.)

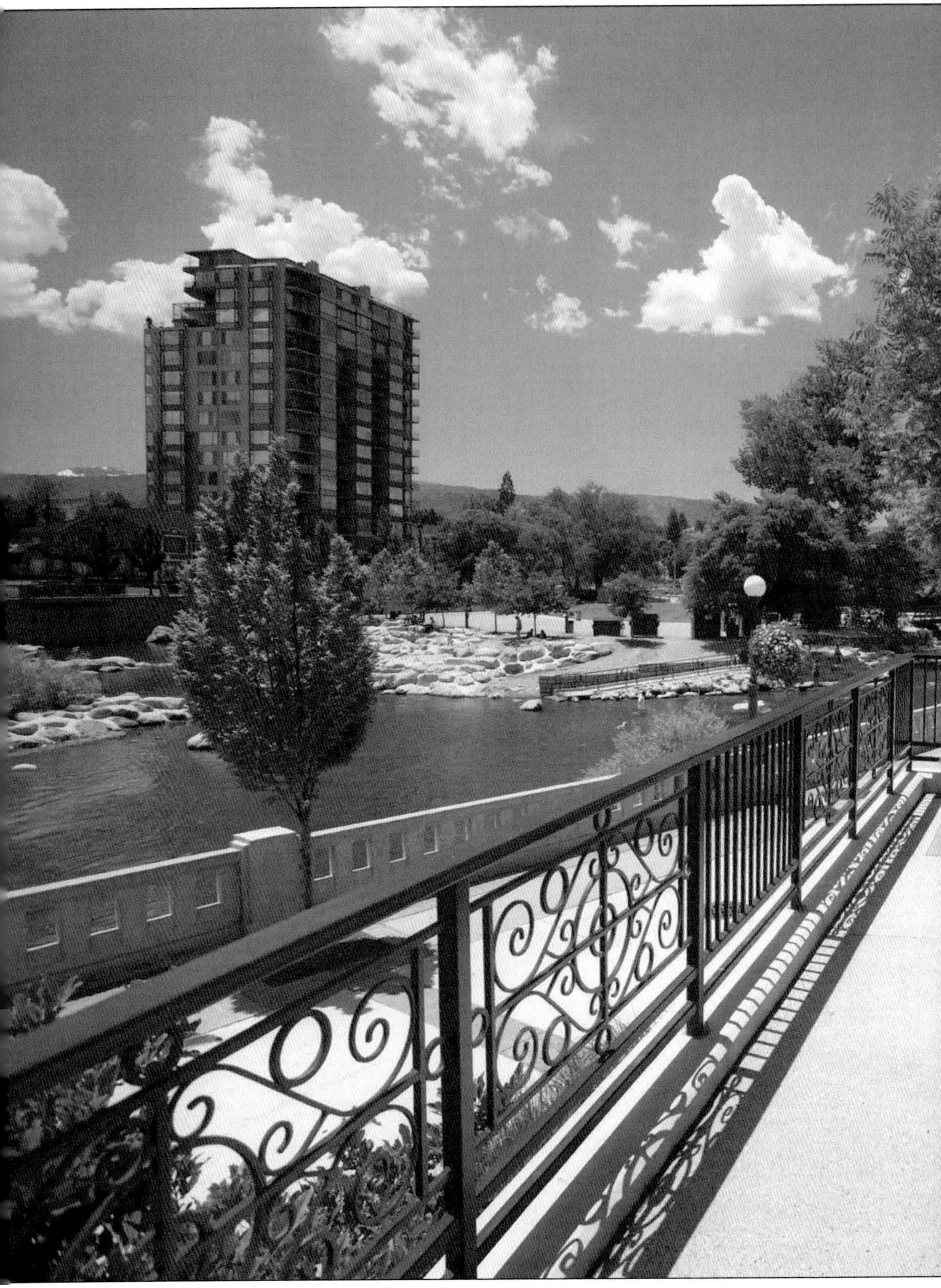

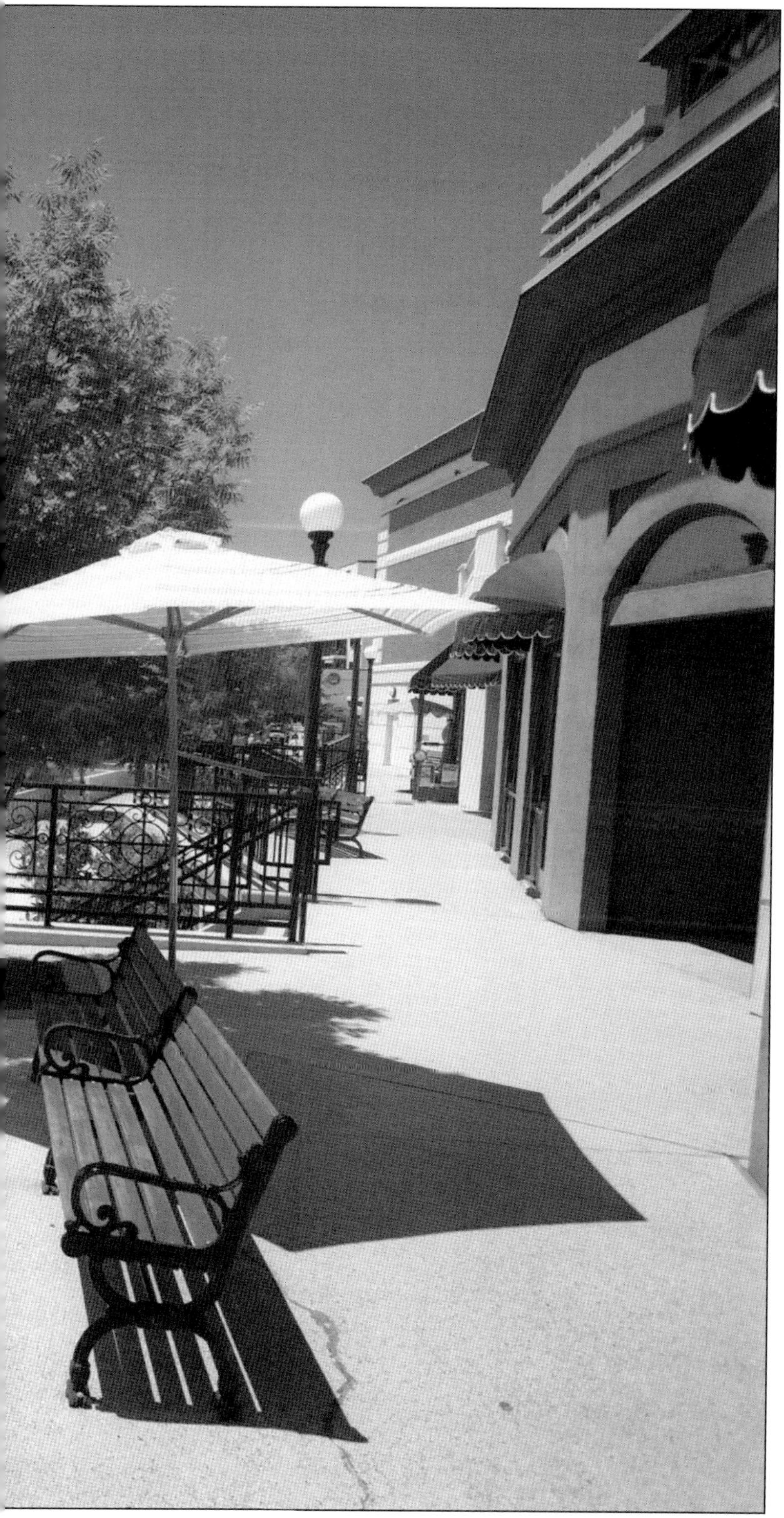

This image, looking north towards the Sierras, shows one of the primary walkways on the Riverwalk. The Park Towers are visible to the left along Island Avenue. The bench is situated near the former site of the Rialto Theater, and below it is a portion of Wingfield Park.

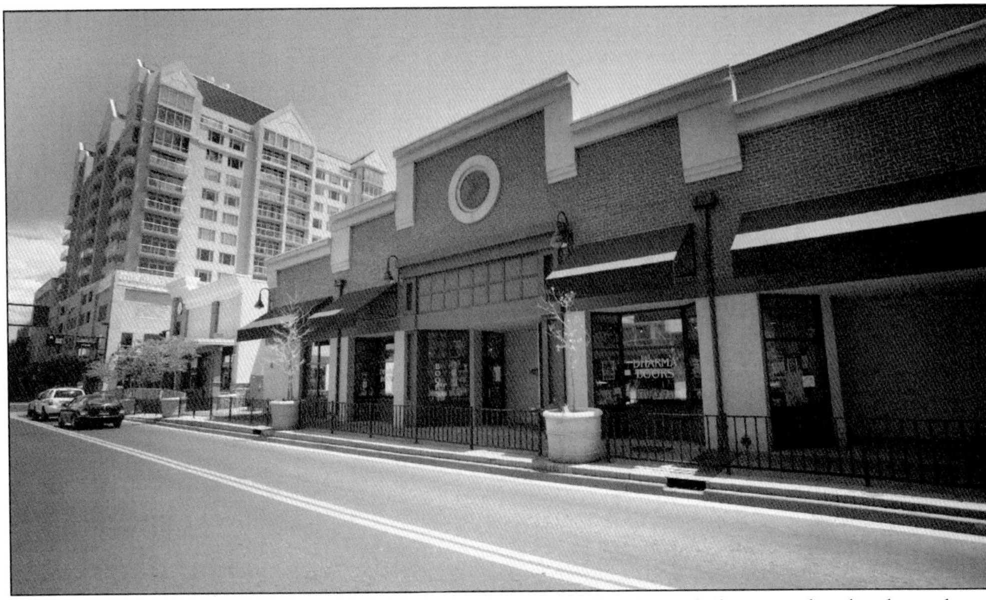

Since its beginning, the Riverwalk Merchants Association has extended its membership boundaries to encompass other historical buildings, including the old *Reno Gazette-Journal* building (which had subsequently become the Merry-Go-Round Bar, famous for its moving bar stools). Other well-known buildings include El Cortez, the Lake Mansion, and the buildings erected in 1940 along Granite and Sierra Streets. These areas are considered part of the larger Riverwalk District. The photograph above features the currently redeveloped area on First Street with the Palladio and old Masonic lodge in the background. The image below features the bottom portion of the historical Riverside and the redeveloped walkways and fountains of the Riverwalk District. (Courtesy of the Riverwalk Merchants Association.)

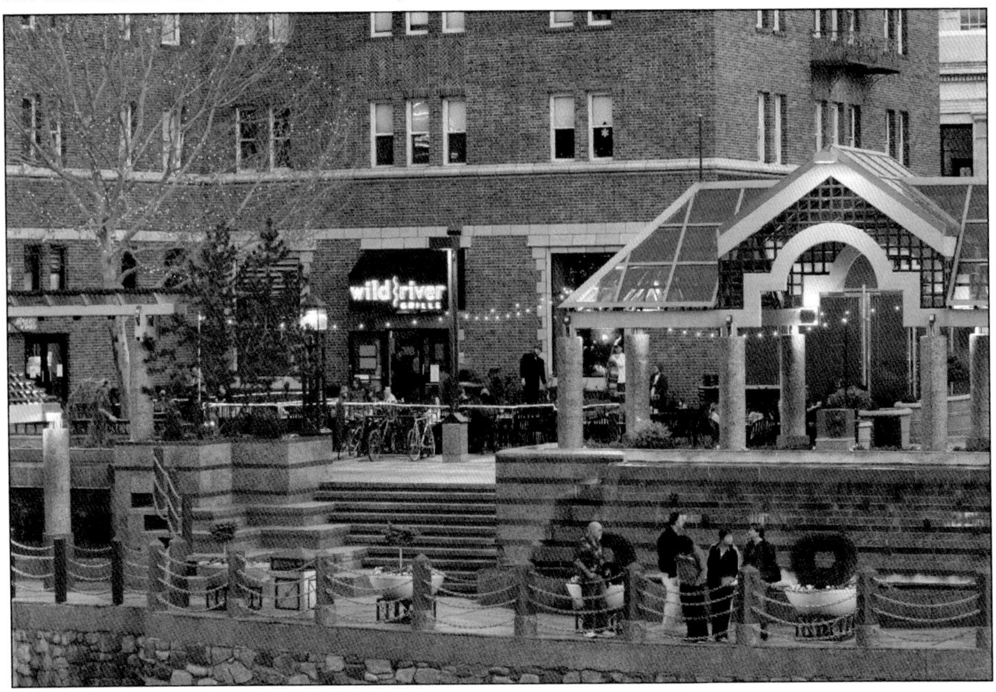

Bibliography

Cafferata, Patty. *Lake Mansion: Home to Reno's Founding Families*. Reno, NV: Eastern Slop Publisher, 2007.

Cafferata, Patty. *Mapes Hotel and Casino: The History of Reno's Landmark Hotel*. Reno, NV: Eastern Slop Publisher, 2005.

Cerveri, Doris. *Reno: A Pictorial History*. Norfolk, VA: The Donning Company Publishers, 1981.

Harmon, Mella Rothwell. *Divorce and Economic Opportunity in Reno, Nevada during the Great Depression*. Reno, NV: University of Nevada Press, 1998.

Nevada Historical Society Docent Council. Images of America: *Early Reno*. Charleston, SC: Arcadia Publishing, 2011.

nsla.nevadaculture.org

onlinenevada.org

renoriver.org

Townley, John M. *Tough Little Town on the Truckee*. Reno, NV: Great Basin Studies Center, 1983.

Zauner, Phyllis, and Lou Zauner. *Reno-Sparks Nevada*. Tahoe Paradise, CA: Zanel Publications, 1978.